Kierkegaard and the Ends of Language

Kierkegaard and the Ends of Language

GEOFFREY A. HALE

University of Minnesota Press
Minneapolis • London

Permission to reprint poetry by Rainer Maria Rilke granted by Suhrkamp.

Published by the University of Minnesota Press
111 Third Avenue South, Suite 290
Minneapolis, MN 55401-2520
http://www.upress.umn.edu

Library of Congress Cataloging-in-Publication Data

Hale, Geoffrey A.
Kierkegaard and the ends of language / Geoffrey A. Hale.
p. cm.
Includes bibliographical references and index.
ISBN 0-8166-3746-6 (alk. paper) — ISBN 0-8166-3747-4 (pbk. : alk. paper)
1. Kierkegaard, Søren, 1813–1855—Contributions in philosophy of language.
2. Language and languages—Philosophy. I. Title.
B4378.L35 H35 2002
198′.9—dc21

2001005617

Printed in the United States of America on acid-free paper

The University of Minnesota is an equal-opportunity educator and employer.

12 11 10 09 08 07 06 05 04 03 02 10 9 8 7 6 5 4 3 2 1

For Frances

Contents

Acknowledgments

First and foremost, this project would not have been possible without the generous support, guidance, and enthusiasm of Werner Hamacher and Judith Butler. Their participation in the project from beginning to end has been invaluable to its completion. I would also like to thank Joanna Klink, who read the entire manuscript in various forms and whose patient but persistent inquiry forced me continually to clarify my thoughts; only her friendship has been of perhaps greater importance. For his constant encouragement, support, and thoughtful reading of the manuscript, I would like to thank Hent de Vries. Especial gratitude is also due to Kevin Newmark, whose thoughtful reading of the manuscript made connections I might not otherwise have seen. Roger Müller-Farguell's careful reading of the work on Kierkegaard has been particularly helpful. I am also grateful to the German department at The Johns Hopkins University for having provided teaching stipends throughout my graduate career. Of course, no thanks to the department would be complete without expression of my appreciation for the remarkable skills, reliability, and organization of Rita Braun. I am particularly grateful to the Dean's Teaching Fellowship program for granting me the opportunity to teach a seminar covering much of the material presented here. I would also like to thank the students in the seminar for their remarkable intelligence and good humor.

The University of Minnesota Press has provided great editorial assistance and support throughout the final stages of the project. In particular, I would like to thank William Murphy for his enthusiasm for the work from the very beginning, and both Richard Morrison and Pieter Martin for their interest and dedication in seeing the publication through to completion.

In addition, the various members of my family, each in their individual ways, have contributed to the project's completion. In particular I would like to thank my mother for her unfailing encouragement and for many thoughtful discussions throughout.

Finally, and most important, I would like to thank the one person whose undaunted patience, faith, support, and encouragement throughout the years, through moments of elation and despair, have been and continue to be absolutely indispensable: Alison Parker.

1

Kierkegaard Who? The Problem for Posterity

The difficulty we confront in reading Kierkegaard begins with the author. Who was Kierkegaard? What sort of work did he write? Philosophy? Theology? Literature? Who decides? And to what end? Is it the author alone who makes this distinction? Under what auspices? Or is it our responsibility as readers to categorize these texts and pave the way for their proper understanding at the start? On whose authority? The question is now conventionally assumed to be resolved by his use of pseudonyms.[1] Kierkegaard's pseudonymous texts, we are assured, are "indirect communications." That is, they are to be understood as merely indirect expressions of the religious truth expressed directly in the theological texts that he signed with his own name. The signature, then, should tell the whole story. As soon as we know "who" wrote each text, we ought to know how to understand it.

Straightforward as this assumption appears to be, however, it amounts to nothing less than the refusal to recognize the problem of authorship altogether. Rather than articulating the inescapable disjunction between "authorship" and "authority" that was so clearly delineated by Kierkegaard throughout his work, the assumption that the signature itself indicates the correct way to understand each text requires that authority concern nothing more than Kierkegaard's ability to determine the meaning of what he had written. The author "Kierkegaard," therefore, always indicated how we ought to understand each text by way of the name he used to sign it. If we accept this premise, there can no longer be any question of the name at all. Regardless of one's conclusions, each attempt to resolve the plurality of Kierkegaard's names under the one name effectively abolishes the difficulty prior to any purported resolution. The array of names simply becomes the matrix for each text's proper understanding. "Kierkegaard" becomes the proper name behind every other name, and each pseudonym, under his control, turns into the cipher for the mode of each authored text's understanding. More than that, to assume that "Kierkegaard" was, directly or indirectly, always the author of each of his texts would result in nothing less than the obliteration of every name's authority, ultimately even his own. "Kierkegaard" would no longer be the name of an author; instead, it would become the sign for the principle of coherence ultimately called upon to secure the intelligibility of each of his texts, and all of his texts together. "Kierkegaard" the name would have no specificity and would simply disappear into the systematic principle of authority. And if "Kierkegaard" the name designates nothing more than the principle of his authority, there is, in the end, no Kierkegaard.

More than a minor point of technical clarification, acknowledging the division between the author and any principle of authority calls into question the very assumptions about what texts mean and how they mean what they mean. For authority to function as the principle of coherence that secures the definitive meaning of every text, it must preexist the very texts that articulate it. As Kierkegaard insisted throughout his work, however, meaning is inseparable from the finite occurrence of language. In spite of all rules of grammar and all the demands of universality in language, we can never know what language means prior to its occurrence. In this way, every text, every act of speech, can only suspend universalizing rules of intelligibility. Otherwise, he insisted, by assuming that all of meaning resides with universal rules of intelligibility, we would always assume we know what language means prior to each of its expressions, and in spite of its finite occurrence. Language would always mean the same thing in its universality. On the contrary, as Kierkegaard argues, we are given language only as it occurs, and whatever meaning it happens to convey depends upon perceiving it as such, not as the illusion of an only presupposed system. For the same reason, therefore, the author can never be assumed to possess authority in advance, and certainly not an authority that guarantees for us what each text means.

Kierkegaard's work continually demonstrates that its categorical determination as philosophy, theology, literature, and so on presupposes a system of coherent signification that can always ultimately be shown to be purely imaginary. In this way, his work calls into question conventional explication in general, and the convention of his commentators in particular. By taking as their task the explication of his work in the identification of, for example, its theological significance, Kierkegaard's commentators effectively work through his texts, erasing them in favor of the principle of their "truth." By calling into question the revelation of "truth" these commentaries in general take as their raison d'être, Kierkegaard's work continually calls into question any conclusions achieved in the conventional mode of commentary. His work invariably shows that such commentary refuses the finite particularity of every text.

By insisting that any understanding of his work can proceed only from an acknowledgment of its finite and material particularity, Kierkegaard opened his work up for a different kind of understanding. And, as I shall demonstrate, just as the conventional mode of commentary can succeed only if it does away with the very texts it claims to explicate, this same mode of commentary can only ignore or more actively exclude understandings of his work that refuse to abandon the uncertainties borne by the finitude no text can do without. As I argue in this book, any understanding of Kierkegaard's work in its specificity requires first the suspension of any preconceived coherence designated in any principle of authority. This understanding of Kierkegaard's significance occurred for the first time at the beginning of the twentieth century in the work of such authors as Rainer Maria Rilke, Franz Kafka, and Theodor W. Adorno. What each of these authors had in common was the refusal to let the identification of what sort of author Kierkegaard may have been determine their understanding of his work and its significance—the refusal, that is, to assume a systematic coherence that his work continually rejects. Whatever significance Kierkegaard's work may be assumed to have for subsequent developments in thought, it cannot be neatly identified with the coherent principle of his "authority" or with any other single principle that would systematically organize and justify the radical incoherence his works demonstrate. On the contrary, what I argue in this book is that, although Kierkegaard's work may be assumed to have had an important impact upon developments in twentieth-century thought, his work can achieve significance only where its resistance is encountered without the prejudices of systematic explication.

The insistence that we can understand Kierkegaard's texts only by way of their signatures seems to result from a more basic confusion. The conventional wisdom seems to fear that, if the "author" is deprived of his "authority," there cannot be any authority at all; and, if there is no authority, one assumes, there can be no meaning. Surely there is meaning, however obscure it might be, so there must be an authority that determines it. That authority must then be the author; it must be Kierkegaard himself. But the crisis in authority that Kierkegaard articulated in his work is not the same as a crisis in meaning. Language still means what it says; it is just that its meaning is not determined solely by a singular principle of authority. Texts can legitimately be understood to mean different things. What texts mean in and of themselves, then, can only bring into question the possibility of any authority called upon to secure that meaning.

The plurality of Kierkegaard's names and pseudonyms indicates at the very least that the identity of the signatory lies properly beyond the realm of textual meaning; at best, it can have only an accidental relation to meaning, not a thoroughly determinate one. The fact that there has never been any clear consensus about how to classify the works of this author in particular, however, suggests that something more fundamental must be at issue. Kierkegaard himself, as we shall see, was most contradictory with regard to any attempt to explain what his work means. Every attempt to claim authority over his authorship is forever embedded in a text written "without authority," as the author himself acknowledged. Every attempt to claim authority over the written word does nothing more than indicate the fact that it is, strictly speaking, impossible. It is by no means certain that what one writes can ever be entirely one's own. No one possesses language in such a way that the author could always be clearly identified as the sole authority as to its meaning. Authority, that is, is not about the author. Rather, it concerns the possibility of conferring meaning upon words in a systematic way. And if the author's authority comes into question through the multiplicity of possible signatories, it is not the author himself who thereby comes into doubt, but any system that would secure an identifiable authority as the source of linguistic meaning.

It is precisely the possibility of a systematically secured meaning that Kierkegaard's work continually brings into question. How can we know that such a system exists? Must it exist? Does language itself require that it does? And, if it does, are there no limits? The more fundamental question, of course, is this: How does language mean what it means? Does it do so solely by dint of an "authority" in whose name it speaks? Or rather, does language itself continue to speak beyond and in the absence of the very authority that would guarantee its meaning?

These questions stand at the center of the study of Kierkegaard's work. To read Kierkegaard is to read the work of one whose works may never be signed with his own name and whose "communication" must always remain "indirect." The written word is forever caught in the unresolvable tension between the singular temporal specificity of its occurrence and the possibility of a meaning held infinitely in abeyance. Although meaning conveyed in language is necessarily "universal," its availability depends upon a language that can take place only in a finite form and thus has no immediate or secure relation to the universal.[2] To speak is to participate in a language already in existence, not to originate that language and its meanings as if from nothing, from nowhere; and every linguistic utterance participates in that existence, partakes of it, and carries it forth without resolving it in any singularly coherent way. This predicament lies at the heart of what we might call the linguistic promise. Language always promises access to a meaning that would be universal and totalizable, although its very occurrence continues to resist complete foreclosure in universality.

That is not to say, however, that language must ultimately remain meaningless. What may initially appear as nothing other than the utter foreclosure of meaning might in actuality form the basis of an explicitly linguistic productivity. That is, as soon as language is understood as not subject to the singular control of any particular "authority," the possibility of its meaning becomes available for what Kierkegaard deemed a kind of posthumous productivity, where textual meaning must continually be produced through subsequent interpretations, "rebirths," and "renewals." Ungrounded as this production of meaning may seem, it is not without its own responsibility.

To read Kierkegaard is to take seriously the impossibility of this task—an impossibility religiously avoided by the convictions of coherent explication that characterize more canonical and conventional commentaries. From its very beginnings in nineteenth-century Denmark, Kierkegaard scholarship has tended to follow what have now become thoroughly predictable patterns. Virtually all commentaries on Kierkegaard, as I shall demonstrate, fall into at least one of four categories: biography, literature, religion, or philosophy. Each has sought, in one way or another, to organize Kierkegaard's papers posthumously in terms of one or another principle of coherence. They have all attempted to explain in terms of a principle of coherence what would otherwise appear to make the whole of Kierkegaard's authorship thoroughly inexplicable. In one way or another, each of these conventional assessments has attempted, as it were, to force Kierkegaard finally to sign his own name.

Recognizing the sheer prolixity of Kierkegaard's work, his numerous pseudonyms, his use of various styles and genres, and the various contradictions and paradoxes exhibited in his work, many commentators have turned to Kierkegaard's life—as psychology or biography—in order to explicate and organize what appears thoroughly beyond any possible conceptual organization. This tendency had already begun with the first publication of Kierkegaard's journals in 1869,[3] though the first full-length biographies of Kierkegaard would not appear until the end of the century. Notable in this regard are Heiberg's biography of 1895,[4] which proposed a psychological profile of Kierkegaard, and Rosenberg's 1898 biography, which attempted to correlate Kierkegaard's life with his literary production.[5] This tendency continued as Kierkegaard scholarship took a more serious turn at the beginning of the twentieth century, as, for example, with Christoph Schrempf's monumental two-volume work, *Sören Kierkegaard: Eine Biographie* I (1927) and II (1928). In the early twentieth century, the attention to Kierkegaard's life also led to a decidedly philosophical account, as in the early Lukács essay "The Foundering of Form against Life: Søren Kierkegaard and Regine Olsen" (1910), where Kierkegaard's life was taken as philosophically significant in itself.[6] Lukács condensed Kierkegaard's philosophy into the "gesture," represented in his famous refusal to marry Regine Olsen, which, for all its certainty, can never be certain of its effects.[7] Yet, in principle, such psychologies or biographies inevitably miss the very texts they claim to explicate, ultimately conjuring up a life nowhere present as such within the texts, or, as the author A of Kierkegaard's *Either/Or* objected, "poetizing the personality" along with them.

Refusing the complexity invoked in Kierkegaard's "prodigious" authorship, the other earliest strain in Kierkegaard scholarship tended to concern itself exclusively with his explicitly theological texts. Initially, these accounts focused primarily on the polemical debates against the official church of Denmark that were carried out in the journals *Fæderlandet* and *Øjeblikket* from the end of 1854 until Kierkegaard's death several months later in 1855. It was this early polemical and theological interest in Kierkegaard that would eventually lead to a more serious reception of his work outside of Denmark. For it was these polemical tracts that first prompted translation of his work into German and garnered broader interest in the German-speaking world near the turn of the twentieth century.[8] And it was these early German translations through which others became familiar with Kierkegaard as well.[9] Although responses varied in terms of the degree to which they took Kierkegaard's critique of the church as more or less polemical and even satirical, his opposition to the church and his deeper rejection of systematic theology ultimately formed the basis for conceptions of dialectical theology or neoorthodoxy in the work of such twentieth-century theologians as Karl Barth, Paul Tillich and Friedrich Gogarthen.[10]

At the same time, and for reasons similar to those motivating the psychobiographical explications, there were also various significant studies that recognized Kierkegaard's prolific literary talent, pointing to the ostensibly "masterful" technique he displayed among the various aesthetic and religious texts. The first major study of Kierkegaard, and certainly the first to have a profound effect upon Kierkegaard reception more generally, was Georg Brandes's *Søren Kierkegaard: En Kritisk Fremstilling i Grundrids* (Søren Kierkegaard: Outline of a Critical Appraisal) (1877), translated in 1879 as *Sören Kierkegaard: Ein Literarisches Charakterbild* (Søren Kierkegaard: A literary portrait). Seizing upon elements in Kierkegaard's life and offering his own version of a psychological explanation, Brandes ultimately concluded that Kierkegaard's primary significance lies in his "artistry," thus dismissing any question as to whether the texts address issues of more substantive concern.[11] Although this approach had the notable effect of "de-Christianizing" Kierkegaard and expanding his reception to those interested in more than purely theological concerns, it also suggested that the work was not to be treated as more rigorously philosophical.[12] Kierkegaard's work was viewed either as symptomatic of a more or less disturbed personality or as the display of a "masterful" aesthetic technique. Similarly, in the German context, Rudolf Kassner, whose first interest in Kierkegaard was guided by a consideration of his explicitly theological texts, concluded in his essay, well known at the time, "Sören Kierkegaard: Aphorismen" (Søren Kierkegaard: Aphorisms) (1906), that Kierkegaard should be regarded primarily as an "artist" among philosophers whose "genius" consisted primarily of his "humor."[13]

Finally, in the early twentieth century, Kierkegaard's commentators began to take his work seriously as philosophy and as opposed to "literature," though the theology was never far behind. The first significant account of Kierkegaard's philosophy was *Sören Kierkegaard und die Philosophie der Innerlichkeit* (Søren Kierkegaard and the philosophy of interiority) (1913) by Theodor Haecker, who was otherwise best known for his work with the polemical journal of social satire *Der Brenner*. Haecker's text amounts to a more or less uncritical appropriation of Kierkegaard's "spheres" or "stages" of existence and presents them in a rigidly schematic hierarchy, moving from the "aesthetic" through the "ethical" to the "religious." This early book on Kierkegaard did much to set the stage for what would become the thoroughly conventional understanding of Kierkegaardian "existence" and the religious "truth" about subjectivity.[14] In spite of their differences, philosophical interpretations of Kierkegaard that see the truth about Kierkegaard as embodied in the primacy of the "religious" sphere remain fundamentally related to theological discourses that use Kierkegaard to argue for the "subjective truth" of "Christianity," however dialectically or paradoxically it may be construed. Rightly regarded as having established the conventional assessment of Kierkegaard that has become so predominant and unproblematic during the course of the twentieth century, this conception of Kierkegaard—the one who prized the "self" at the same time that he prioritized the religious "stage" of existence toward which this self was oriented—likely has more to do with Haecker than it does with Kierkegaard. More concerned with establishing an easily transmitted "truth" about Kierkegaard, it can only avoid those aspects of Kierkegaard's work that resist such a normative assessment.

Nonetheless, Haecker's account of Kierkegaard laid the groundwork for the vast majority of commentators who take Kierkegaard's analysis of "existence" as his central contribution to philosophical thought. In this regard, Kierkegaard's work is taken as the primary impetus behind philosophies of existence, most notably in the work of Karl Jaspers.[15] "Philosophy of existence," as Jaspers describes it, "is the tendency of thought which makes use of material knowledge and transcends it, so that man can once again become himself."[16] Thus, existence is construed essentially as a problem of subjectivity to be explicated in one or another manner of "becoming a self." The vast majority of Kierkegaard's commentators, particularly in the Anglo-American context, are devoted to the explication of the "self" in Kierkegaard.[17] Even Jaspers, in a late essay on Kierkegaard, is careful to maintain that, although philosophies of existence may rely extensively on Kierkegaard's work, it remains by no means certain wherein precisely Kierkegaard's significance lies. His importance for various modes of "existentialism" does not make of him an "existentialist."[18]

With the realization that Kierkegaard's "indirect communication" must somehow be about language, more recent Kierkegaard scholarship appears to have come full circle and praises Kierkegaard for his decisively literary technique. Still, in the absence of any discovered or revealed principle of coherence, Kierkegaard's notion of "indirect communication" is called upon to explain the true relationships among the texts, such that the "aesthetic" or "philosophical" texts illustrate "indirectly" the truth "directly" related in the theological texts. In the wake of the more structural and systematic accounts of Kierkegaard—which certainly have not disappeared—and ostensibly in response to recent developments within continental philosophy, Kierkegaard is again being praised as a "poet," a great writer of "literature," and is appropriated under the name of "postmodernism." The shift began most notably with Louis Mackey's *Kierkegaard: A Kind of Poet* (1971), which asserts unabashedly: "Kierkegaard is not, in the ususal acceptation of these words, a philosopher or a theologian, but a poet" (p. ix). And: "Whatever philosophy or theology there is in Kierkegaard is sacramentally transmitted 'in, with, and under' the poetry" (*Kierkegaard,* xi). What Mackey seems to mean, though, is that Kierkegaard's work is still about "God" and "existence"; but it has to be read as "poetry" and interpreted as "literature"—which apparently simply means rhetorically. Mackey concludes his book with the explicit identification of "poetry" with "indirect communication," claiming that "any philosophy which deals with matters vital to human beings must communicate itself indirectly" (*Kierkegaard,* 295). Still, Mackey maintains the illusion that this "vitality" precedes its communication and that one simply chooses to communicate it indirectly in order to communicate it at all. It is only because of the "subject" of communication that it must somehow be indirect. That is, this still assumes that "indirect communication" seeks to resolve a problem imposed by a desired content of communication rather than one of communication as such. In this way, "indirect communication" becomes a principle of figure or metaphor, saying one thing and meaning another. Therefore, Mackey continues, "his [Kierkegaard's] philosophy *is* poetry because it centers on man," and "poetry," then, becomes a "reflection" of what Mackey calls "the ambiguity of human existence" (*Kierkegaard,* 295). Not to forget the ultimately theological purpose of even this philosophy of existence, Mackey continues: "For although Kierkegaard's thought centers on man, it does not in the last analysis find its repose in him . . . God is the ultimate reason of poetry as of all things: His Being everywhere imagined in the creation makes poetic communication possible; His image everywhere distorted by the creation makes the obliquity of poetry necessary" (*Kierkegaard,* 296).

Mackey's subsequent work on Kierkegaard, collected in *Points of View: Readings of Kierkegaard,* repeats this gesture. Here, too, "language" continues to be seen as rooted either in the "self," as "self-love" or "the agency of human self-assertion," or in "God" as exhibiting "*in language*" traces of "solemn divinity" (p. xvii). But in this account, perhaps differently from Mackey's earlier text, where "indirect communication" was a matter of metaphor, all language is seen as a matter of "irony" and "indeterminability," where the significance is not just that Kierkegaard's texts do not mean literally what they say, but, further still, they might not mean in only one (metaphorical) way: "philosophy and theology are signed with the mark of undecidability and thrust into endless closure. And he [Kierkegaard] blames it all (ironically?) on ... Christianity" (*Points of View*, xviii; Mackey's ellipsis). Thus, the question seems to have become one of neither philosophy nor theology, but a resolutely anti philosophical and antitheological "literature": "their [Kierkegaard's texts'] literary form barely masks (because it incarnates) their profound offensiveness to the normal and normative modes of philosophical and religious discourse" (*Points of View*, xix). Still concerned with the relationship "between God and man," however, Mackey insists upon the primacy of religion in Kierkegaard's work—even if he must find it ultimately "inexplicable." He asserts that it is precisely Kierkegaard's "Christianity" that makes him "anti-philosophical" (*Points of View*, xxi).

In Mackey's view, "indirect communication" is nothing but the intentional deception of a thoroughly "ambivalent" and "duplicitous" subject. Quoting the Kierkegaard of *Practice in Christianity* (the "communicator" is "nobody, an absentee ... null, a no man"), Mackey continues to insist that the texts are the work of a somebody, "the work of an *ironic* subject who lurks behind a barricade of pseudonyms" (*Points of View*, xxiii), as if this "irony" now allows Mackey to expose this subject who must already have been there from the very beginning. From this, Mackey feels compelled to conclude that the texts don't really mean what they say: "By virtue of his authorial self-restraint, his texts exhibit an almost complete abstention from determinate meaning and an almost perfect recalcitrance to interpretation" (*Points of View*, xxiii). "Almost," that is, because he has now been found out. Thus, the "self" is still construed as the "subject," and its communication can be indirect if and when he so chooses simply by deciding whether they are intended to mean what they say. Yet, as I shall demonstrate, what Kierkegaard's "indirect communication" exhibits is not that one can choose to communicate directly or indirectly in a thoroughly calculable way, but rather that all communication is necessarily indirect—which is not the same as "meaningless." What Kierkegaard demonstrates in the very matter of indirect communication is not that there is a subject "lurking" somehow "behind" it, even if only ironically, but that the structure of indirect communication is already constitutive of any conception of subjectivity and, hence, already undermines any contention that this subject would exist wholly and already in such a way as to guarantee for this subject singular control over its language. It would appear that it is not the subject who controls the communication, but rather the inverse.

Resolving or praising the "obliquity" or even "meaninglessness" of

Kierkegaard's "poetry" has become the cornerstone of various attempts to incorporate Kierkegaard into some conception of the "postmodern."[19] Though such studies acknowledge the functional significance of language in Kierkegaard's work in principle, they tend by and large to construe indirect communication in language as a problem of "irony"—the possibility of meaning what one says and not meaning it at the same time, or simply the possibility of meaning more than one thing at a time, and possibly even meaning nothing. Irony, thus, is enlisted in an effort to empty language of meaning in "poetry" and to understand that as its primary challenge to both philosophy and theology. In that sense, Pat Bigelow, in his *Kierkegaard and the Problem of Writing,* claims that this unavoidable irony—what he calls "the Kierkegaardian gambit"—"means that there is a way of saying that is not *about* anything" (p. 5). In the same way, studies of Kierkegaard that identify themselves as "postmodern" take up the problem of linguistic indeterminacy in Kierkegaard as one of "arbitrariness" and its "meaninglessness," forgetting at the same time that meaning, even in irony, is the very condition of language in general and in Kierkegaard in particular.[20] In all of his numerous discussions of language, Kierkegaard never said that language is only meaningless.

Perhaps in response to the impossibility of offering a coherent account of what Kierkegaard's work means in a definitive sense, attempts to chronicle the progressive development of his "influence" in the twentieth century inevitably seem to lapse into a kind of idiosyncratic personalism. In the end, we are assured, interest in Kierkegaard remains a profoundly personal affair, and that must be why his work has apparently spawned such a plethora of diverse and divergent responses. "Kierkegaard is a captivating figure," Mark C. Taylor staunchly asserts. "His probings drive the reader even more deeply into himself."[21] Roger Poole, in an essay outlining twentieth-century uses of Kierkegaard ("The Unknown Kierkegaard: Twentieth-century Receptions"), announces with emphatic banality: "Every thinker who falls under Kierkegaard's sway does so for his own reasons" (p. 53). His point is simply that one relates to Kierkegaard on a purely personal level and that Kierkegaard becomes relevant only on the basis of an existing personal predilection. As he also says of Kafka's response to Kierkegaard: "Kierkegaard's influence can only be decisive within a personal problematic that exists already" ("The Unknown Kierkegaard," 50); Kafka, too, refused to marry. Or, with ostensibly greater conceptual pertinence: "Kierkegaard's effect on theologians has usually been because of the existential nature of his own theological thinking" ("The Unknown Kierkegaard," 53). Similarly, in his more exhaustive account of Kierkegaard's reception through the first third of the twentieth century *(Receiving Søren Kierkegaard),* Habib C. Malik concludes of all those who took up the Kierkegaardian banner that they responded to Kierkegaard on an experiential level: they all "exhibited at least one Kierkegaardian trait: they allowed their personal lives to be affected by their reading of Kierkegaard, especially the religious writings. Thus they reacted *existentially* to his thought, and this alone credits them with a significant degree of seriousness and depth" (*Receiving Søren Kierkegaard,* 395). But to respond "personally" or "existentially" is no longer to respond to what Kierkegaard wrote. It is no longer to respond to the work at all, because it absolves one of the responsibility to read. Kierkegaard is emblematically reduced to the vehicle for coursing individual, personal, and experiential crises of "faith"—and this in the name of the one author for whom the availability of "faith" and "experience" for the understanding remains, at best, questionable.

This is not to say, however, that all studies of Kierkegaard are somehow condemned to failure; rather the condemned are those that take as their presumptive point of departure the explication and hence the affirmation of given modes of subjectivity and the self, on the one hand, or given conceptions of "God" and "Christianity," on the other. Contrary to such conventional wisdom, there have been several attempts in recent years that have found in Kierkegaard neither the acclaimed value of "self" and "God" revealed, nor the sheer praise of his "ironic" and "poetic" "meaninglessness," but rather a substantial challenge to the presumed centrality of precisely these preconceived notions. Two in particular are worth noting here: Peter Fenves's *"Chatter": Language and History in Kierkegaard* and Sylviane Agacinski's *Aparté: Conceptions and Deaths of Søren Kierkegaard.* Significantly, both take as their point of departure particularly Kierkegaardian motifs of language—"chatter" in Fenves's and "irony" in Agacinski's—not for the appraisal of emptiness and meaningless in language for its own sake, but rather for the concrete articulation of the ways in which the unavoidable possibility that language somehow also communicates nothing poses the greatest challenge to the very centrality of notions of subjectivity and divinity in Western philosophical and theological traditions. Fenves explains: "The idleness of the ones who talk and the meaningfulness of their idioms serve to challenge the very concepts of a *given* language and *already* constituted subjects to such an extent that the operations of both given languages and already constituted subjects are suspended—in idleness" (*"Chatter,"* 2). Agacinski, on the other hand, takes her departure from Kierkegaard's notion of irony, where the negativity of irony undermines the possibility of positing the subject as such and even the possibility of positing itself. Irony, in Agacinski's reading, is not a position; it "posits nothing" (*Aparté*, 35). And this negativity can never exactly be overcome. "A thesis can always be haunted by irony" (*Aparté*, 78).

In a more conventional sense, however, contemporary commentary has not gotten very far away from the same debates that characterized Kierkegaard scholarship in its nineteenth-century beginnings. At base, the question remains: What sort of author is this? When we read Kierkegaard, are we reading theology, philosophy, or merely the literature of a crafty and cunning author? In view of what schematic matrix do his otherwise erratic and unconventional texts become explicable or intelligible? Does Kierkegaard show us the truth about God and Christianity or the truth about the subjective individual? Or does he perhaps show us no truth at all, but rather a facile and satirical irony? The question will likely never be resolved, and certainly not within its own terms. Indeed, what characterizes virtually all studies of Kierkegaard, and apparently compels them to pose such a question in the first place, is rather a profound incomprehension, an incomprehension demonstrated rather than resolved by the affirmation of one or another truth in one or another categorical determination.

The paradoxical situation of writing a text that one can never author with one's own authority was explicitly thematized from the beginning of Kierkegaard's "authorship." Already in the first volume of *Either/Or*, published pseudonymously in 1843, the anonymous, pseudonymous author A, in an aside that interrupts a larger discourse entitled "The Tragic in Ancient Drama Reflected in the Tragic in Modern Drama," describes a certain method, such as it is, for writing. Subtitled "An Effort in Fragmentary Endeavor," mirroring the volume's subtitle, "A Fragment of Life," the direction here might apply as much to the discourse it interrupts as it would to the work of the unnamed author of this and other texts in the philosophical, literary production claimed by Søren Kierkegaard. Not only does the passage reflect the problem of the conceptual and epistemological disruption posed by an always finite existence that in one way or another marks and informs virtually all of Kierkegaard's work, even the expressly theological texts, but the interpretive method prescribed in response to such limitation would continually haunt the work he himself produced—both within the work itself and throughout its history, the history of its "productivity."

The method prescribed here hardly proves reassuring. Rather than overcoming textual fragmentation with a principle of coherent unification, it seeks to articulate the ways in which fragmentation is itself already the ground for any possible signification. Opening the interruption with the assertion that "it is at variance with the aims of our association to provide coherent works or larger unities," A quickly makes it clear that this is not exactly an elected position: "it is not our intention to labor on a Tower of Babel that God in his righteousness can descend and destroy since ... such confusion justly occurred" (*Either/Or* I, 151). This image is descriptive. The confusion has already occurred. The author does not exactly suggest that there would once have been a prior moment of complete coherence. There is only the confusion of a destroyed "Tower of Babel"—and the "justness" of this occurrence is in turn the uncohesive multiplicity with which any possibility of justice must contend rather than overcoming it.

The discord that comes to affect all that an author produces is grounded in nothing other than existence itself. Indeed, as A says, "since it is not granted to human beings to live with an eternal view like the gods'," there is no possibility of a foothold outside of the text that would secure for it its own universal truth in a singular way. Thus, A concludes that it is "characteristic of all human endeavor in its truth that it is fragmentary, that it is precisely this which distinguishes it from nature's infinite coherence, that an individual's wealth consists specifically in his capacity for fragmentary extravagance *[Ødselhed]* ..." (*Either/Or* I, 151). Indeed, it is not simply because this author would be ideologically opposed to "coherence" as such that this text is fragmentary. All texts are fragments because, like everything in existence, they are finite. And because they are finite, they must be incomplete—broken off prior to a more formal or ideal resolution—not because of some failure or inadequacy, but simply because they are.

Insofar as language has meaning, as Kierkegaard insists, only to the extent that it exists, the very contingencies of existence necessarily affect its capacity to mean. If linguistic meaning is inextricably bound to its finite occurrence, language cannot, therefore, be merely some instrument of deictic reference, referring only to some other reality that it itself is not; nor can it simply be the means of conceptualization, continually absolving itself into the infinite and eternal realm of the idea.[22] Language neither vanishes before the referent nor fulfills itself in the truth and presence of the idea. The very existence of language as such will always suspend or interrupt the possibility of such "infinite coherence." To write, therefore, is to risk the utter suspension of intelligibility, which is not the same as having to abandon intelligibility altogether. If, as A writes, it is "characteristic of all human endeavor in its truth that it is fragmentary," then the meaning of any text must remain forever uncertain, not just because any attributed meaning might not be true or its truth would remain undecidable, but because the text is already finite, so no meaning can ever present itself as the final one. The "truth" of the text is its fragmentation, its incompletion within itself, not some ideal and therefore external meaning. This "truth"—the fragment—thus is not the goal of meaning, but its condition. And as its condition, it must also be understood paradoxically to condition the very meaning it cannot secure. There can be no language without meaning, and yet there can be no meaning that is not already fragmented in and by the finite occurrence of language. Any assumed system or method can never secure for what is fragmentary a "truth" that would be any less of a "fragment" itself.

No one, therefore, can determine with absolute certainty what a text means. No author—least of all Kierkegaard himself, whose work is characterized not by a singularity of authority but rather by the multiplicity of its pseudonymous "authors"—can free the text from the necessity of its own finite distinction, which forever separates it from the singular control of any authority. Although this may, in turn, motivate psychobiographical interpretations, for example, it also makes clear why such interpretive gestures inevitably fall short: "because of the disjointed and desultory character *[det Afbrudte, Desultoriske]* of unfinished papers, one feels a need to poetize the personality along with them" (*Either/Or* I, 152). All texts, as unfinished, render the author as authority unavailable within them. Recourse to authorial control, as to any universalizing system or methodology, will always fall outside the realm of textual interpretation, because the author one thus produces is, in a certain way, only a product of the text, not the other way around. There is no *authority* there, in the text. The author A is clear about this. All texts are unfinished. All texts, therefore, are "disjointed" or "interrupted" and "desultory"—falling, that is, without rule.

This does not mean, however, that these texts become available for a merely random attribution of meaning. Attributed meaning, however apparently responsible, will always have just as accidental a relationship to the text as any biographical interpretation. It cannot supplement and complete what is already in itself incomplete. Texts are not destined to become fragments; they are fragments already. At no point does A suggest that a fragment might be construed as merely part of a whole; he never suggests that there would be something like wholeness or completeness that would be available as such. And the object of interpretation, accordingly, can never be understood as having to restore a totality that has never existed. Language is fragmentary only with respect to its own incompleteness. Its own incompleteness, not that of some imagined totality, thus renders every text its own self-interruption, self-disjoining. Being "disjointed" and "desultory," therefore, might better be understood as functions of textual fragmentation rather than as its result. "Unfinished papers," A says, "are like a ruin," because they are already of themselves ruinous (*Either/Or* I, 152).

The process of fragmentation, we must be clear, is simply the logical effect of its finitude. For a text to be finite means that it cannot contain its own end. All texts are "ruins," forever "desultory" and "disjointed," not because they have become that, but because they are texts "left behind," without hope or promise of completion. Accordingly, no authority can free a text of the imperative of interpretation by guaranteeing for it a place and a meaning outside of its finite occurrence. The text cannot refer to or represent a totality of which it would once have been part; its being forever "left behind" can only prohibit such totalization. Put another way, we might also say, if the text is incomplete, never itself a totality, then there must be something more than language alone whenever it appears, something more than language that is not the same as language but without which language would not exist. As opposed to any imagined conception of the infinite as the whole, the fragment can define itself only with and against what it itself is not. Every text posits itself as itself at the same time that it posits itself against what it is not. Every text, thus, remains positive and negative at the same time, and positive and negative in different ways. The negative of language can be conceived only as the incalculable void that continually undoes every attempt at purely positive delineation. Each text turns upon its fragmentariness into fragmentation. In this way, the fragment is always itself and its continual fragmentation at the same time.[23] It can present itself only as both itself and its own self-fragmenting ground; it breaks apart in its breaking apart.

That is the rule of all writing: "The art, then, is to produce skillfully the same effect, the same carelessness and fortuitousness, the same anacoluthic thought process" as the fragment itself (*Either/Or* I, 152). The "art," not artifice, is to produce fragments, because one cannot avoid producing texts that would not simultaneously risk their own desultory fall. Because language as fragment inherently lacks any guarantee of its own intelligibility, texts are already breaking apart, falling. Without any universalizing rule of intelligibility, texts can only fall apart. "Desultory" then comes to describe the self-interruption of any attributed meaning in universality. But this does not mean that language is ultimately unintelligible; it just means that its intelligibility can always be presented in another way.[24]

The doubling of the fragment in and through its finitude is carried here by what A calls the "anacoluthic thought process." "Anacoluthic" refers to a technical term of rhetoric, *anacoluthon,* "pertaining to a changing from one grammatical construction to another without completing the former."[25] It is the rhetorical term for grammatical interruption, the raising of expectation of one type of completion only for the expression to be suspended and interrupted by another. For the fragment we have understood thus far, this interruption can amount only to the continual self-interruption and self-suspension of every linguistic utterance. But here the author A is more specific than that. He speaks of an "anacoluthic thought process" that, even in the attempt to formalize methodical production, amounts to the impossibility of any such formalization. In the performative fragmentation of this text, itself a "fragmentary endeavor" interrupted by a fragmentary digression on the fragment, the term denotes the radical suspension or fragmentation of rhetorical coherence as such.[26] Because the fragment always speaks in at least two languages, any attempt at meaningful, coherent unification will always be undermined and suspended by the fragmentary duality already maintained by the finitude that inaugurates it. Its incoherence already inheres in the text. Thus, *anacoluthon* describes not just a shift from one grammar to another, but a shift in thought itself that is motivated by the very grammar of its expression; it describes the radical irreconcilability of rhetorical presentation with the universalization of the thought bound indissolubly to it. As such, however, the anacoluthic suspension is available never within rhetorical presentation itself, but only in its disruption.

This question remains, however: If language and its meaning are produced rather than given in advance and as a totality, in what sense can a text avoid the apparently inevitable possibility of its own absolute meaninglessness? Without the guarantee of what language must mean, is there equally no imperative that it mean anything at all? How can it not disappear in an apparently nihilistic self-elimination, vanishing into the void of its own utter meaninglessness? Again, the author A offers some suggestion. If language means anything at all, what it means it means only in its equally incalculable effects, registered indirectly in the relationship between the author's text and its reader. It is in part the dream of a common and shared understanding, and yet, in the same way that language in its anacoluthic fragmentation is always somehow more than it appears and always speaks another fragmented and fragmentary language, there is always something beyond the merely common meaning:[27]

> ... and what is the producing individual's enjoyment is the receiving individual's also, not the laborious and careful accomplishment of the tedious interpretation of this accomplishment but the production and the

> pleasure of the glinting transiency, which for the producer holds much more *[et Mere]* than the consummated accomplishment, since it is a glimpse of the idea and holds a bonus *[et Mere]* for the recipient, since its fulguration stimulates his own productivity .... (*Either/Or* I, 152).

In each case, the author acknowledges an excess on the part of the text directly related to its finite occurrence; and in each case, this excess is something for which the text itself cannot entirely account. Whatever "glimpse" and "fulguration" there may be, it is available only insofar as it passes away; it is available, that is, only in its passing away, its disruption.[28] If a text does offer "a glimpse of the idea," this can occur only through its inevitable transience, its coming into existence and coming to an end. Yet, this "glimpse of the idea" might be available only to the text's "producer" or author, not to its "recipient" or reader. The "more" for the "recipient," also available only in a moment, a flash or "fulguration," is retrievable—if we might still speak in this way—only in the author's own "productivity," writing, or rather rewriting and interpretation. That is, in spite of the fact that language is always accompanied by the unavoidable absence of any guaranteed meaning or guarantor of meaning, one cannot not account for it. But this account, no matter how direct or apparently responsible, is never a kind of supplementary conclusion, never itself totalizable in terms of a systematic and scientific explication. On the contrary, the legible effects of one text are nothing more than texts themselves, continually suspending any promised meaning even as its meaningful promise.

In this way, a text's fragmentation is simultaneously its paradoxical "prodigality" or "extravagance": its finitude exceeds itself in itself. Because it is finite, it is never whole, complete. And because it is finite, it can never cease becoming. Yet, as in its "anacoluthic thought process," what exceeds the text's own fragmentation is never knowable as such within that fragmentation, but always falls outside of it. In this sense, language always exceeds itself in the incalculable void of its own indeterminability, the impossibility that one might know in advance what it means and the terms by which it operates.[29] The "prodigality" of linguistic fragmentation is the inevitable encounter in language with the unknown and unknowable alterity that language also is, and, hence, the unavoidable nonauthority of every authorial endeavor, in spite of every intention to the contrary.[30]

This is the sense of "nonauthority" that emerges throughout Kierkegaard's work, the sense in which he repeatedly attests to writing "without authority." Because of this, and because of its very "prodigality," Kierkegaard's work resists all attempts at categorical organization, even, ultimately, his own. Taking seriously the unavoidable finitude of language, all of Kierkegaard's work consists, in this sense, of posthumous papers, papers "left behind," without hope or promise of completion. Fragmentary and incomplete, the work is assigned neither systematic coherence nor definitive, totalizable meaning. As we have said, this is precisely its condition, not an undue complication to be clarified or resolved in each of the work's commentaries.

That does not mean, however, that he is also not obliged to account for his work in some way, just that such an account, like all others and like the work it would attempt to organize, can never be definitive, never complete—enough. Kierkegaard's first attempt to acknowledge his authorship occurs in the unnumbered pages at the end of the *Concluding Unscientific Postscript to Philosophical Fragments* under the title "A First and Last Explanation," signed by "S. Kierkegaard," although the *Postscript* itself is attributed to "Johannes Climacus." He begins simply by claiming responsibility for the production of all of the texts previously published under his various pseudonyms:

> For the sake of form and order, I hereby acknowledge, something that really can scarcely be of interest to anyone to *know*, that I am, as is said, the author of *Either/Or* (Victor Eremita), Copenhagen, February 1843; *Fear and Trembling* (Johannes de Silentio), 1843; *Repetition* (Constantin Constantius), 1843; *The Concept of Anxiety* (Vigilius Haufniensis), 1844; *Prefaces* (Nicolaus Notabene), 1844; *Philosophical Fragments* (Johannes Climacus), 1844; *Stages on Life's Way* (Hilarius Bookbinder—William Afham, the Judge, Frater Taciturnus), 1845; *Concluding Postscript to Philosophical Fragments* (Johannes Climacus), 1846; an article in *Fædrelandet*, no. 1168, 1843 (Victor Eremita); two articles in *Fædrelandet*, January 1846 (Frater Taciturnus). (Postscript, [625])

In claiming responsibility for these texts, "in a legal and in a literary sense" (*Postscript*, [627]), however, he is not thereby trying to assert any authority over their meaning or content. "To *know*" that he is their author ought to be, as he says, of no interest whatsoever. This "knowledge" would alter nothing of what is presented in and as the text. With regard to these texts, he explains simply:

> I am impersonally or personally in the third person a *souffleur* who has poetically produced the *authors*, whose *prefaces* in turn are their productions, as their *names* are also. Thus in the pseudonymous books there is not a single word by me, I have no opinion about them except as a third party, no knowledge of their meaning except as a reader, not the remotest private relation to them, since it is impossible to have that to a doubly reflected communication. (*Postscript*, [625–26])

In spite of the fact that he himself has written the texts of his pseudonymous authors, in spite of the fact that he personally has given them their names, there is not a single text by him, and he, as the "author," can have no authoritative "opinion" about their contents; even the pseudonyms are not from him, but are themselves products of pseudonymity. And if the pseudonyms are themselves produced pseudonymously, then pseudonymity, even in this account, must itself be the condition of authorship, not the other way around.

The inability to control textual meaning, as we have seen, is effected by the texts themselves, not because they would declare as much, but because, no matter what they declare, they communicate this impossibility everywhere communication takes place. To say that they are "doubly reflected" does not amount to their categorical classification, as if one might imagine other texts, for example, that do not meet this criterion. To say that these texts are "doubly reflected" is a statement about language rather than an attempt to classify them in terms of any identifiable genre. Every text is a "doubly reflected communication," and a "doubly reflected communication," as readers of the *Postscript* will already have been informed, is an "indirect communication."

At first glance, "indirect communication" would appear to describe the double separation of the "form" of communication from its "expression": "When thought has gained proper expression in the word, which is attained through the first reflection, there comes a second reflection, which bears upon the intrinsic relation of the communication to the communicator and renders the existing communicator's own relation to the idea" (*Postscript*, 76). Yet it is not exactly the case that "reflection" here implies adequation, as if, after finding an adequate word as the "form" for some idea, the "communicator" has to see that the word now also reflects both himself and the idea, perhaps choosing a different word more appropriate to this double condition. No, the communicator's "subjectivity" does not thereby come to bear on the possibility of communication as a secondary reflection upon a primary one. If the finitude of all linguistic communication already severs the possibility of an exclusive and exclusionary "authority," then no subject can assume authority over communication. On the contrary, the indirection of communication is the inevitable consequence of the very fragmentary finitude that characterizes all language in its occurrence, and, accordingly, every conception of the subject.[31] Climacus, hence, is impelled to assert here that it is this "second reflection" of "indirect communication" that first "renders" and thus establishes "the communicator's own relation to the idea."

In this sense, the "communicator's own relation to the idea" is never entirely proprietary, never entirely his or her own. When Climacus describes "inwardness" as a kind of "possession," it can never be entirely certain who ultimately possesses what. "Inwardness" as such can never be regarded as the exclusive property of the subject. Rather, "inwardness" becomes precisely the quality that effectively severs any possibility of proprietary relationship to subjectivity. In response to the assumption that there must be a subject in existence for language or thought to occur in the first place, every attempt to claim authority for this subject continually devolves into the impossibility of precisely this presupposition. The way of language in thought—and in thinking "the universal"—continually removes this subject from any possibility of exclusive, proprietary, and authorial control. "In thinking, he thinks the universal, but, as existing in his thinking, as acquiring this in his inwardness, he becomes more and more subjectively isolated" (*Postscript*, 73). And becoming a subject is precisely a matter of becoming isolated—becoming, that is, distinct, finite. This is what Kierkegaard/Climacus means by having this "subjective thinker" exist "in his thinking," which is not the same as having one's existence subsequently reflected in the thought. If thinking is always structured by language and the subject must express itself in language, then language must already structure the existence of the subject in and as its expression. Existence as such never preexists its occurrence, so the "existing in thinking" of the "subjective thinker" can amount only to a kind of declension of thought. More than that, all "subjects" as such always occur in this declension. It is, he later insists, communication that holds subjects apart. The "doubly reflected" form of communication "is the subtlety that the subjective individuals must be held devoutly apart from one another and must not run coagulatingly together in objectivity. This is objectivity's word of farewell to subjectivity" (*Postscript*, 79). And objectivity in communication can do nothing but issue this word of farewell to subjectivity. Objectivity bids farewell to subjectivity, and, in so doing, turns subjects out, exposes them, under the sign of the negative that is there with all of communication. "The wound of negativity," as Climacus also calls it (*Postscript*, 85), means the exposure of the subject to the negative in communication, to which each subject owes its own particularity, "isolation," "solitude," and, hence, "existence."

If subjective existence is a form for Kierkegaard/Climacus, it cannot be construed as a kind of Platonic ideal. It is rather an antiform and a deforming form that, in making the subject subjective in the first place, does nothing other than separate, divide, and isolate this subject beyond all communication. That is, the subject cannot assume, as Kierkegaard repeatedly insists, a universally communicable form or expression in reflection, but rather the opposite: "doubly reflected communication" reflects the subject only under the sign of its own impossibility and, hence, the impossibility that it might be reflected in any communication. "Doubly reflected communication" can reflect the subject only away from communication. "Rendering" the "communicator's own relation to the idea" in communication, thus, can amount only to the wrenching of this subject from the idea as its own negativity.

It would appear, then, that there should be two kinds of communication: a subjective communication that ought to be "doubly reflected" and therefore always indirect, and an objective one that, spared the necessity of the "double reflection," is thankfully capable of communicating itself directly. But, Climacus implicitly asks, is direct communication still communication? Can there be such a thing? The answer, quite simply, is no. "Double-reflection is already implicit in communication itself" (*Postscript,* 73). If communication occurs only where subjects are concerned and communication always "reflects" the incommunicable inwardness that masks and expels every subject, then there can be no communication that is not "doubly reflected" and, hence, no communication that is not already "indirect" prior to any claimed "direction." Where there is no subject, there is no communication. "Objective thinking," Climacus explains, "is aware only of itself and is therefore no communication" (*Postscript,* 75–76).[32]

Climacus insists, therefore, that there is no communication that is not always "aware" of more than itself and that does not always give way to something other than itself in communication. Communication, in this sense, always communicates, and it communicates more than one thing, in more than one way. It is always, to use Kierkegaard's terms, direct and indirect at the same time. It always expresses at least the possibility of communication in the content of communication, and it always expresses the impossibility of communication—which breaks communication apart—in the communication of existence as the existence of communication. For this reason, he insists that "inwardness" or "subjective existence" amounts to a "contradiction" in communication and that it is impossible "for this contradiction to become manifest in a direct form" (*Postscript,* 73). Lest one assume too quickly that, of course, communication always relates back to an "inwardness" and "subjectivity" positively available, he explains that it is precisely the "negativity" of communication that turns communication into communication. "Negativity," Climacus says, in a footnote, "transmutes the positive into the negative" (*Postscript*, 76). In doing so, it "transmutes" an assumed direct communication into "an illusion." Or, where this negativity is heeded in communication—in indirect communication, that is—communication appears to be "nothing." The two moments, Climacus suggests, are in fact the same. The negativity of communication that invariably defines communication by dividing it always makes (of) communication (a) nothing. But to say that communication is always nothing is not to say that it is only nothing: it is always also nothing. The negative of communication is that which for every act of speech always defines what is posited in communication against the positing at the same time of what it also is not. In other words, the negativity of communication is always imparted by its finitude. And every communication imparts its own fragmentation at the same time.

The "secret" of communication, which cannot be perceived or communicated as such, is the fragmenting in and of communication that all communication owes to its finitude and the negative with and against which it determines itself. The "secret," this "knowledge which cannot be stated directly, because the essential in this knowledge is the appropriation itself" (*Postscript*, 79), has nothing to do with the content of communication positively understood. Its "secret" *is* its "appropriation," but appropriation here means something more like apportionment, the dividing up of subjectivity into isolated subjects. "Indirect communication," thus, is not necessarily the same as "irony." The negative in communication is not the ironic negativity that always undermines the self-certainty of every assertion. The negative of communication rather refers to the more fundamental finitude of all language in communication to which the merely ironic negativity owes its existence. The finite negativity of communication does not ironically say "maybe/maybe not," but, more fundamentally, "yes—or no." In this way it always says "yes" and "no" at the same time and, hence, suggests that this is not exactly a choice. Whereas Climacus appeared to claim that the difference between "objective" and "subjective" communication, or the difference between "direct" and "indirect" communication, had to do with whether one might recognize the negative in communication, it now becomes clear that the negative is always there with communication, even if one does not recognize it as such. Whether or not you recognize it, we might say, it always recognizes you.

"Indirect communication," therefore, cannot be a rule of communication. It does not amount to the insistence that successful communication is *merely* "indirect," that is, that it follows a more or less circuitous though nonetheless calculable route. Communication cannot be direct because it can be only finite, it can be only fragmentary. Insofar as "communication" concerns the possibility of rendering "truth" in language from an "author" or "producer" to a "recipient," it must account for more than simply the content of expression and more than simply the means of a proper and correct understanding. And because communication is never direct, it can never communicate its own end. It always opens up and suspends in advance the possibility that language might adequately "communicate" any "truth" at all. The "secret," that is, is there with language, not intentionally held in reserve by some devious "authority." In this sense, "Kierkegaard" can be only the "reader" of his own texts, rendering all of his work, in a certain sense, the product of "pseudonyms."

Nonetheless, Kierkegaard, in acknowledging his "authorship," does attempt to give that authorship a certain order—an order, however, that does little to clarify the "careless" and "desultory" quality of the work he can only have "left behind." In *The Point of View of My Work as an Author: A Report to History*, which was written in 1848, several years after the *Postscript*, but not published until 1859, four years after Kierkegaard's death in 1855, he claims that the entirety of his "authorship" has but a single purpose, a single goal. He begins *Point of View* in this way:

> "The contents of this little book affirm, then, what I truly am as an author, that I am and was a religious author, that the whole of my work as an author is related to Christianity, to the problem 'of becoming a Christian,' with a direct or indirect polemic against the monstrous illusion we call Christendom, or against the illusion that in such a land as ours all are Christians of a sort (*Point of View*, 5–6).

The "pseudonymous" texts would thus appear to be "ambiguous" and "duplicitous" for the sole purpose of rendering indirectly the "truth" of the "religious" texts. They would be seen as attempting to make the reader "aware" of this truth, to bring the reader to the point at which this truth might "directly" be communicated. And for this reason, the most conventional of Kierkegaard scholarship refers to this text in order to justify the hierarchical ordering of the "spheres" from the lowest point in the "aesthetic" to the highest in the "religious," which then becomes the paradigm for every "self" directed toward the "truth" of the "religious." Yet, even this normative account raises more questions than it answers. What is a "religious author" as opposed to, say, a "poet"? What is "Christianity" here? Assuming that we know the answers to these questions, there remains the question of perceiving the "truth" of Kierkegaard's authorship in this way. At what point might we believe ourselves to be sufficiently "aware" to perceive this truth "directly"? How do we know? Who tells us?

On the contrary, *Point of View* is no claim of authorship in any direct or conventional sense. It offers no revelation of a hitherto unacknowledged secret; it does not attempt in this way to correct an otherwise misled readership. In it the author never explains or supplies the meaning for texts previously written. "What I write here," Kierkegaard claims, "is for orientation. It is a public attestation; not a defense or apology. In this respect, truly, if in no other, I believe that I have something in common with Socrates" (*Point of View*, 6). "Orientation," that is, is not the same as explanation. And whatever "orientation" he supplies at this point can never overcome the very fragmentariness of all that he has written in such a way as to provide a clear principle of coherence. As this is an "attestation," Kierkegaard can only bear witness to what he has produced and bear witness to the fractured "yes" and "no" of its communication. In spite of all appearance to the contrary, he—like all readers—is in no position to alter or explain his texts in any way. His "orientation" or "direction" here can never render as "direct" what can remain only finite and fragmentary and, hence, always incomplete and indirect. He cannot claim, for example, that his work would simply have been misunderstood and thus "defend" what he has written by explaining its true, proper, and ostensibly direct meaning. Nor can he simply disavow the texts, "apologize" for one or another of them, and hence assert that, properly understood, one would have to dismiss their assertions or ignore them altogether. There is no grand interpretive schema that would make these interpretive gestures more comprehensible than others. Apology and defense can never apologize or defend enough, can never reach those earlier assertions completely enough, to alter them and in this way correct or subdue their possible effects.

So what, we might ask, is the connection to Socrates? Is it actually the case that Kierkegaard seeks to eliminate the difficulty posed by "indirect communication" by substituting a corrective and explanatory "direct" one? Does the assertion "I am and was a religious author" suddenly clarify the difficulty of pseudonymity? Does the sudden explanation of what Kierkegaard is "as an author" amount to the explication of the authorship with regard to who he is as a person? Is it an attempt to integrate the Kierkegaard who writes with the one who lives and breathes—"to poetize," that is, "the personality," as the author A might object? And, with regard to what is explained here, can we assume that we know what a "religious author" is and how the work of such an author would "relate" to

"Christianity"? What, then, is "Christianity"? Who can presume to know in advance what it means to be a "Christian," if, as Kierkegaard says, "Christianity" is a condition of becoming as opposed to being? Is not such a presumption precisely the sin of "Christendom"?[33]

Even here, in this book signed "Kierkegaard," and with the claim that it offers an "orientation" through the whole of his "authorship," Kierkegaard never confuses the coincidence of his own name with that of the signatory and never confuses "authorship" with "authority" (*Point of View*, 75).[34] This distinction is made even more explicitly in a text of 1851, "My Activity as a Writer": "*Without authority* to *call attention* to religion, to Christianity, is the category for my whole activity as an author, integrally regarded. That I was 'without authority' I have from the first moment asserted clearly and repeated as a stereotyped phrase. I regard myself preferably as a *reader* of the books, not as the *author*" (*Point of View*, 151). Yet what "reader" can "call attention" in the work of any "author," for any "author," to its proper "category" without calling into question the propriety of that very authorial gesture in whose name it speaks? Is it not the case that any reader who claims to identify a text's proper category and proper mode of meaning actually obviates and reneges the very principle he or she claims to assert, even in the author's own name? Can even "Christianity" here appear in any other way than already subject to doubt?

Kierkegaard's work "as an author" is unavoidably qualified by the absence of "authority," which is by no means restricted to the pseudonymous works alone, but applies equally to everything he has written. There can be no confusion on this point for Kierkegaard. As an "author" he can only be "a nothing." He is neither part of the text nor part of its meaning, and merely assumes an "accidental" relation to it. As he explains in *Point of View:*

> An author is often merely an *x*, even when his name is signed, something quite impersonal, which addresses itself abstractly, by the aid of printing, to thousands and thousands, while remaining itself unseen and unknown, living a life as hidden, as anonymous, as it is possible for a life to be, in order, presumably, not to reveal the too obvious and striking contradiction between the prodigious means of communication employed and the fact that the author is only a single individual.... But all this, which deserves the most serious attention on the part of one who would study the demoralization of the modern state—all this I cannot enter into more particularly here. (*Point of View*, 45)

Entering into it more particularly would precisely be prohibited. Indeed, the very communicability of language, its repeatability and iterability to "thousands and thousands," prohibits in advance the possibility of completely successful communication in any "direct" sense.[35] The principles of Kierkegaard's own claims about authorship, about the relationship between author and text, and his understanding by way of "indirect communication" of the impossibility of a subject to be made present in and through language, thus continually disrupt his own claims of authorship. The point, however, is neither to decide once and for all to whom these texts properly belong nor to deny them their otherwise proper author or authority—this question is, after all, undecidable, nor would such definitive attribution clarify the problem to any degree—but rather to "call attention" to the space inevitably opened up in the delineation of authorial responsibility. There can exist, in this sense, nothing other than "contradiction" between the "means of communication" and "the fact that the author is only a single individual." As the author A has already suggested, there is an always disproportionate relation between the work and its author. The respective fragmentations of "the single individual" and linguistic expression do not render them wholly communicable among themselves.

Even at the time when Kierkegaard was busily "orienting" his readers toward the singularly "religious" teleology of his entire literary production, he continued to harbor doubts about the feasibility and efficacy of such a project. His doubts were related to the very fact that he was writing in the first place. In a journal entry from 1849, for example, Kierkegaard enumerates the reasons why he cannot issue a personal statement taking responsibility for the pseudonymous works and direct the reader toward their proper understanding:

> About my personal life, and directly, nothing is to be said: (1) because after all I am essentially a poet; but there is always something mysterious in a poet's personality and therefore he must not be presented as, and above all he must not confuse himself with, an authentically ethical character in the most rigorous sense. (2) Insofar as I am a little more than a poet, I am essentially a penitent, but I cannot speak directly of that and therefore also cannot discuss any possible extraordinariness granted me. (3) I cannot guarantee either in the case of myself or in the communication that the emphasis will fall strongly enough upon God. (4) It is an inconsistency in connection with self-denial. (*Journals and Papers,* 139)[36]

That is, as far as any poetic text is concerned—and it is by no means certain that there is any other kind—it is and remains precisely that: a text. There will always be something "mysterious" or enigmatic and unknowable, that will not be presentable with language in the same way that language is present. There is always something unutterable about every linguistic utterance, something unfathomable and unknown. This has only partially to do with the singularity of the author, to the extent that saying something about the author personally amounts to a kind of "self-denial." What is "mysterious" about a text is not the singular "subjectivity" of its author. The problem also concerns more than the reflexive failure of self-representation, indicating nothing more than a blind spot within the field of discourse, outside of which all "communication" would continue in a more or less direct fashion. In each case, the difficulty referred to has to do with the "I" in communication and the possibility that "I" might control the communication. "I am a poet," and thus not just "I"; therefore, "I" cannot be self-identical as "an authentically ethical character"; "I" "cannot speak about any extraordinariness granted me" that both is and is not "my" "extraordinariness"; "I cannot guarantee ... that the emphasis will fall strongly enough upon God," because this might very well be the definition of both "God" and "myself" in communication—that upon which emphasis can never fall enough, adequately, or sufficiently; and, finally, whatever "I" might want to say about "myself" can only amount to "self-denial"; if it could ever be equated with "myself," there would no longer be any "self" there. In each case, furthermore, what is unfathomable about any text is also not accountable in any other form; it has to do with the finite actuality of the text itself and the impossibility that its fragmentary form might ever be overcome with any certainty. If Kierkegaard's orientation for the reader requires a personal statement of responsibility and intention on his part for his texts, it is precisely this requirement that confounds the possibility of its success.

Kierkegaard's pseudonymity is no aberration of language. It is not a trick he is playing as an authoritative author to seduce his readers into one or another belief. Rather it is already inherent in language itself; it is the very requirement of language. Thus, as he explains in another journal entry from 1849, his own work will always remain pseudonymous: "The difficulty with publishing anything about the authorship is and remains that, without my knowing it or knowing it positively, I really have been used, and now for the first time I understand and comprehend the whole—but then I cannot, after all, say: *I*.... But this is my limitation—I am a pseudonym" (*Papirer*, X^2 A 89). Language and subjectivity remain irreconcilable, and this irreconcilability itself exceeds the delimitations of cognition. It cannot itself be known within language, because it is already the effect of language. Language produces the subject as its own excluded outside. To say "I," in this sense, is to be used by language without knowing it. And the moment it appears to be known and understood by the speaking subject, this subject itself would be occluded by the very language it speaks and by which it appears to "know." To say "I" is to be unwittingly deployed by language; and to know of this deployment is to know of the impossibility of saying "I" in the first place. In this sense, "I" cannot not "be used." Every time "I" write, every time "I" seek to communicate or otherwise use language, "I" relinquish any possibility of complete authority; "I" relinquish the possibility that "I" might say "I." This is true, moreover, for the whole of language, not just in those moments when "I" would claim authority over it. Every time "I" use language, language in turn uses "me." Every time "I" speak, "I" cannot help but give myself over to the unknown that language also is.

Conventional appropriations of Kierkegaard, therefore, can never sufficiently account for what Kierkegaard's writing, in its most finite particularity, means by attributing it to the author "Kierkegaard" in the name of his authority. Every attempt to claim authority for him continually exposes the impossibility of such authority and, accordingly, undoes the very meaning ostensibly secured in the name of authority. By separating the author of the work from its authority, Kierkegaard opens up the question of meaning as always the effect of an encounter rather than the result of discovery. To ask about the work's possible meaning in this way is to ask about the possibility of inheritance. What can the work mean—for us? And if, as is true of Kierkegaard's work, its only meaning must already be contained within the fragmentary form through which it is presented, whatever it means can never escape the possibility of its own uncertainty. In a certain way, language as fragment makes us responsible for establishing a significance that cannot be given to another authority. What we inherit by way of Kierkegaard's work, then, looks less like property or "real estate," to borrow a phrase from the *Philosophical Fragments*, than it does like a certain debt or obligation.[37]

So, then, what sort of debt do we inherit with Kierkegaard? A's "fragmentary endeavor" in *Either/Or* offers some suggestion. The digression about the fragment takes place at precisely that moment where the possibility of conventional literary history emerges in the account of the transition from the "ancient" to the "modern." The essay attempts to reconstruct what can be understood now as the radically fragmentary history of "the tragic" in literature. No ordinary account of conventional periodization, the relationship between "ancient" and "modern" tragedy turns into an account of the impossibility of "modern" tragedy ever to free itself from the debt of its ancient precursor. Articulated in terms of the tragic figure of Antigone, we might take A's account of Antigone's modern "rebirth" as one of the peculiarities generated by a certain fragmented heritage.[38]

Immediately following the digression on the fragment, and as if to exemplify what has been more formally articulated in that interruption, A attempts to distinguish "the tragic" in the Greek Antigone from that in the "modern" one that can somehow only be imagined, by way of an inherited "debt." Who Antigone is has everything to do with what she has inherited, a "secret" that possesses her as much as she possesses it. Her "secret" is one of an intergenerational guilt transmitted from Oedipus to his daughter Antigone only under the condition that it cannot as such be known. But this is precisely what makes Antigone Antigone. "She is proud of her secret," A explains, "proud of the fact that she has been selected in a singular way to save the honor and glory of the lineage of Oedipus." Antigone's "secret," however, is nothing other than her mortality, the fact of her death inherited indirectly through her father and his own death. "Our Antigone," as A says of the "modern" one, "although alive, is in another sense dead; her life is quiet and concealed" (*Either/Or* I, 157). Her death, literally and figuratively, is this "quiet" "concealment," the finite end of her own life that she already embodies in her "secret" debt.

That is to say, her end and limit is the very finitude of her existence, beyond which no thought can reach and no word can, directly, communicate. To inherit a secret in this way, however, as "our" Antigone has done, is to inherit the debt of an incommunicable nonknowledge. "Our" Antigone, A tells us, lapsing now into a more general rhetoric of the "individual," inherits her debt "in such a way that the individual participates in his own guilt" (*Either/Or* I, 160). The secret, that is, singles her out—in the same way that communication always also singles out, isolates, and exposes—making her responsible for the inherited guilt as her own. And her responsibility is directly related to the secret's incommunicability: "But for our Antigone it is different. I assume that Oedipus is dead. Even when he was alive, Antigone knew this secret but did not have the courage to confide in her father. By her father's death, she is deprived of the only means of being liberated from her secret." Yet it is not as if she simply chooses not to "confide in her father," as if doing so would absolve her of her guilt rather than generate another. Even while he was alive—alive and dead, as she also was—"she could not confide her sorrow to him, for she did not know if he knew it. . . ." And "knowing it" is precisely the one thing always prohibited, proscribed in advance as the very limit imparted by the finitude of death that marks all of existence and every "human endeavor" in an unknowable and incalculable way. "But," A continues, "our" Antigone is (no) different: "she knows everything; yet within her knowledge there is still an ignorance. . . ." The nonknowledge of her father's guilt/death, to which/whom she owes her own birth/death/rebirth, will always inhabit her existence. "Her father is always in her thoughts, but how—that is the painful secret"—what we might also call the "wound" of her own "negativity" (*Either/Or* I, 161).

Antigone's secret is, in other words, never knowable as such—which, like the very fragmentariness in this endeavor, is not without its effects. Just as the unavoidable finitude of all communication turns every act of communication into its own fragment and, hence, into indirect communication, so, too, "our" Antigone's death in life turns every understanding of her into an understanding of the effective indirection in and of communication. What distinguishes "our" Antigone from the Greek one, A explains, is the way of "our" understanding. At the moment in Sophocles' *Antigone* when she realizes that she is to be buried alive with the fallen brother she has buried already, she exclaims that she is to be delivered "alive to the place of corpses, an alien still,/never at home with the living nor with the dead." A insists that "our" Antigone can say the same thing and "can say this of herself all her life." But because "our" Antigone is already in some sense fragmentary, what she says cannot be understood in the same way. "If our Antigone were to say the same thing, it would be figurative," A explains, "but the figurativeness is the factual pain." What makes figures of language, then, is not that it means something other than what it says. Rather, it is the very facticity of the finite—Antigone's "pain," after all, is the "secret" of her and her father's death in life—which in turn renders every linguistic utterance incomplete within itself. In this way, the "figurativeness" *(uegentlighed)* of discourse is nothing other than its very "factualness" *(egentlighed)*. This "factualness" in turn means that every figurative expression in communication owes its figurality to its finite literality: "when, however, our Antigone feels pain in her solitude, it is only figuratively that she is alone, but for this very reason, only then is her pain truly literal" (*Either/Or* I, 159). Figurality cannot escape its literalness.

Yet, in this careful and paradoxical delineation of an inherited guilt, A never loses sight of his own responsibility—guilt/death. "Our" Antigone, he insists from the very beginning, is the product of his own imagination, his own "productivity." Yet, precisely because of this awareness of responsibility and the paradoxical limit of indebtedness, any attempt to account for the source or principle of "authorship" inevitably confounds the conventional lines of heredity it seeks to secure:

> She is my work, but still her outline is so indistinct, her form so nebulous, that each and every one of you can *forliebe sig* [fall in love] with her and be able to love her in your own way. She is my creation, her thoughts are my thoughts, and yet it is as if in a night of love I had rested with her, as if she in my embrace had confided a deep secret to me.... I put words into her mouth, and yet it seems to me as if I abused her confidence; it seems to me as if she were standing reproachfully behind me, and yet it is the reverse—in her secrecy she becomes ever more visible. She belongs to me, she lawfully belongs to me, and yet at times it is as if I had cunningly crept into her confidence, as if I always had to look behind me for her; and yet it is the reverse, she is always in front of me—only as I lead her forward does she come into existence. (*Either/Or* I, 153)

It is impossible here to tell to whom Antigone actually belongs. Even the "lawful" right of ownership generated by the actual fact of literary production does little to account for the "debt" that production actually entails. Possession is not reducible to signification or significance. For A to claim "our" Antigone as his own is at once to claim the utter impossibility of any ownership in this way at all. The moment he claims Antigone, she claims him. The moment he claims the words he has put into her mouth, she in turn claims his. Thus, she becomes his as he becomes hers in a way that will confound every attempt at proper identification such that she will always be behind him when he looks in front, and always in front of him when he looks behind. The claim of ownership in this way is precisely the acknowledgment of a debt or guilt that can never fully be absolved, and, conversely, the acknowledgment of indebtedness is at once the claim of ownership or responsibility from which one's "authorship" is never entirely free. More than that, however, his "lawful" ownership of her, as the "producing individual," simultaneously gives "her" up to others, although in such a way that one is never entirely free to choose or refuse the debt as given.

Kierkegaard's pseudonymity, then, is not a refusal to assume authority over what he has written. It is the logical effect of every text's finitude. Because of this finitude, pseudonymity also concerns the possibility of reading and understanding what he has written. This possibility, however, is avoided or eliminated only if the task of reading becomes one of discovering or supplying some other principle of authority. On the contrary, the only possibility of reading Kierkegaard exists where the absence of authority is encountered, not corrected. The first reader to recognize pseudonymity in this sense, as the basis for any possible understanding of Kierkegaard, was Franz Kafka. He says as much in a letter from 1918 to his friend Max Brod when he compares Kierkegaard's texts in general to "The Seducer's Diary," the final section of the first volume of *Either/Or:* "They are not unequivocal, and even when he later develops a kind of unequivocality, even this too is only part of his chaos of spirit, melancholy and faith.... Besides, his compromising books are pseudonymous and pseudonymous nearly to the core. They can, in their totality and in spite of their contents, just as well be understood as the misleading letters of the seducer, written behind clouds."[39] Their meanings are not, as Kafka insists, unequivocal, because the same fragmentariness and incompletion that removes any illusion of the author's authority also refuses to grant authority to a single principle of coherent organization. The texts might always mean something else. This does not mean, however, that Kafka would therefore dismiss them. On the contrary, it is acknowledgment that their "cloudiness" is part of what they are.

If Kierkegaard's work exhibits anything, it is that language, because it is inescapably bound to its finite occurrence, can be understood only as fragmentary and that anything understood as meaning can be construed only as the very effects of this fragmentariness rather than as its resolution. At no point is it possible to offer an ultimate, coherent rationalization as its singular and necessary meaning. Any claim of authority, either Kierkegaard's own or another's, can ultimately demonstrate only the impossibility in every instance of precisely this form of authority.

Because it always insists upon its own fragmentation, Kierkegaard's work, in all its pseudonymity, will always elude any commentator's attempt at coherent unification. Any commentary that presents itself in this way can always be shown to have missed the finitude and, hence, the incompletion, that inevitably characterize and qualify each of Kierkegaard's texts. In this way, Kierkegaard's work will continue to resist any canonical and conventional assessment. Such an assessment, as canon or convention, depends upon a universalization, as rule or agreement, that Kierkegaard's work continually calls into question and cannot therefore support. Its fragmentation, thus, will thwart any attempt to establish a conventional understanding in any traditional sense so that it might be transmitted without any transmutation. It cannot be passed on, as Climacus says, "like real estate." Because it is fragmentary, it cannot as such be passed on; it resists.

That is not to say, however, that Kierkegaard cannot have had any significant effect upon subsequent thought. Simply, such influence can only have occurred where the work's fragmentation has been acknowledged and encountered rather than resolved and, hence, avoided. Given Kierkegaard's own suggestion that the meaning of a work might appear first in the "productivity" of others, we have to look beyond the realm of scholarly commentary. We must shift our attention, that is, from "secondary" to "primary" literature.

This book is not an attempt to provide an exhaustive account of those influenced by Kierkegaard in the twentieth century. On the contrary, it argues that any attempt to determine the significance of his work for later thought must in some way account for its fragmentation rather than overcome it, and understand this fragmentation as the very means of its transmission at the same time. Such an understanding, we might also argue, first became possible with the developments in literature and philosophy in the early twentieth century. At the same time that the conventional Kierkegaard was solidified through the efforts of Haecker, Schrempf, Brandes, and the like, another Kierkegaard began to take shape in the work of Franz Kafka, Rainer Maria Rilke, Walter Benjamin, and Theodor W. Adorno. For the first time, his work's insurmountable finitude was identified as the source of both its greatest significance and its greatest difficulty. In his first published book, *Kierkegaard: Construction of the Aesthetic*, Adorno argued that it is Kierkegaard's insistence upon the inescapability of the finite that saves him from disappearing into the universalizations of speculative idealism. For Kafka, the finite particularity isolated in Kierkegaard's work causes every normative conceptual or ethical presupposition to founder. For Rilke, on the other hand, it is the "seriousness of death" that fragments and thus transforms all of existence. In this way, the reflections of these early twentieth-century authors force us to reconsider the function and significance of what have become commonly accepted Kierkegaardian motifs—existence, indirect communication, death, and anxiety. The readings of Adorno, Kafka, and Rilke in this book, then, alternate with rereadings of the Kierkegaardian texts to which they refer.

The point here is not to articulate lines of causality or "influence" more generally. Rather, accepting an already fragmentary relationship to Kierkegaard on the part of these authors, we must investigate the terms of the appropriation in their most particular appearance. We must ask how that interest affects our understanding of their work, particularly if understanding in this instance resists direct conceptualization. What does it mean to understand their work by way of Kierkegaard as the continued or renewed productivity of Kierkegaard's own "fragmentary prodigality"? And what, in turn, does it mean for our understanding of Kierkegaard that his work might engender such literary permutations? If the authors we thus discover are less familiar than their names lead us to believe (Rilke, Kafka, Adorno, Kierkegaard), that is precisely the point. We cannot know their work before we read it.

The grounds for the necessity of such intervention have already been clearly, if negatively, laid in Kierkegaard's more canonical reception. While tracing out and ordering the voluminous responses to Kierkegaard's work, studies of Kierkegaard's "influence" almost invariably avoid Adorno's book on Kierkegaard, though it clearly falls within their general historical trajectories and, if disliked, might easily be dismissed as yet another personal reaction to Kierkegaard.[40] Not just a mere oversight, it seems that something more critical is at stake. At the very least, returning to the general, guiding question of whether Kierkegaard's work would be properly understood as philosophical, theological, or literary, Adorno's book serves to remind these commentators that this question misses the point. To claim the works for one or another genre— that is, to claim in advance that there is a predetermined way in which these texts must be understood—is to miss what Adorno calls their "truth content." Claims of their purely philosophical intent presuppose a kind of speculative universalization that the works themselves cannot support. And claims of the purely literary quality of the texts refuse in advance their rigorous and (perhaps more disturbing) conceptual challenge to philosophical thinking in favor of the easy pleasure of their "poetry."

Perhaps of even greater pertinence, however, is Adorno's more general argument against idealist interpretations of subjectivity and the self in Kierkegaard. According to Adorno, the focus on concepts of the self in Kierkegaard remains caught within idealist conceptions of totality. In this view, Adorno claims that the "self" in Kierkegaard is nothing other than the interiorization—the turning inward—of Hegel's philosophy of history. Yet, what prevents Kierkegaard from disappearing entirely in pure idealism is his conception of the aesthetic not as a "sphere" but as a radically discontinuous dimension of actuality that pervades all of his philosophy and disrupts every systematic ordering of the "spheres" themselves. More specifically, the aesthetic emerges in Kierkegaard's discussions of language not as the realm of free play and dissociation now prized by those commentators who would claim Kierkegaard as a kind of protopostmodernist, but precisely as the condition of finitude upon which meaning is infinitely founded. To read Kierkegaard, in Adorno's view, is to encounter the aesthetic finitude of language. And to read language's finitude is to read its figures and allegories not metaphorically, but literally.

Like studies of Kierkegaard himself, studies of his "influence" are abundant. Yet each of these, in one way or another, assumes that "what" Kierkegaard means can simply be separated from the occurrence of his "influence," so that what "belongs" to Kierkegaard can thus be "identified" in Heidegger, Sartre, existentialism, Kafka, Nietzsche, Wittgenstein, postmodernism, and so on. In this way, studies of his influence inevitably assume that we already know what Kierkegaard means and that it remains simply to apply that meaning to any one of a number of subsequent authors to secure the relevant points of agreement. Yet, if that connection is to be formative in a material way for developments in later thought, to assume that the canonical Kierkegaard of the late twentieth century is the one and only Kierkegaard ever read inevitably misses the connection altogether. If we assume, as most commentators happily do, that there is a connection and that we already know what Kierkegaard means, then we can only rediscover the same Kierkegaard we already assume we know. Any discussion of his "influence" in this instance lapses into tautology; we find only what we believe we already know, and thereby contribute yet another external support to the growing conventionality of Kierkegaard reception.

In turn, the conventional assessment can only mask and obscure the particularity of any of the authors identified as having been "influenced" by his work. Kafka, Ibsen, Rilke, Heidegger, Wittgenstein, Sartre, and so on—they all become simply imposters standing in for the one, true Kierkegaard.[41] We want to know "how the book turns out," as Kierkegaard's Johannes de Silentio complains in *Fear and Trembling*.[42] And then we let the result retrospectively determine all prior significance. Such an approach, as Kierkegaard continually reminds us, is "backwards," offering at best a caricature of understanding.

Before we can begin, and without knowing how the book turns out, we must ask ourselves one question, the same question Adorno posed with his *Kierkegaard*: What exactly does one read when one reads Kierkegaard? And, given the absence of any secure "authority," what does it mean *to read*?

2

Learning to Read: Adorno, Kierkegaard, and *Konstruktion*

If the difficulty of Kierkegaard's work concerns the extent to which it both articulates and is founded upon the particular strictures of an always only finite language, then any attempt to understand his work might best begin with the attempt to define the relationship between the linguistic expressions of the work and the philosophical ideas they are said to represent. In this sense, Theodor Adorno's work in philosophy proves doubly useful, not only for his early interest in Kierkegaard, but also because his approach toward philosophy is related explicitly to the understanding of language. "All philosophical critique," he proclaims in his "Thesen über die Sprache des Philosophen" (Theses on the language of the philosopher), "is possible today as language critique *[Sprachkritik]*" (p. 369).

This essay is one of several early texts in which Adorno attempts to articulate a more programmatic assessment of the task of philosophy that he would attempt to pursue in his own work.[1] Yet it is by no means clear what, precisely, Adorno's assertion means in terms of a philosophical project. That is, what does it mean to pursue "language critique" as opposed to a more formal "philosophical critique"? What exactly does one pursue in this instance? What does philosophy have to do with language? What is language for philosophy? Is there a difference between "philosophical critique" and "language critique"? Yes—and no. If "philosophical critique" is possible as "language critique," then there must, at the same time, be a separation between the two forms of "critique" such that the ideas of philosophers can be seen as distinct from their merely linguistic presentation, and, within this separation, there must be an intersection between the two realms such that the ideas at no time exist apart from their expression and, moreover, their expression in some sense determines in advance the adequacy of the ideas they express. Philosophy and language, then, must follow different but related grammars. To speak here of "ideas," however, is already to assume that these constitute the proper object of philosophical work and that they are available in and through philosophy, that philosophy can, in some sense, lay them bare. And yet, it is by no means certain that philosophy has such an object, by no means certain that one can grasp it by means of its concepts. On the contrary, what philosophy means as philosophy, its language must also mean as language. Or rather, and perhaps more pertinently, what language means as language, it must also mean as philosophy. If philosophical critique and linguistic critique are deemed coextensive, language must itself be philosophy, not just philosophical.

There is perhaps no better place to begin exploring these questions than in the work of the one "philosopher" who took seriously the possibility that different languages mean different things, whose work was presented through myriad pseudonymous "authors," in innumerable "poetic" forms, ranging from "philosophy" to literature, theology, and beyond—in the work, that is, of one Søren Kierkegaard. It should come as no surprise, then, that Adorno, in light of his declaration that philosophical critique is the critique of language, began his own career as a philosopher with a book on Kierkegaard, on which he was working when he wrote the "Theses on the Language of the Philosopher." Adorno's first published book, *Kierkegaard: Construction of the Aesthetic,* written in 1929 for his habilitation and published, after extensive revision, in 1933, is, in this regard, exemplary. If nothing else, the book is the very execution of Adorno's proclamation. And yet, it is also more than this, for what Adorno presents as a reading of Kierkegaard is indeed first and foremost a reading of Kierkegaard and not some other philosopher. To this extent, it is also a testament to the importance of Kierkegaard's work for Adorno's understanding of philosophy.[2]

When Adorno began to work on Kierkegaard in the late 1920s for his habilitation, after having withdrawn an earlier manuscript on Kant and Freud that had been intended for the same purpose, he began to work in relatively uncharted territory. Kierkegaard had only recently been translated into German, there was little in the way of a critical assessment of his work, and the criticism that was available tended to appropriate directly and uncritically Kierkegaard's claims about his "authorship."[3] Moreover, the work on Kierkegaard in German, produced under the assumption that Kierkegaard was a "philosopher" and not an author of literature, tended to define his philosophy in the most "scientifically" complete and systematic way possible, no simple task indeed. Hence, most discussions of his work developed explications of a "doctrine" of "spheres" or "stages of existence"—aesthetic, ethical, religious—that are organized systematically in a hierarchical order, from the "lowest" (aesthetic) stage to the "highest" (religious) stage of existence. Such uncritical assimilation, however, inevitably misses its mark. Unable to produce a schematic totalization of Kierkegaard's work solely in terms of its "systematic" deployment, each of these early works lapsed into affirmation of Kierkegaard's "genius" in a merely stylistic sense. Kierkegaard was, as he himself attested, a "poet." To take this affirmation as the critical evaluation of the work's proper categorization, however, is to abandon the responsibility to pursue a critical assessment of the works as "philosophy."

Adorno took this as his point of departure in the opening sentence of his book on Kierkegaard: "Whenever one strives to grasp philosophical texts as poetry, one misses their truth content *[Wahrheitsgehalt]*."[4] That is, to read "philosophy" merely as "poetry" is already to circumvent and dislocate the possibility of reading—reading seriously. What, then, does it mean *to read*? Adorno does not intend to establish an absolute distinction between the genres of art and philosophy, one that would allow the true assessment of their respective purposes, functions, uses, meanings, and so on, as if, simply by knowing whether a given text was intended to be either poetry or philosophy, one would then be able to formulate an adequate understanding of its assumed philosophical meaning or simply be able to take pleasure in its merely poetic artistry.[5] The point for Adorno is that this distinction cannot be drawn, or at least cannot be drawn to this conclusion. There is no point at which one would be able to delimit and know a work's philosophical intentions, beyond which its expressions would be free of any adherence to philosophical rigor.

The moment one identifies Kierkegaard's "genius" as "poetic," one forgets that his work, whether in spite of or because of its "poetry," continues to serve a philosophical purpose, to serve as or rather *to be* philosophy. Adorno treats the common appraisal of Kierkegaard's "poetry" rather as an indication of the failure on the part of his readers to understand it as philosophy. What the work means, however, is by no means reducible to its said philosophical intentions. As opposed to those interpretations that cease to understand the work the moment they admire the poetry, Adorno insists that the work's meaning is in no way contingent upon its categorization within a given genre; even if it is poetry, one still has an obligation to read it and to understand it. Because one cannot know in advance what a text means, one accordingly cannot attribute it to one genre as opposed to another or make its meaning contingent upon classification by genre. The difficulty, however, is not one of correctly identifying a text's genre, but rather of always understanding the meaning of a text prior to developing any concern for genre. To read the "writings" of philosophers as "poems" instead of "philosophy" is to miss their "truth content" *(Wahrheitsgehalt)*. This "truth content" is directly related to their capacity not merely as philosophy, but, moreover, as "writing" *(Schrift)*. Philosophy is in search of "truth," and its only access to truth is through words, through concepts. There must be a relation between the words one uses and the truth one hopes to find or reveal. Adorno continues without interruption: "The law of philosophy's form *[das Formgesetz der Philosophie]* demands the interpretation of the real in adequate connection to concepts *[im stimmigen Zusammenhang der Begriffe]*" (*Kierkegaard,* 9; 3). However, Adorno does not exactly say that philosophy refers to the truth per se in an absolute sense, nor does he identify "truth content" as "reality" *(das Wirkliche)*. The "law of philosophy's form" is not one of "reference." Rather, he insists that philosophy is primarily "interpretation" *(Deutung)* and that only as interpretation is it concerned about the relationship between "reality" and "concepts." Thus, the only way to assess the "truth value" of any philosophy is through the reality presented in "adequate connection" with its concepts. The praise of poetry, whatever that might mean, would separate the word from its "reality" and would disrupt the "connection."

So what is this "adequate connection"? The coincidence or concurrence Adorno seeks between philosophical texts and their "truth content" is one of simultaneity, in which concepts *(Begriffe)* and the reality *(das Wirkliche)* they would interpret are irreducible to one another and yet, at the same time, inseparable from one another. The "real" does not amount to the "meaning" of the concept, nor is it the supplementary completion of the concept that would make it whole. Philosophy, and therefore also its "truth," is neither determined nor guaranteed either by reference to some other conceptual order or by the supposition of its systematic totality. It is rather opposed to any such ideally or referentially construed meaning, but nonetheless ineradicable in relation to "truth," the truth of the "concepts." Adorno continues:

> Neither the declaration of the thinker's subjectivity nor the pure coherence of the work determines its character as philosophy, but only: if something real *[Wirkliches]* entered into its concepts, proves itself in them, and comprehensibly grounds them. That is contradicted by the conception of philosophy as poetry. By tearing philosophy away from the standard of the real, it deprives philosophical work of adequate critique. Only in communication with the critical spirit is it able to be tested historically. (*Kierkegaard*, 9; 3)

To read philosophy as poetry would be to read the text as self-contained and complete within itself, without need of anything other than itself. On the other hand, in Adorno's view what makes philosophy philosophy is the openness of its terms to another "reality," irreducible to conceptual form. The "truth content" of philosophy is directly related to the extent to which this other "reality" *(Wirkliches)*—that is, neither the "truth content" itself nor its expression as concept alone—enters into and grounds the concept. What, exactly, we must ask, is this "reality" if it is expressible neither as truth nor as conceptual idea? How does it show itself? Does it show itself? If it is available—and this is by no means certain—it is available, Adorno insists, only through "critique." Adorno is specific here: only in "communication" with "critique" can reality be fathomed "historically"—as an adverb, take note, not "history," as a noun. "Communication" with "reality" is communication in history, not with history.

What, first of all, is "critique" if it is a form of "communication"? If the "law of philosophy's form" is also a law of "communication," in accordance with what rules does it operate? What, we must continually ask, is philosophy? It is, first of all, not a science. The rules of philosophy are never as such determinable; nor could they, once specified in a particular occurrence, continue to function prescriptively with respect to an as yet unknown object. Adorno distinguished philosophy from science in "Die Aktualität der Philosophie" (The Actuality of Philosophy) (1931), and retained this distinction virtually throughout his life. Science is not distinguished from philosophy under the assumption that philosophy concerns a "higher degree of generality *[Allgemeinheit]*." That is, "science" *(Wissenschaft)* and "philosophy" are not two different versions of the same thing—the same, in this instance, generalizability. Rather:

> The central difference lies in that science regards its results, at least its ultimate and deepest results, as whole and indissoluble, whereas philosophy conceives the first result it encounters already as a sign *[Zeichen]* which it must decipher. Simply put: the idea of science is research *[Forschung]*, that of philosophy, interpretation *[Deutung]*. Here the great and perhaps eternal paradox remains: that philosophy must always, again and again, proceed

> interpretatively and with the demand for truth, without ever possessing a certain key of interpretation; that it is given nothing more than fleeting, disappearing hints in the enigmatic figures of being and in their marvelous intricacies. ("Actualität," 334; "Actuality," 126)

Science, in this sense, is still focused by a desired generalizability that determines in advance its objects as pure objects, in some sense, "whole and indissoluble" *(unauflöslich und in sich ruhend)*, unaffected by and sealed off from their contextual situations. In opposition to this, the openness toward "reality" that defines the philosophical task assumes that its objects are "signs" *(Zeichen)*. "Signs," however, are not in and of themselves meaningful, but must be interpreted. Their meaning is neither given nor permanent. What is "given" is nothing other than the signs themselves out of which the understanding will still have to be constructed through the interpretation of their "reality." And, given that the elements at hand are irredeemably temporal, this "construction" can only begin, and begin again from scratch.

That is, "interpretation" cannot *result* in "sense." Neither, Adorno claims, is such a meaning available or "given," nor is "reality" *(Wirklichkeit)* ever to be "justified" *(rechtfertigt)* as "meaningful" *(Sinnvoll)*. "Every such justification of what exists *[des Seienden]* is prohibited by the friability *[Brüchigkeit]* in being itself" ("Actualität," 334; "Actuality," 126). The task, then, is not to correct the "Brüchigkeit" or to restore to it some sense of completeness, but to read and interpret in this open-ended friability a kind of "truth" *(Wahrheit)*. In their transience and meaninglessness, the elements of reality are not subject to systematic order. On the contrary, these elements remain forever incomplete and uncompletable, subject to unpredictable alteration—which necessarily confronts the task of philosophical "interpretation" with the possibility of contradiction, the possibility of its own aporetic paradox. The task is to understand what they mean in their own reality, not what they can be made to mean through the subsumption to or the deduction of another order, another system. Philosophy must learn to read: "The text which philosophy is given to read is incomplete, contradictory and fragmentary, and much of it may be consigned to blind demonics; yes, perhaps reading is precisely our task . . ." ("Actualität," 334; "Actuality," 126).

We return to the point from which we began, to the "Theses on the Language of the Philosopher":

> All philosophical critique is possible today as language critique. This language critique is not merely concerned with the "adequation" of words to things, but rather equally the status *[Stand]* of words in themselves; it must

> be asked of words to what extent they are capable of bearing the intentions attributed to them, to what extent their power is historically extinguished, to what extent it might be preserved in configuration. The criterion for this is essentially the *aesthetic* dignity of words. Noticeably powerless are words which, in the linguistic work of art—which alone preserves the unity of word and matter *[Sache]* over against the scientific duality—are rightly subjected to aesthetic critique, while hitherto having enjoyed unimpaired philosophical favor. Thus results the constitutive meaning of aesthetic critique for cognition. Accordingly: true art today no longer has the character of the metaphysical, but immediately turns toward the presentation of real contents of being. The growing meaning of philosophical language critique can be formulated as the beginning convergence of art and knowledge. ("Thesen," 369–70)

One might suspect, however, that this "growing meaning" and this "beginning convergence" describe only the momentary asymptotic relationship, not necessarily the possibility or the inevitability of its achievement. Adorno is concerned with the relationship between aesthetics and "cognition," not with the dissolution of one into the other. This, however, as already acknowledged, presents philosophy with the paradoxical task of seeking "meaning" where none can be permanently secured. The paradoxical task of philosophical interpretation has to do with the simultaneous concern for the "adequation" of words and things and for the status of the words in themselves, in their "aesthetic dignity." Philosophical critique as the critique of language has continually as its task the formation of meaning with and out of the very elements that, in and of themselves, resist or even destroy the possibility of meaning in an ideal—or, as Adorno writes here, "metaphysical"—sense. For this reason, then, Adorno insists that, as far as philosophy is concerned, there can be no "scientific duality" that would unite a word with its (intended) meaning.

Philosophy is always presented with only one thing: the word. This is not to say that the word dissolves into the one thing it would mean. On the contrary, the word in its "aesthetic dignity" is always more or less than one thing. As things, words have an existence irreducible to, if not wholly separate from, what they mean. As existent, they are also historical. This is the material given to critical evaluation. The aesthetic presentation of the word itself, in turning toward the "presentation of real contents of being," disrupts the intended completion of the word in its intended meaning. To what extent, now, Adorno asks, can words carry their intended meaning? Furthermore, given their historical situation—their situatedness—to what extent has their "power" been effaced or even obliterated *(erloschen)* by history? And, as opposed to this, to what extent can that power be preserved? Far from stabilizing any intended meaning, words, in their "aesthetic dignity," open up that meaning into temporality, into a temporal existence, in which this meaning can no longer be guaranteed by any reference to an eternal value, an eternal truth. If this is to be secured at all, according to Adorno, then it can be secured only in "configuration." So what, now, is the "power" of words? And what does this have to do with figuration?

Adorno's insistence that philosophical critique as "language critique" is concerned with the "aesthetic dignity" of words and his repeated insistence that this "language critique" is "aesthetic critique" are directly related to the work on Kierkegaard. If the "aesthetic dignity" of words extends beyond their intended meanings and their intended representation, then the concern for the aesthetic itself is more than merely categorical. If aesthetics is concerned with appearances, and not with what might grant appearances a certain value or meaning, then aesthetics itself cannot be described as one category unified within itself. In his reading of Kierkegaard, Adorno traces out the multifarious and ultimately inconsistent and contradictory usage of aesthetics. Hardly grounds for condemnation pure and simple, it is in the very discrepancies of its various appearances and its inability to be contained within any single, unifying category that Adorno finds the Kierkegaardian aesthetic most liberating.

Adorno begins more or less methodically by isolating and summarizing three apparently distinct ways in which Kierkegaard uses the term "aesthetics." First, it describes the realm of art criticism in the discussions of tragedy and comedy in *Either/Or.* Second, "the aesthetic" describes the first of the three "stages" of existence. In comparison to "the ethical," Kierkegaard explains in volume II of *Either/Or* that "the aesthetic in a person is that whereby he immediately is what he is; the ethical is that whereby he becomes what he becomes. Whoever lives in and of the aesthetic, by and for the aesthetic, lives aesthetically" (*Kierkegaard,* 25; 14–15).[6]

Given the already divergent uses of the term "aesthetics," in Adorno's reading the term becomes most productive in Kierkegaard's work when it carries these inconsistencies already within itself. Here, admittedly, Adorno reaches "beyond conventional Kierkegaardian usage" (*Kierkegaard,* 25; 15). Not surprisingly, for Adorno this inconsistent use of the term appears explicitly in relation to language. Located exclusively in the *Concluding Unscientific Postscript,* aesthetics is "related to the form of subjective communication and justifies Kierkegaard's concept of existence" (*Kierkegaard,* 25; 15). "Communication," in Kierkegaard's sense and as Adorno adopts it from Kierkegaard, has to do with the ways in which "subjective existence" appears.[7] This is what makes "communication" aesthetic and what ultimately—in spite of Adorno's belief to the contrary—separates expression from pure formalism.[8]

Kierkegaard's understanding of "communication," in ways related to Adorno's own understanding of language, is not restricted to what words mean. Rather, it must also contend with the particular situation in which the words occur. Adorno cites, for example, the following passage from Kierkegaard's *Postscript*, which describes the "double reflection" inherent in communication. Here Adorno is most interested in what makes "communication" "art":

> The "double reflection" of subjective thought, namely of the thing and the inwardness of the thinker, must "also express itself in the form of communication. That is to say, the subjective thinker will from the beginning have his attention called to the requirement that this form should embody artistically as much of reflection as he himself has when existing in his thought. In an artistic manner, please note, for the secret does not lie in a direct assertion of the double reflection; such a direct expression of it is precisely a contradiction." Accordingly, aesthetic means precisely the way in which interiority appears as the How of subjective communication.... (*Kierkegaard*, 25–26; 15)[9]

Communication is first and foremost a work of art; it is the "artistic" expression of "interiority." The "secret," as Kierkegaard describes it here, is that this "communication" cannot be direct. It concerns more than simply finding a merely adequate "form" in relation to both the "matter" or "issue" and the "subjective inwardness," in which they would, directly, be communicated. As Adorno himself has already noted, communication for Kierkegaard is not just about the presentation of interiority; rather, "the dialectic among the things *[in den Sachen]* is for him simultaneously the dialectic of communication" (*Kierkegaard*, 11; 4). To express directly what is by definition necessarily indirect is clearly a contradiction. There is, however, no point at which communication, even at its most indirect and circuitous, would not run the risk of contradiction, no point at which a "form" of indirection could be found that would render the "double reflection" on the "thing" and in the "interiority" directly apparent. "Inwardness," even as Adorno describes it here, is nothing other than a mode of appearance; it is not the "content" of any communication. Aesthetics, as the "How of communication," is nothing other than what makes communication communicate, what makes art work.

Adorno's interest in the aesthetic in Kierkegaard is twofold. First, the aesthetic, because of its lack of predetermining, formal organization, is the place of contradiction, the place where contradiction is not alread precluded:

"Kierkegaard's category of the aesthetic comprises disparate manners of usage. It can no more be added up out of them than won from their abstract resistance" (*Kierkegaard,* 26; 15). Second, because there is no point at which one could summarize the aesthetic, there is accordingly no point at which one might leave it behind. Thus, as Adorno explains later, the fractures and contradictions that occur as aesthetic are everywhere ineradicable, even in the "higher" sphere of the ethical: "Hence the friable ambiguousness of the term 'aesthetic' in Kierkegaard; hence the discontinuity of the aesthetic itself preserved under the 'ethical' aspect" (*Kierkegaard,* 95–96; 65).

In *Kierkegaard: Construction of the Aesthetic,* philosophy, in order to yield the truth Adorno seeks, must contend with the *literal* presentations of a nondiscursive "reality." Adorno separates figuration from the presentation of intentional meaning. Figuration, he says, is "expression" *(Ausdruck),* not content. To understand Kierkegaard, Adorno insists, is to understand the necessity of "language critique" for philosophy—not because Kierkegaard's work is especially in need of straightening out, but rather because Kierkegaard's work itself depends upon the expressive capacity of words beyond desired intentions. Kierkegaard, now, teaches Adorno something about reading. By insisting on maintaining the discontinuities of the aesthetic throughout Kierkegaard's philosophy, Adorno stands in opposition to the systematic organization of Kierkegaard's work in accordance with the differences between the pseudonymous authors and the systematic organization of the "spheres." Adorno insists simply that Kierkegaard's philosophy cannot be read schematically, either as oriented through the presupposed constancy of Kierkegaard's pseudonyms or in terms of a rigid and deterministic progression through a strictly hierarchical "system" of "spheres." Rather, the very expression of the philosophical "system" continually ungrounds the otherwise "deceptive consistency of the pseudonyms." To take the desired constancy of either as constitutive of the philosophy as a whole rather than as clarifying and explicating Kierkegaard's philosophy "blocks the way" (*Kierkegaard,* 20; 11) and obstructs the very purpose of that philosophy.

Adorno, on the contrary, pits one against the other: "Critique must first understand the expressions of the pseudonyms according to their philosophical construction; it must understand how this construction may be demonstrated in every instance as a dominating schema." Critique not only allows for the comparative evaluation of the separate pseudonymous claims against the whole of their philosophical construction, but also enacts the separation of the claims from the construction. The understanding of the construction for critique is possible only on the basis of its own destructibility. The separation of the "expressions" from the "schema" does not result in the deduction of the construction from the claims that would constitute it, but rather makes possible the disclosure of the "concrete" "secrets" of the claims themselves: "What the pseudonyms then say beyond what is imparted by the philosophical schema: its secret and concrete core is subjected to interpretation in the literalness *[Wörtlichkeit]* of communication" (*Kierkegaard,* 20; 11). And, insofar as the pseudonyms do speak, they will always say more. Words are excess. In the literal appearance is given both the coincidence and the separation of the desired philosophical intention and its concrete representation. Accordingly, something always remains beyond intentional or conceptual content, something not exactly identifiable as "truth," but rather the "secret kernel" at the heart of its presentation, which, itself unknowable in terms of a conceptually ordered schema, always resists and disrupts conceptual representation, the very "schema" that would otherwise conceal it.

The "power" of words to resist systematic representation, no matter how carefully or artfully the words might be chosen, lies in their literal unpredictability: "The selection of words, whose stereotypical (if not always planned) return indicates contents which even the deepest intentions of the dialectical method would rather hide than expose." Thus, it is in the repetition and return *(Wiederkehr)* presented in the "Wörtlichkeit" of the word, its "literalness," that difference appears. And because of this difference between the literal and the figurative meanings of linguistic expressions, Adorno maintains that the limit of the system is to be found not within the intelligible coherence of the "system" itself—if such a thing were as such accessible—but within the limits of its expression, the limit as expression:

> The individual utterances of the pseudonyms are to be grasped literally *[wörtlich]* and within their respective "sphero-logical" construction: as expressions of the aesthetic, ethical, religious form of existence which at the same time are limited by their literalness. Faced with the exegete Kierkegaard, exegesis is concerned first of all with metaphor. While Kierkegaard's metaphorically intended objects are to be explicated in terms of the logic of the "spheres," the literal metaphors acquire independence *[Selbständigkeit].* (*Kierkegaard,* 21; 12)

Even as "metaphor" continues to function in a normalizing sense as the representative image of a "logic" otherwise not presentable, the representation, which is also presentation, refuses the reduction solely to the logic it represents or embodies. In this respect, the limit to the logical system is always the limit of its own representability. The moment of metaphorical representation is simultaneously the end of metaphorical representation.

In that moment, the word of metaphor is nothing other than a word, an expression—nothing other than "literal" *(wörtlich).*

Yet Adorno, for reasons still unclear, insists on maintaining the concept of metaphor—or insists at least on keeping this word. Insofar as the recognition that literal expression remains irreducible to and ultimately unaccountable for metaphorical intention, language itself, even as expression, remains figural, but figural in another way. Figuration, Adorno explains in "The Actuality of Philosophy," is not produced solely for the expression of philosophical ideas. On the contrary, figuration first becomes figuration in interpretation:

> True philosophical interpretation is not concerned with a meaning *[Sinn]* lying already and continually behind the question, but rather illuminates it [the question] suddenly and momentarily and destroys it at the same time. And just as the solutions to riddles are formed when the singular and disparate elements of the question are brought into different arrangements until they crystalize into a figure from which the answer leaps out while the question itself disappears—so too must philosophy bring its elements into alternating constellations, or, to use a less astrological and more current scientific expression, in alternating experimental arrangements, until they chance upon a figure which becomes legible as an answer, while at the same time the question disappears. ("Actualität," 335; "Actuality," 127.)

What distinguishes one kind of "interpretation" from another is its relation to the possible (metaphorical) expression of ideas. Any "interpretation" that is based on the assumption that the literal expression is the tangible means for the presentation of an otherwise intangible idea refuses to acknowledge the literal figurality of the word. To take this literality seriously, however, is to recognize that ideas themselves can be only as ephemeral as the words that are used to present them. There can be no constant "sense" that guarantees the meaning of a word. There is still meaning, still "*Sinn*"; it simply cannot be secured. Philosophical interpretation can "illuminate" it only "suddenly" and "momentarily" while at the same time and just as suddenly "consuming" words, exhausting them and using them up.[10] Yet "*Sinn*" as such is apparently not available in a singular relationship with words. If it is available, it is available only in its "literal" figural presentation. "Figures" in this sense are primarily about relationships among words, not about one thing representing another. "Figures," like the "answers to riddles," appear in the constantly changing formations of "constellations." Their legibility as figures amounts simultaneously to the disappearance of the "riddle." Figuration is simultaneously its own disfiguration.

The disappearance of the "riddle" does not unfold into linear, chronological progression, as if one moment there would be a question, then next maybe a "figure" that would answer the question followed by the disappearance of the question altogether. The "riddle" is itself already the figure of its own solution; and, accordingly, it is already, if it is a "figure," the means of its own dissolution. Articulating again the opposition between "research" *(Forschung)* and "interpretation" *(Deutung)*, Adorno insists, even much later in the *Negative Dialectics* (1966), that what separates the one from the other is the simultaneity of question and answer in the figural construction: "[I]n philosophy, the authentic question almost always contains its answer in a certain way. It does not know, as does scientific research, a first-and-then of question and answer. It must model its question on what it has experienced so that it may be received. Its answers are not given, made, created: the transparent, unfolded question turns into them."[11] The figural displacement from question to answer, no longer conceivable in terms of linear progression, occurs in the "moment"—"momentarily," as Adorno has already described in "The Actuality of Philosophy." This event, this occurrence, is marked by the concurrence of conflicting temporalities. If the answer is already contained "in a certain way" in the question and this relationship is, strictly speaking, not chronological but simultaneous, the answer also cannot be "contained" in the question as its "secret core" that is in need only of explication in order to become explicit. This "moment," then, rather than securing a durable and persistent "answer," appears as the collapse into temporal dissolution.[12] The answer is simultaneously the question in its configuration, and must, at the same time, be the destruction of the question. In the figure, the question is also its own self-negating destruction.

If, for Adorno, philosophy as philosophy is always philosophy as language, philosophy occurs only in its own disintegration. Returning to the "Theses on the Language of the Philosopher," Adorno insists that words themselves are already words in disintegration. They are not simply isolated among themselves from one another, but are already disintegrating, decaying, crumbling, in themselves: "Today the philosopher is confronted with a fallen language. His material is the ruins of words to which history binds him; his only freedom is the possibility of their configuration toward the force of truth in them. It is just as impossible to think a word as given as it is to discover a word" ("Thesen," 368–69). Language is neither given, purely and simply, nor does it lend itself to the spontaneous "discovery" of new words, free of historical determinations. It is, moreover, "material" for philosophy, and as such is necessarily historical; it exists in history. Yet this history is not one of continuity or teleological progression toward a given end. The language available to the philosopher is a "fallen" language, one consisting almost entirely of "ruins." Almost. Adorno does identify one "freedom"—we might also say "power" *(Kraft)* in language: configuration. The "ruins" that are language can be related to others. It is here that the relation to "truth" is to be found, and thus it is of this "possibility" that philosophical critique must avail itself. There must be, according to Adorno, a "dialectical" relationship between the historical reality—that is, the temporal collapse or ruination—of the elements of language and the "truth" sought in philosophy. Philosophical "truth" cannot be the attempt to eliminate the inevitability of its own ruination, but can be configuratively constructed only from ruination.

The "power" and "freedom" of words consist in their availability for "construction," the formation of "configurations" and "constellations"—that is, by referring not to an external reality *(Wirklichkeit)*, but through each other to their own reality, the reality of their own "decay" *(Zerfall)*. As such, however, the process or act of philosophical "interpretation" is inevitably aporetic. If its "task," as Adorno understands it in *Kierkegaard: Construction of the Aesthetic,* is "to construct *[konstruiern]* ideas," "which illuminate and partition the mass of what merely exists *[des bloß Seinden]* and about which the elements of what exists crystallize for knowledge" (*Kierkegaard,* 10–11; 4), and if the elements of "construction" are available only as language in "decay," then philosophy itself inevitably runs the risk of its own destruction. That is, the possibility of philosophical interpretation is simultaneously the delineation of its impossibility. Adorno is aware of this paradox from the very beginning, as he explains in the lecture "The Actuality of Philosophy":

> Just as precisely aware I am of the impossibility of carrying out the program which I have given to you—an impossibility which does not simply stem from the brevity of the hour, but is rather more general, since, precisely as a program, completely and universally, this program cannot be carried out—: so clearly do I see the obligation of suggesting: philosophy does not shrink back from that liquidation.... ("Actualität," 339; "Actuality," 129)

The impossibility of philosophical "interpretation" is endemic. It is, moreover, its only possible goal. It cannot be systematically presented as the generalizable and repeatable program for a new philosophy, but remains forever incompatible with any system, any totalization or generalization. "Interpretation" hardly functions as formal methodology. Its attention is rather focused on what exceeds any notion of prescribed and eternal meaning, or "*Sinn*," and seizes as truth what is necessarily ephemeral and nonlinguistic, or "*sinn-los*." That is, words are embedded in a nonlinguistic, historical reality and this ultimately silent reality informs the possibility of their meaning and informs their relation to "truth." The intervention of this ephemeral, historical, and, for Adorno, material reality in any constructed meaning interrupts the possibility of any ideally construed "*Sinn*." All meaning is constructed, yet construction (in principle) cannot conform to the presupposition of eternal meaning. If "interpretation" is still to define a "methodology," it can be construed only as nonsystematic and antimethodological.

Precisely this conviction of the antimethodological task—or even obligation—of philosophical interpretation persists throughout Adorno's work. In this sense, as he explains in the *Negative Dialectics*, the function of dialectic in critique, precisely because of its construction out of an always only discontinuous reality, is neither "method" nor "reality":

> Dialectics is actually neither merely method nor something real in the naive understanding. Not a method: for the unreconciled matter lacking precisely that identity which substitutes for thought is contradictory and resists every attempt at its unequivocal interpretation.... Not merely reality: for contradictoriness is a category of reflection, the confrontation of concept and thing in thought. Dialectics as procedure means thinking for the sake of contradiction once experienced in the thing and thinking against it in contradiction. (*Negative Dialektik*, 148; 144–45)

The elements of "reality," discontinuous and contradictory in themselves, allow for nothing other than an equally contradictory thinking. Or, rather, this discontinuous and contradictory reality always eludes a thinking conceived under the rule of noncontradiction. Unable to overcome the contradictions in "reality" in the unification or universalization of concepts, the dialectical thinking of critique is reduplicated and, in its reduplication, is paradoxically opposed to itself. Recalling the earlier formulation from "The Actuality of Philosophy," philosophical critique not only does not "shrink back from" its own "liquidation," but would be impossible without the continual possibility of its own collapse. In this absolute suspension of any potential universalization—suspension precisely as irreducible contradiction or paradox—Adorno identifies the "reality" that philosophy would seek. Unable to conclude the paradoxical reduplication of the critical "procedure," philosophy, as he says again in "The Actuality of Philosophy," "remains standing where irreducible reality breaks in" ("Actualität," 343;

"Actuality," 132). Given that the elements of critique are already themselves the elements of reality, there is no other possibility than that the "irruption of the irreducible" is itself, in its breaking in, the very reality of which Adorno speaks, not simply some other thing, one more thing among others.

If this "reality" appears anywhere in Adorno's interpretation, then, it appears only in the realm already torn apart by its own "friability" and "contradictoriness." It appears, that is, in the aesthetic. And precisely because of the aesthetic resistance to any "unanimous *[einstimmig]* interpretation," it will inevitably persist beyond any attempt to align it with a more methodological and systematic coherence. Yet, if the "reality" with which philosophy must be concerned is still to be understood, it can be understood only in its very resistance to conceptual coherence, through an interpretation that takes into account the paradoxicality of appearance without any attempt to do away with it. This is not merely a question of perceiving in general, regardless of any attempted systematic presentation, the point at which the system breaks down and admits the reality irreducible to it.

In his book on Kierkegaard, Adorno attempts to read the traces of "reality." These traces begin where intentional meaning, whether properly philosophical or not, comes to a halt. Hence, Adorno is interested in the "figures" of philosophy that exceed any system of explication. In this, however, he cannot assume in advance that he knows how they mean. He must, rather, follow the possibility of their meaning first through their aesthetic appearance. That is, he must follow the very particularity of the aesthetic:

> Not what is abstractly removed from time truly endures in works of art—in its emptiness, it most nearly succumbs to it. Motifs are maintained whose hidden eternity is most deeply embedded in the constellation of the temporal, most faithfully preserved in its ciphers. Works of art do not obey the power of the universality of ideas. Their center is the temporal and particular towards which they are directed as its figure; what more they mean they mean only in the figure. (*Kierkegaard*, 34; 21)

And *that* these "figures" mean something "more" seems indisputable. The difficulty concerns rather *what* "more" they mean. Because they are "temporal and particular," however, they indicate first and foremost nothing other than themselves as they appear, nothing other than their own temporality and particularity. And yet this particularity alone can never account for the possibility of a text's meaning. Figures, in this sense, are "ciphers," for which meaning, indeterminable in advance, has yet to appear. What Adorno finds, however, in isolating figural presentation in the temporal particularity of the "cipher" is that the figure itself remains still irreducible to a single temporality. Maintaining the paradoxical temporality of the Kierkegaardian "moment," Adorno still speaks of a "hidden eternity" that exceeds aesthetic immediacy and particularity. This excess is expressed only in the figure, in the paradoxical configuration of textual constellations.

And yet, for both Adorno and Kierkegaard, even this "hidden eternity" cannot be construed as the eternal meaning of any given text. Rather, "hidden eternity" amounts only to one piece among others with which the reading of the text must contend. In this sense, what appears written within textual "ciphers"—that is, "figures"—is never, strictly speaking, reducible to one thing, not even to an exclusive temporal particularity of aesthetic appearance. This particularity is already the coincidence of several different aspects, only one of which might be construed as "eternal." Language itself is already figural: "Kierkegaard's metaphor of writing *[Schrift]* contains: the unalterable givenness of the text itself; its unreadability as that of 'secret writing' *[Geheimschrift]*; its schema as that of 'ciphers'; its origin in history." If there is something of the "eternal" attached to textual "ciphers," it must concern the "reality" of the text itself. Even if the text itself might be perceived as unchangeable, its meaning is not: "But the invariable meaning of the invariable text is incomprehensible in Kierkegaard: the fullness of divine truth for the creature distorts" (*Kierkegaard,* 39; 25). The legibility of the text is never immediately available, but plays itself out between its said "unchangeability" and its historical existence. Rather than making the text legible, however, by constituting its equally unchangeable meaning as the disclosure of a now known and, hence, unconcealed *(unverborgene)* "eternity," Kierkegaard's insistence on the "divine truth" present within it is precisely what disrupts the possibility of meaningful continuity. The illegibility of the text as of "secret writing" is ineradicable, and there would be no text without it.

That is, what constitutes a text's legibility is something in and of itself inexpressible and unknowable. The paradoxically illegible legibility of the text—what opens it up to the possibility of linguistic critique—is the irreducible historicity, if not "materiality," of its expressions. To understand Kierkegaard's texts (or texts in Kierkegaard's terms), according to Adorno, is to understand that, insofar as they consist of the expression of the inexpressible, they must be read as "ciphers," where reading "ciphers," then, is not construed as searching for the particular "key" to "unlock" their meaning. Although "ciphers" remain meaningless in themselves, they are equally uncompletable by any particular meaning attributed to them. In this sense, borrowing Walter Benjamin's interpretation of allegory from the *Ursprung des deutschen Trauerspiels (The Origin of the German Tragic Drama)*, Adorno insists that "ciphers" are more than simply "signs": "Paradoxically the utterly hidden is communicated in the cipher. As in Benjamin's interpretation, every allegory is not merely a sign *[Zeichen]*, but an expression *[Ausdruck]*" (*Kierkegaard*, 40; 26). The "absolutely hidden" is maintained in the paradoxical communication of "ciphers," not absolved into "communication." This is what separates "expression" from "sign" in Adorno's account: the persistence of paradox within and beyond the "communication" of "ciphers."

"Allegory," however, is not simply one kind of figuration among others. When Benjamin declares that allegory is "expression," he equates it in the same gesture with all language. It would be impossible for language not to be allegory. Speaking of baroque allegory, Benjamin claims: "Allegory ... is not a playful technique of images, but expression, just as speech is expression, and, indeed, writing is. This was the *experimentum crucis*. Precisely writing appeared as the conventional system of signs beyond all others."[13] The point is not only that language is concerned with meaning, but that linguistic expressions are subject to their own historicity, the historicity of their conventional usage. In this sense, allegory exemplifies, even as figuration, a discrepancy, or even an aporia, in which all language as language participates.[14]

What Adorno understands in Benjamin's association of "allegory" and "expression" he does not explain in *Kierkegaard: Construction of the Aesthetic*. He does, however, in "Die Idee der Naturgeschichte" (The idea of natural history), which was written during the same period as the book on Kierkegaard. Allegory, he says, quoting Benjamin again, "is not a random sign for a contained contents; rather between allegory and its meaning is a substantive relationship, 'allegory is expression'" ("Idee.", 358). Allegory disrupts the otherwise singular relationship between "signs" and their said "content." What makes allegory more than simply a "sign," in Adorno's understanding of Benjamin, is that what is presented allegorically, its "expression," is not simply reducible to "contents," but what is presented as allegory is always separate from but related to what is allegorically presented. Allegory "happens" in this relationship. Adorno continues:

> Conventionally, allegory means the sensible presentation of a concept, and it is therefore called abstract and random. The relationship of what appears allegorically and what is meant, however, is not a random and symbolic one; but rather something particular takes place, it is expression, and what occurs in its sphere, what is expressed, is nothing other than a historical relationship. The theme of the allegorical absolutely is history. ("Idee," 358)

History, however, does not "appear" as the "content" of allegorical presentation; rather, it "occurs" in the relationship between "allegory" and "the allegorized."[15]

The separation of "allegory" and its meaning is a temporal separation, the separation of one temporality from another. Insofar as this relationship "occurs" in allegory—insofar as the specificity of one particular temporality is coupled with a desired constancy, the temporal constancy and generality of "symbolic" meaning as opposed to allegory—the occurrence of this relationship, its "play," is inevitably that of "transience" *(Vergänglichkeit)*. Adorno now cites the following passage from Benjamin's *Ursprung des deutschen Trauerspiels (Origin of the German Tragic Drama)*:

> Within the decisive category of time . . . the relationship between symbol and allegory can be incisively and formally determined. Whereas in the symbol, with the transfiguration of destruction, the transfigurative face of nature is fleetingly revealed in the light of redemption, in allegory the observer is confronted with the *facies hippocratica* of history as a petrified, primordial landscape. Everything about history that, from the very beginning, has been untimely, sorrowful, unsuccessful, is expressed in a face—or rather in a death's head. And although such a thing lacks all "symbolic" freedom of expression, all classical proportion, all humanity—nevertheless, it significantly expresses not only the nature of human existence as such but also the biographical historicity of the individual in this figure most subjected to nature as a riddle. That is the core of the allegorical view, of the baroque, secular exposition of history as the Passion of the world; its meaning resides solely in the stations of its decline. The greater the significance, the greater the subjection to death, because death digs most deeply the jagged line of demarcation between physical nature and meaning. (Benjamin, *Ursprung*, 144–45; *Origin*, 166, cited in Adorno, "Idee," 358–59)

In Benjamin's sense, then, the possibility of allegorical meaning, as opposed to symbolic meaning, appears only in the moments of its disintegration—the very disintegration and decay that constitute the allegorical image. This image, as Benjamin explains, is in itself already discontinuous: "By its very essence classicism was not permitted to behold the unfreedom, the incompleteness, the brokenness of sensible, beautiful *physis*. But beneath its extravagant pomp, this is precisely what baroque allegory proclaims, with unprecedented emphasis" (Benjamin, 154; 176). The very "brokenness," "unfreedom," and "incompleteness" of the allegorical image stand in direct relation to any possible meaning, resisting as much as supporting any desired meaning. Thus, as Adorno emphasizes, what the image means, it means only insofar as its discontinuous reality suspends the possibility of any constant meaning secured outside the temporality of "decay." Adorno describes a double movement in allegorical interpretation, so that "as its meaning becomes clear, so does its transience *[Vergänglichkeit]*" ("Idee," 359). Meaning appears in and as its own collapse.

Allegory, as both Benjamin and Adorno point out, requires a particular understanding of history. If "meaning" appears where any desired continuity with its expression is suspended, insofar as each belongs to a separate temporality, then to understand history is to understand that history as well is not merely about the continual teleological progression of a singular temporality. Even with such a singularly progressive conception of historical time, what appears in history is also bound to another temporality. What appears present as history, appears already in decay; it appears already as "ruin." Benjamin explains: "In the ruin, history moved perceptibly onto the stage. And in this form, history does not assume the form of the process of an eternal life so much as that of incessant decay. Allegory thereby declares itself to be beyond beauty. Allegories are, in the realm of thoughts, what ruins are in the realm of things" (Benjamin, 155–56; 177–78). That is, history cannot be conceived solely in terms of its progression—a progression, moreover, understood as of one in and of itself "eternal," as "the process of an eternal life." Rather, its progressive presentation appears only insofar as it falls away, insofar as it disappears. In this sense, Adorno, together with Benjamin, stresses not the possibility of any sort of historical continuity, but rather the isolated moments of historical particularity, "singularity," together with its inevitable "transience." Thus, when Adorno speaks of an "originary history of meaning" *(Urgeschichte des Bedeutens)* in Benjamin's notion of allegory, he explains that historical meaning—meaning in history—is not just about the repetition and inclusion of prior historical moments in later events, but is simultaneously something more than this: "It is not enough merely to say that originary historical motifs continually appear in history itself, but rather that originary history itself as transience contains within it the motif of history" ("Idee," 359–60). "Urgeschichte" in this sense is what constitutes the historical character of "history," what all history has in common and what makes history history, not the nostalgic restitution and repetition of an originary event in history preserved in each subsequent occurrence. History is itself already and only conceivable as ephemeral, as "transience" *(Vergänglichkeit)*, not as "the past" *(Vergangenheit)*.

Yet what is significant about such an understanding of the transience of history does not end there. History itself is never as such presentable—which is not to say that it is not somehow present. Adorno continues: "Originary history *(Urgeschichte)* is absolutely present as transience, and is so in the sign of 'meaning'" ("Idee," 360). What "meaning" means, it means only in its own historical transience—transience not just in the sense of temporal mutability, but in the sense of mutability always under the sign of its inevitable disintegration. The presentation of an always paradoxical originary history as history in meaning accordingly determines its own interpretive strategy. If meaning is available (present-able) in history—and it can be nowhere else—and that history remains irreducible to the universal, unilateral development of an "eternal" progression, then the momentary presentation of meaning involves more than the relationship of a "sign" to its "meaning." It involves what brings this "sign" into a temporality of disintegration; it involves its relationship to others. Isolated, but never singularly isolable—meaning in history, as meaning in allegory, appears in constellations. Adorno's commentary on the citation from Benjamin in "The Idea of Natural History" reads:

> What is all this talk about transience supposed to mean, and what does "originary history of meaning" mean? I cannot develop these concepts from one another in the conventional way. What we are concerned with here is of a form in principle different from the development from a "hypothesis" upon which the general conceptual structure is constitutively based. This other logical structure itself here is not to be analyzed. It is that of the constellation. We are not concerned with the explication of concepts from one another, but with constellations of ideas, and in particular the ideas of transience, meaning, nature, and history. ("Idee," 359)

Neither history nor allegory follows the trajectory of organic development *(Entwicklung)*. "Constellation," as "this other logical structure," is not a development and, hence, remains opposed to a conventional development of concepts not only because it is not one of a collection of traditional concepts, but, more important, because its very form, its very structure, remains opposed to tradition itself in the sense that it pays homage not to originary intentions but to present, momentary occurrence.

Adorno's understanding of such an opposition to the "traditional" has as much to do with Kierkegaard as it does with Benjamin. Kierkegaard, too, as Adorno describes in *Kierkegaard: Construction of the Aesthetic*, breaks with the traditional use and definition of concepts. In spite of the apparently systematic presentation of "existence" in terms of (astrological) "spheres"—a systematicity that, in Adorno's view, still connects Kierkegaard with the abstraction and universalization he associates with idealism—the figural presentation itself remains "paradoxical" and continually disrupts an otherwise unchecked tendency toward the universal. At the same time Kierkegaard succumbs to the "idealist system compulsion," the discrepancies isolated within any given category continually subvert its totalization:

> Even if he always ridicules Hegel's "system of existence," he succumbs to the same idealist system compulsion insofar as existence *[Dasein]* for him is reduced to consciousness; insofar as the spontaneous act of freedom for him always becomes the innermost determination of subjectivity; insofar as the image of the individual as "total" organizes pure thought for him. But at the same time, he must strive to express systematically what always opposes the system in his project: Being which bears thought; ontological sense which is not dissolved into thought; fissures which cannot be closed by the continuity of deduction—all this nevertheless settled in precisely that spirituality which effectively posits the system. (*Kierkegaard*, 124; 86)

Adorno's critique insists upon the inclusion of both the systematic presentation and that which in the presentation itself cannot be exhausted within the system. This has everything to do with the central figural importance of the "spheres": "Kierkegaard elaborated the paradoxical system of existence *[Existenz]* in the theory of the spheres" (*Kierkegaard*, 124; 86–87). The "spheres" themselves, for Adorno particularly in their astrological connotations, refuse any desired resolution in universality.

Intended as the articulation of various possibilities of subjective existence, the figurality of the "spheres" themselves both betrays and circumvents their "idealist" origins:

> Hence, the doctrine of the spheres is more and less than a material demonstration of the "project" *[Entwurf]* of existence. Less: because it is not limited to pure actuality, but produces the obligation for becoming present precisely where Kierkegaard would prohibit it. More: because subjectivity, once obliged to construe itself materially without merely losing itself in productive unity, arrives at assertions about existence which are supported nowhere in the Kierkegaardian doctrine of existence in the depths of its concentration. (*Kierkegaard*, 126; 88)

The "actuality" of subjective existence always exceeds any systematic presentation. At the same time, and together with this insufficiency, on the one hand, this figural, or "material," presentation exceeds in another direction its own apparently systematic intention. In this sense, according to Adorno, the figural presentation continually exhibits something about "subjective existence" that is unsupportable by Kierkegaard's said "doctrine."

Ultimately, in Adorno's analysis, it is the very figural reality of the "spheres" that separate Kierkegaard from his idealist predecessors. After tracing similarities with Hegel in each of the various "spheres," even where

Kierkegaard explicitly criticizes and opposes Hegel, Adorno claims: "The true difference from Hegel lies not in the 'leap,' so much as in the resistance of the spheres to any synthesis ..." (*Kierkegaard*, 129; 90). Finding little evidence for an absolute separation between Hegel and Kierkegaard, either in Kierkegaard's own opposition to Hegel or even in the "logical" opposition to Hegel in a new concept of the "leap" *(Sprung)* that would resist the orientation toward synthesis of Hegelian dialectic, Adorno rather identifies the same opposition not on the level of conceptual operation, but solely in terms of figural presentation. Even in the apparent "totality" of the "system" of "spheres" as a whole, the "spheres" themselves remain incompatible with the "existence" they are intended to explicate and disclose. Even where it seems to appear as a "process," as perhaps in the "stages on life's way," Adorno insists that "the 'sense' never supports the continuity of the process," and the "system" itself never comes to completion; "thus the totality of the spheres ... does not result in the completion of the system." Instead, there is "totality" here only in another sense: "It is a totality layered out of ruins" (*Kierkegaard*, 130; 90). A totality, that is, that is never as such totalizable and never adds up to the universalized subjectivity it might otherwise seek.

In this way, reading the central importance of Kierkegaard's philosophy not in terms of the primacy of subjectivity but rather in terms of the allegorical figure that ought to articulate the concept of subjectivity, Adorno situates Kierkegaard at a crucial turn in the history of philosophy. The figure of the "spheres" both connects Kierkegaard with an understanding of idealism extending from Platonic "forms" through the Kantian deduction of a priori principles and, at the same time, separates his work from an idealism no longer supported by its figural presentation: "All of its nomenclature is astral; and just as the most secret experiences are always deposited in the terminological figures of philosophy, the word sphere does not in vain awaken the memory to the mythical harmony of the Pythagoreans" (*Kierkegaard*, 130; 91). This recollection, however, serves only to disarticulate any potential "harmony." More than simply recalling an ideal of musical and mathematical purity, the "spheres"—this word and this figure—record "secrets." That is, the figure no longer simply directs and determines the possible understandings of "subjectivity." Moreover, the figure itself, at its most secret, no longer lends itself a priori to description, but, refusing this, lends itself only to critical interpretation. In this way, even Kant's mention of the "starry heavens" in the second *Critique* finds its way into Adorno's reading of Kierkegaard's "spheres":

> The Kantian formula of the starry heavens above and the moral law within us appears with Kierkegaard's "spheres" in baroque contraction; the starry sky is collapsed into the blind self, and the law of its freedom has been transformed into natural necessity. The moral life is oriented through categories of nature. Not in a causal way: but certainly astrologically. They always return in Kierkegaard. (*Kierkegaard,* 130–31; 91)

In the "contraction" of the Kantian "formula" and its collapse into the "blind self," the Kierkegaardian subject appears not as an autonomous and free agent, but always in conflict with "categories of nature." The astrological figure in relation to the subjectivity it would describe always appears at the limit between freedom and necessity. Hence, the figure can never bear a purely "causal" relation to the subject, even in its bond with "nature."

The figural function of astrology separates "categories of nature" from their otherwise "causal" determinations. "The constellations *[Sternbilder]* of the spheres are always signs of conjuring, utterly allegorical" (*Kierkegaard,* 131; 91). And their allegorical function is not distinct from their categorical one. Here, Adorno's description of Kierkegaard comes perhaps closest to his understanding of Benjamin. It is precisely the allegorical appearance of the "spheres" that avails them to "constellation." What separates Kierkegaard from his idealist predecessors is—in and through the "spheres"—his use of concepts. Rather than following a perhaps more "traditional" method of "developing concepts from one another," Kierkegaard "loves 'to put concepts together'" (*Kierkegaard,* 131; 92). Thus, thought does not follow an organic developmental process through progressive conceptual formation, but rather occurs in the differences within their combinations. This is true not simply for the more abstract understanding of the concepts, but more particularly for each individual subject understood in relation to philosophical concepts. The particularity of the subject refuses the universality of concepts:

> Individual existence is interpreted in terms of constellations in order to avoid definitions. What remains obscure to mere observation; what resists transparent, categorical form as content: this actuality *[dies Eigentliche]* is to be read by thought from figures which are inscribed in the object by the connection of relevant concepts as whose focus it [the object] dictates its figural law without coming to rest on one of the curves. As opposed to mathematics, dialectics is not able to formulate the laws of figure and focus conclusively. Constellations and figures are ciphers to it and its "sense," embedded in history, cannot be calculated arbitrarily. (*Kierkegaard,* 132; 92)

Unlike mathematical figures, which describe the formulaic relationship between "focus" and "figure" prescriptively, whereby "figures" would be produced in relation to a given "focus" in accordance with mathematical formulae, the calculations in linguistic (literal) "figures" never conform to an ideal and programmatic linearity.

The point is not simply that this "individual existence" refuses the ideality of prescriptive figuration, but rather that figuration itself, at least as far as the "spheres" in Kierkegaard are concerned, continually yields results irreducible to any figurative intention. For Adorno's reading of Kierkegaard, this has as much to do with the inevitable inaccessibility of any individual subject through conceptual presentation as it does with the complex and ultimately aporetic function of the figure itself, which is aporetic in its own finitude, its own missed totalization. Each of the spheres—aesthetic, ethical, religious—describes its own "dialectic," which is both distinct from and constitutive of the "dialectical" relationships between them. So, in the "aesthetic sphere," for example, there is one kind of dialectical "movement," which, complete in itself, is at the same time only one pole in relation to another. Adorno explains:

> "Aesthetic earnestness" is in itself dialectic insofar as it is both "harmful and of use"; by way of the "ideal," it completes itself as totality, and in the "leap" of the decision, it inaugurates the next sphere. That clearly implies a doubled conception of dialectics: for Kierkegaard there is both a dialectic immanent to the spheres and a dialectic between the spheres. Thus, Kierkegaard is not merely formally distinguished from Hegel, to whose schema the "sphere-immanent" dialectic would correspond, while that of the "leap" between the spheres would contradict it. The duality of his conception expresses the aporia of the dialectic of the spheres. (*Kierkegaard*, 140; 98)

More than simply two kinds of "dialectic," one interspherical and the other intraspherical—the two forms refuse all compatibility; the intraspherical dialectic is not simply one stage in the progression of that between the separate spheres. Although the movement of thought within each of the "spheres" may be "dialectical," properly speaking (which would explain Adorno's suggestion that here there is nothing to separate Kierkegaard from Hegel), there exists no "mediation" *(Vermittlung)* between the separate "spheres." The juncture from one to another occurs only in the "leap"—that is, outside the dialectical logic of "mediation." (And the "leap," furthermore, as Adorno claimed already, is not what separates Kierkegaard from Hegel.) The two concepts of "dialectic," if not exactly contradictory, remain mutually incompatible. The respective dialectics within each "sphere," taken together, never amount to the "totality" the figure of the "spheres" might otherwise indicate. This happens, however, not because something is still missing—some as yet unknown piece, which, when added to the rest, would complete the picture. Rather, one kind of dialectical movement continually and inevitably interrupts the other. Where there is "dialectic," there is no "leap," and where there is a "leap," there can be no dialectic: "The 'leap' as movement is no longer commensurable with that within the sphere, no longer demonstrable in an act of consciousness" (*Kierkegaard,* 142; 99). If this is no longer properly "logical," what is it?

"Nothing better distinguishes this dialectic from the total dialectic between the spheres than the claim that it is a movement in place" (*Kierkegaard,* 142; 100), Adorno declares. He takes the image from *Sickness unto Death* where Kierkegaard, under the pseudonym Anti-Climacus, uses it to distinguish the "movement" of "becoming oneself" from the simple process of "becoming" as one of changing from one thing to another. Adorno quotes: "'To become is a movement from the spot, but to become oneself is a movement in place'" (*Kierkegaard,* 143; 100).[16] This figure, in Adorno's reading, inscribes the distinction between the two kinds of dialectic, two kinds of "movement." Movement in place, however, is not taken as the "leap" from one "sphere" to another. The movement of becoming oneself as the movement in place—an impossible movement—describes the "dialectical" movement within each "sphere," the one kind of "dialectic" Adorno wants to maintain as dialectical in the Hegelian sense. The dialectical movement within each "sphere" occupies the same (logical) space. Incapable of making a progressive movement from one "sphere" to the other, "leaping" from one to another, each would occupy the same space without, however, and this is accounted for in the absence of any "mediation"—negation. This movement is one of repetition, which, as repetition, continuously withdraws any ultimate conclusion, refuses to close the circle or, rather, the "sphere."

This simultaneity, however, lends itself to no sense of constancy. With respect to the repetitive suspensions of "movement" within each "sphere," no longer resolvable in "dialectical" synthesis, the movement from one "sphere" to another—still within the figure, as the figure—can appear only as a "leap." In the absence of logical progression, no continuous "process" can "move" from one "sphere" to another. "Leap" appears only as breach:

> With each sphere, dialectics begins anew: its continuity is broken. The discontinuity of the greater movement, however, is produced by the "in place" of the individual, psychological movement, and the project of an "intermittent" dialectic, whose true moment is not the continuation, but the suspension, not the process but the caesura, is, at the center of the Kierkegaardian philosophy of existence, opposed to the mythical omnipotence of the spontaneous subject as the objection of trans-subjective truth. (*Kierkegaard,* 143; 100)

The "movement in place" is nothing other than the perpetual self-interruption of dialectical progression. Unable to complete itself in any "mediated" "synthesis," the movement breaks down. What remains is only dialectic in fragment. Yet, in Adorno's reading of Kierkegaard, the discontinuity of the figure of the "spheres" is not limited to the figure as a whole, as if a properly dialectical movement would be preserved within each separate "sphere." Rather, the discontinuous relations among the spheres are themselves products of the movement within each. Condemned in advance to self-repetition, even the more confined "dialectic" breaks down prior to any synthetic resolution. It is precisely in the image of such self-contradictory movement—but movement nonetheless—that the figural explication of subjectivity breaks down as well. This does not mean, however, that the Kierkegaardian "spheres of existence" ultimately cannot account for the "truth" of a subjectivity that really ought to be explicable and really ought to appear through dialectical mediation, as if this would "justify" the function of the figure in the first place. On the contrary, discrepancy, as evidenced in the inevitable self-contradiction of the figural framework, separates the singularity of each "existing" subject from the "mythical omnipotence" of an otherwise purely universal and abstract "subjectivity."[17]

Incompatible with conceptual mediation, the "true moment" *(wahrer Augenblick)* of subjective existence appears only where its figural presentation comes to a halt, where it ceases becoming a figure—as suddenly, perhaps, as the legible figures in constellations. Beyond the general incompatibility of any individual with an idealized concept of subjectivity, Adorno attributes primary significance to its figural presentation. Yet, whatever "truth" *(Wahrheit)* might be disclosed in the figural presentation appears only when the figure no longer offers metaphorical representation. The truth of the figure is confined to the figure itself and appears only there, and only momentarily, where the figure breaks down, revealing "truth" only in and as breach, "caesura."

And yet, even here where the figure stops, where it breaks apart, we are still within the realm of figurality. (Indeed, Adorno's entire reading of Kierkegaard is grounded in the impossibility of leaving figurality behind, the impossibility that one might finally arrive at a "truth" that would render the "figure" superfluous.) The difficulty is always one of knowing how to read figures—of knowing what cannot be known in advance and of knowing what in the end perhaps cannot even appear as knowledge. How, in this instance, for example, are we to understand this "figure"—still as the figure of the "spheres"? Can this figure still "represent" subjective existence? Can it still "explicate" subjectivity? If it cannot, what is the relationship between the figurality of the "spheres" and the "subject" that all along has been the focus of the philosophical work, for both Kierkegaard and Adorno continually insist that there is a relationship, an intersection between one and the other? In the interstices and suspensions of a more teleological figurative understanding, a progression toward understanding as commanded in the figurative interpretation, one "figure," one image, would lapse into another. The movement within and between the "spheres," impossible as anything other than discontinuous, self-annihilating repetition, however, becomes another image. The impossible movement described in and by the "spheres" as "movement in place" is the movement of "breath" *(Atem)*.

This figure—this image—Adorno explains, supplants and suspends the Hegelian "mediation" between "necessity" and "freedom." That is, there is an intersection between the "image" and the idea, but it is not entirely clear how this intersection occurs. Is it more than merely another kind of depiction, another kind of representation? Adorno, however, insists: "The metaphor of breath is to be taken literally *[buchstäblich]*." But what exactly does it mean to take this metaphor "*buchstäblich*," or as he said earlier, "*wörtlich*"? Adorno continues: "Namely as the reestablishment of the body in the rhythm of absolute spirituality." Yet, after all Adorno has explained about figurality so far, "absolute spirituality" never appears "absolute," never appears at all, not even metaphorically in some other form. Adorno emphasizes, rather, the "rhythm" alone that inevitably prevents any "subjectivity" from gaining control as "absolute." The "literal" intervention of the rhythmic image of "breath" is at once the literal and the real appearance of "nature" and at the same time the emptying out of the image of any content other than its pure and purely rhythmic "reality":

> In place of the Hegelian "mediation" between freedom and necessity, intermittence enters as breath which pauses, contracts, and resumes again; it is a movement in place, not one of progress or continuity. The metaphor of breath is to be taken literally. Namely as the reestablishment of the body in the rhythm of absolute spirituality. The turn of spiritualism into a corporeal doctrine of organs has found its place in the dialectical movement itself. For the moment of the pause, where dialectics is suspended, is the same one in which its mythical ground echoes: nature in the depth of the tolling hour. Its appearance assures humanity of its transience like the caesuras of time for the deathly ill. Yet its empty figure, the rhythm of time by itself, without any other expression than that of itself, indicates the silent *[sprachlos]* intervention of reconciliation. The ceaselessly repeated tolling of hours paradoxically contains the uncertain certainty of the end. (*Kierkegaard*, 144; 101)

The "moment of the pause"—the "true moment," as Adorno claimed earlier—is at the same moment the "echo" of its "mythical ground": "nature." But nature appears here in a specific sense and marks a specific occurrence. Nature in the rhythm of breath, as "nature" in Benjamin's notion of baroque allegory—is the "nature" of temporality. The rhythmic repetitions of breath appear not as repetitions within constancy, but, as the very image of fracture and discontinuity, insist upon an inevitably ephemeral temporality where an otherwise synthetic dialectical logic would seek permanence.

In the end, Adorno adopts an even more explosive image to explicate the same rhythmic movement. "In vino veritas," the "aesthetic" section of Kierkegaard's *Stages on Life's Way*, ends with an image that Adorno takes as that of aesthetics itself. Comparing the image here to the more conceptual discussions of "the aesthetic" offered by Kierkegaard's Judge William in *Either/Or* and *Stages*, Adorno explains:

> At the end of "In vino veritas," Kierkegaard offers a metaphor of the aesthetic sphere which captures it more precisely than any of Judge Williams' conceptual efforts ever could, because it grasps the realm of images itself in an image.... "So it is that a skyrocket is propelled upwards in one shot, stands still for one moment as a coherent whole, in order then to explode in all directions." The idea of the aesthetic sphere is no different: free of subjective dialectic and vastly outshining it, suspended in the eternity of the moment as an apparent whole, decaying the light of hope over the things to which it belongs like the rocket to the modern antiquity of pyrotechnics. (*Kierkegaard*, 186; 131)[18]

In each case, the image follows the same trajectory, moving alternately between progression and suspension—progression presumably toward "totality" *(Ganzes)* and suspension presumably as "totality." Yet, as this second image makes pointedly clear, this "totality," if it is one, is inconceivable outside the relentless movement of temporality, which is not the same as the climbing of the rocket or the taking in of "breath." This "totality," already in its suspension, is not one of duration, but one of explosion. Finding no support outside of its own time, the aesthetic presentation of the aesthetic inevitably breaks apart.

The same is true of "breath." Condemned in advance to an always only self-destructive repetition, the rhythm of breath is one of exhaustion, exhalation, and expropriation. It is, as Adorno maintains, nothing other than the rhythm of "time itself" *(bloßer Zeit)*, with no expression other than itself, and, thus, a figure already of its own emptiness. Yet, even here,

Adorno wants to attribute to this figure an ideal of "reconciliation" *(Versöhnung)*, as if even here, at the limit of figurality—where figurality ends in nothing other than its own emptiness—the repetition promised in breath might still be one of recuperation. Perhaps all is not lost: "Nature, as temporal, dialectical in itself, is not lost" (*Kierkegaard*, 145; 101). Perhaps. However, Kierkegaard himself, in spite of Adorno's apparent optimism in this regard, withholds all promise of reconciliation. Or at least he withholds the possibility of its fulfillment.

If "nature" is itself nothing other than its own disintegration in its own ephemeral temporality, what exactly is saved, if, in the image, "nature" is kept from being lost? Can this still be conceived as "reconciliation"? Adorno cites the relevant passage from volume II of *Either/Or*, in which Kierkegaard, under the pseudonym Judge William, describes "*Reue*" (repentance, or simply regret or remorse) as the "expression" for the "reality" of "reconciliation": "'Repentance, it is true, is an expression for reconciliation, but it is also an absolutely irreconcilable expression'" (*Kierkegaard*, 145; 101).[19] What exactly does this "reality" express? If "remorse" or "regret" is "real," there must equally be something regrettable, something over which one would express remorse, some lapse or mistake one would, in the expression of remorse, see reconciled, repaired, or made good again. Yet this is not the case. Kierkegaard, however, does not say here that some given lapse over which one would express remorse—for which one might even be repentant—is no longer reconcilable. "Reconciliation," even in its "real" expression, can only be withheld, even as it is promised. It is the very expression itself—the very reality that is remorse—that is already irreconcilable. Reconciliation is possible only as it is, paradoxically, irreconcilable.

The irreconcilable expression, remorse for reconciliation, can be read only as the irreconcilability of all expression. "Breath," "rocket"—images in "miniature" for the questions posed in Kierkegaard's work—refuse all restriction to the realm of the merely "aesthetic." On the contrary, Adorno points out, the very discontinuities that mark the "concretion" of aesthetic images persist throughout the whole of Kierkegaard's "system of spheres," ultimately obstructing any possibility of systematic regularity and cohesion. The system of spheres, in its aesthetic and figural determinations, must fall apart:

> Thus, ultimately even the system of spheres disintegrates about the question of concretion which had originally distinguished it from Hegelian systematic universality. Labyrinthically convoluted, the dialectic of the spheres offers more and more room for the entrance of concretion in its intermediating caesuras, in the shafts of light of concrete illumination. Yet the figure which

> it collectively forms indicates, as a cipher, the greatest contradiction: its own collapse. Autonomous spirit, infinitely moved and without exit, can, for Kierkegaard, only be truly salvaged in death. (*Kierkegaard*, 149; 105)

The very function of figurality in Kierkegaard, as Adorno reads it, is continually directed toward its own paradoxical disfigurality, its inevitable disintegration coupled, as its figure, with that of the system.

If the goal of Adorno's text were merely to criticize Kierkegaard, he would need to go no further. If Adorno only wanted to explain that Kierkegaard, in spite of his persistent opposition to Hegel, remained simply a kind of belated adherent to an all too idealist philosophy, that, in its closed systematicity, failed to reach the very subject Kierkegaard himself identified with truth, he might simply end here with the declaration of the inadequacy of all idealism.[20] Or he might not even have had to go this far. If the problem is simply one of the inadequacy of Kierkegaard's philosophy as "system," he would not need to follow that "system" through to its collapse. If, in his reading of Kierkegaard, Adorno repeatedly follows Kierkegaard's figural expressions to their inevitable self-contradiction and self-interruption, why does he speak here still of "salvaging"—no, "truly *[wahrhaft]* salvaging"—what the figure itself prohibits or excludes?

At two moments in his text, Adorno declares the end of the "spheres" as system—the point at which the "system" in its literal expression no longer functions in accordance with its said conceptual intentions and, moreover, produces effects beyond and opposed to those same intentions. In the first, cited earlier, he reads the interstices and breaks of the dialectical movement described by the "spheres" in opposition to their apparently systematic presentation. They never add up to the "whole" the "system" seems to promise. The second, related to the first, concerns the presentation of "subjectivity" within a system in collapse. If, as Kierkegaard insists in the *Postscript*, "truth is subjectivity"—and Adorno marks this as the central "theme" throughout Kierkegaard's work—then this "subjectivity" cannot remain unharmed by its presentation. That is, for Adorno, the two run parallel, "system" and "subjectivity." If the "system" that describes this subjectivity is only system in decay, so too must be the subjectivity presented by it. If the system as system ultimately breaks apart, so too must its subject: "Subjectivity disappears, professing its essence as transience" (*Kierkegaard*, 145; 101).

The same transience that constitutes the literal "reality" of the "spheres" is also inscribed in the subject presented by them. And yet, Adorno is suggesting more than the mere parallel between two independent spheres. He is not suggesting simply that the "decay" that constitutes the literal figurality of the "spheres" indicates or refers to a similar disintegration on the part of a subjectivity contained within them, within their figure and thus figured by them. No, in the same way that "language critique" is "philosophical critique," there is no separation between subjectivity and its expression. If there can be a subject, it can be only its expression. If there is a "subject" in any form, one has to read it literally. Unpresentable as universal ideal, "subjectivity" appears only as "affect": "Subjectivity moves dialectically in its affects; but in them it also allows the displaced truth to be acknowledged in the cipher. Of course, not in the continuation of dialectics, but where it stops" (*Kierkegaard,* 145; 101). And one "affect" above all others: melancholy. This is the second moment of figural inversion: "Defeated melancholy is meaningful in an entirely different way. Its ruins are the ciphers which Kierkegaard traces and hope is placed in the nonsense *[Widersinn]* of its wishes. The order of the spheres is inverted" (*Kierkegaard,* 176; 124).

Adorno is concerned with what "melancholy" means. Even if the "order of the spheres" is intended to describe completely the "truth" of "subjectivity," does melancholy still mean in some sense that same subjectivity? Adorno insists here, as he has all along, that what melancholy means as "affect" it means only in its literal expression and, thus, can never entirely be traced back to any universal concept of "subjectivity." This, however, does not mean that it cannot mean anything. On the contrary, what it means, it means "otherwise" *(ganz anders)*, so that, if melancholy still means something—and it does—it can be read only in opposition to the conceptual order of an only ideal understanding of the spheres. The "truth" of melancholy begins only with its literal presentation; it does not end there. This "truth," as its meaning, is already situated in its own disintegration, its own ruination: "But it is the schema of that truth with which Kierkegaard's originary question is concerned: the ciphered and distorted truth, which though unable to establish autonomous subjectivity, is still able to read the melancholy subject; here melancholy restores what existence *[Existenz]* had destroyed" (*Kierkegaard,* 178; 125). The "truth" of "melancholy" does not result in the creation of an "autonomous" subjectivity; it does not result in creation at all. Rather, its truth lies in its legibility, which, in the shadow of an always only impossible "subjectivity," appears in the traces of its own inevitable loss. In Kierkegaard's work Adorno "reads" the subject of melancholy; he "reads" the legible traces of subjectivity's ruin.

But why, in the end, does Adorno read, even within loss, "hope"? What is "hope" for him? What does it mean for Kierkegaard? Again, if Kierkegaard really had been only the idealist Adorno condemns and nothing more, Adorno's work would be finished and there would be neither anything left to hope for nor any reason to speak of "hope." If Adorno reads "hope" in the expressions of subjectivity's collapse, the traces of this collapse cannot be directed toward "subjectivity" as the ideal object of Kierkegaard's philosophy. Their disintegration prohibits any possible reconciliation with the lost ideal. In this way, Adorno's critique of the legible traces in the interstices of an ideal subjectivity already in collapse amounts to more than the condemnation of an idealism to which Kierkegaard could never be returned. To read the remaining fragments of ruination—their only possible expression—is not only to read the impossibility of the persistent operation of the autonomous ideal, but also to read beyond it: "The order of the spheres is inverted." And: "Thus, the system of spheres ultimately decays...." Furthermore: "Its ruins are the ciphers which Kierkegaard traces, and hope is placed in the nonsense of its wishes." "Hope" turns the direction of Adorno's reading away from mere criticism and ultimately toward "construction."

Adorno situates this "hope" precisely in the legibility of "ciphers," in the legibility of "melancholy": "In the face of the claim to mastery of his systematic idealism, irreducible to the spontaneous center of subjectivity, what breaks apart into disparate and, among themselves, incomparable definitions of the aesthetic, that crystalizes in the gaze of melancholy—irregularly, certainly, but still in a meaningful way" (*Kierkegaard,* 180–81; 127). If melancholy is indeed legible, it is legible only in its expression as already determined by its aesthetic presentation. As such, it is no longer regulated by any schematic systematicity. If there is "hope" in the aesthetic—and for Adorno, it seems, there must be—it resides in the very failure of aesthetic images to conform to ideal regulation and the failure of these images simply to remain closed within the aesthetic. The "hope" of the aesthetic is that of its "irregularity." For it is in this irregularity that the fragments of the aesthetic become legible.

In the same way that Adorno finds the most accurate expression of the aesthetic in an aesthetic image, that of the "rocket," he seeks the most "faithful" presentation of "hope" in an image as well. The image is one of "decay," and it occurs as an image of "reading" from *Either/Or,* "where writing is presented as a model of despair in order to be quietly transformed into that of hope" (*Kierkegaard,* 178; 125). Adorno cites the following passage, in which reading itself is the image and figuration of the despair of Marie Beaumarchais:

> And thus she will pass her time until at last she has consumed the object of her grief which was not the cause of her grief, but the occasion through which she always sought an object for her grief. If a man possessed a letter which he knew, or believed, contained information bearing upon what he must regard as his life's happiness, but the writing was pale and fine, almost illegible—then would he read it with restless anxiety and with all possible passion, in one moment getting one meaning, in the next another, depending on his belief that, having made out one word with certainty, he could interpret the rest thereby; but he would never arrive at anything except the same uncertainty with which he began. He would stare more and more anxiously, but the more he stared, the less he would see. His eyes would sometimes fill with tears; but the oftener this happened the less he would see. In the course of time, the writing would become fainter and more illegible, until at last the paper itself would crumble away, and nothing would be left to him except the tears in his eyes." (*Kierkegaard,* 178–79; 126)[21]

Here reading does not amount to understanding. Even at the moment where the key to any possible "*Sinn*" might finally appear, its very certitude does little more than throw the rest into absolute uncertainty, turning the "end" into nothing more than another beginning. The only possible end is the inevitable and irreconcilable decay of the text itself.

Here the image of reading is the image of the temporality of the aesthetic. Unable to yield any certain knowledge, in time the text disintegrates; it consumes itself in reading. Adorno reads in this image of an always only fleeting and inaccessible meaning an image of "hope." Here "hope" is Adorno's. His commentary on Kierkegaard's image reads: "But no truer image of hope can be thought than that of true ciphers, legible in traces, fading into history, which elude the overflowing eye in whose tears they are still preserved; to which the tears of despair appear bodily in figures, dialectically, as emotion, consolation and hope" (*Kierkegaard,* 179; 126). What one reads, even in the image of reading, is only "ciphers." Thus, reading cannot be about understanding a fixed, unchangeable text and finding its equally fixed "*Sinn.*" To read, itself never more than a possibility, is to encounter the delimitation of meaning in the "cipher" as necessarily fragmented and incomplete and, at the same time, uncompletable in anything other than itself. Thus, reading is possible only through the "traces" of what is already only receding, already its own disappearance *(Entschwinden).* "Ciphers" disappear, and can appear in no other way. If they are available to reading, they are available only in their departure, their waning in history. Adorno now finds "hope" in their disappearance, as opposed to any certain "sense." Thus, if "hope" itself is to appear as image, it can only recede before every promised appearance: "The hope which dwells in the aesthetic is that of the transparency of figures in decay" (*Kierkegaard,* 187; 132). Accordingly, where "hope" appears even in the image, it cannot reside in any sort of static figure. On the contrary, "hope" enters only where the figure breaks apart; "hope" is already its own breaking apart.

In spite of all appearances to the contrary, every figure, even as it "crystallizes" in view of melancholy, can only feign its own permanence. "Crystallization," then, neither guarantees nor secures the figure as figure; on the contrary, its figurality is already its own fragmentation. Yet it is precisely the impermanence of images, their failure to retain any fixed meaning, that opens up the possibility of "hope." "Hope," in this sense, is nothing other than a kind of empty promise. It exists only where the possibility of positive meaning has been cut off, suspended in "the senseless *[widersinnig]* caesura which hope places in existence through its decay" (*Kierkegaard,* 189; 133). Thus, "hope" promises within the figure only the collapse of the figure as the proleptic demarcation of its legibility, irreducible to any one thing in particular. In this sense, the significance of "hope" for Adorno is, again, primarily temporal. In self-negation and self-destruction, "hope" opens figural meaning up to the possibility of a future. But it can do this only insofar as any meaning granted to a figure is prematurely suspended in the figure's decay.

The "hope" of images, however, is not itself an image, even paradoxically when it is given in the image. For Adorno, it emerges where images themselves no longer reach, that is to say, where images are more than simply images; they enter into "reality." The image always remains in some sense "unreal," as Adorno quotes Kierkegaard explaining in *Practice in Christianity:* "For the imaginary image, or the image which the imagination reproduces and fixes, is after all, in a certain sense, unreality, it lacks the reality of time and duration and of the earthly life" (195–96; 138).[22] This has more to do with the untranslatability of the image into reality than with the irreality of the image itself. If "reality" is represented aesthetically in an image, then the "reality" contained in the image as represented there is no longer real. What remains "real" is only the image itself in its aesthetic appearance. The connection to reality appears only where the unreal image stops, and this has everything to do with the effects of the reality of the image (as opposed to an only ideal reality in the image). What Kierkegaard discusses as a limitation of the "imagination" *(Einbildungskraft),* Adorno identifies as the limitation of the image *(Bild).* "Hope" enters in this limit: "The unpresentability *[Unvorstellbarkeit]* of despair in fantasy is its guarantee for hope" (*Kierkegaard,* 196; 136). "Hope" because, where there can be no image of reality, there must be reality.

"Hope" has nothing to do with what is represented in images; it has to do only with the necessarily incomplete reality of images—the reality of the image only as its very incompletion. There is, even for Kierkegaard himself, no totalizable construction in reality, neither in the totality of the figure nor in the totality of what the figure would describe, neither in the "spheres" nor in the subject's own "self." And it is only in the abruptly incomplete finitude of the image that reality comes into play. Reality, as Adorno says, "happens." The difficulty is that, if "reality" happens, it happens only at the limits of the image as what constitutes its finitude, not its content. To understand images, to read them, even as "ciphers," is to read and understand precisely what delimits their own legibility: "Therefore, it is not the total self and its total image, but only the fragment of existence in decay, devoid of all subjective 'meaning,' the sign of hope, and its fissures are the true ciphers, historical and ontological in one" (*Kierkegaard,* 197; 139). What is legible is no longer "*Sinn*" as the possible content even of fragments, but rather the "fissures" that break the fragments apart. These fissures, and not the material fragmented, are the "true ciphers." What is legible is only the disruption, only the "caesura."

In the end, even Adorno cannot resist the temptation to read "hope" as the promise of security—the messianic possibility of a certainty yet to come, as soon as one understands well enough the aporetic discontinuity of figural meaning. Meaning, it seems, even within inevitable decay of an only ephemeral reality, still moves toward the possibility of reconciliation. The "cipher," it seems, still promises the confluence of "hope" and "reconciliation": "If the history of fallen nature is that of the decay of its unity, then it moves in decay towards reconciliation, and its fragments bear the tears of disintegration as promising ciphers" (*Kierkegaard,* 199; 139). We read now with Kierkegaard: if the cipher presents the reality of "reconciliation," it is, truly, an "irreconcilable expression." Figures themselves can promise nothing other than their own promising.

3

Affirmation: "Death's Decision" and the Figural Imperative in Rilke and Kierkegaard

Clearly the difficulty with reading Kierkegaard—the difficulty with which Kierkegaard's work presents its readers—has to do with the extent to which and the multiple ways in which language remains inconceivable merely as a system of representations. If what Kierkegaard shows his readers is the instability of representations, this is because the "productivity" of language extends beyond its aesthetic perception; language is never merely aesthetic, and understanding it is not merely about perceiving what it is. In this sense, the rhetorical analysis of linguistic significations will never entirely account for what language means. Insofar as the understanding of language in Kierkegaard's account always concerns more than what it represents or what it means, the understanding of language will always be confronted with what language is not—the point at which it reaches its limit or comes to its end. If understanding language involves the understanding of its own excesses, the ways in which it exceeds even itself, then any descriptive understanding of language will never entirely present an understanding of language. As Adorno has shown, concrete images of linguistic figuration constitute the moment in which reality interrupts the otherwise conceptual functioning of a more direct communication. The very literal reality of figurative presentation thus constitutes the moment in which language is not language: it is itself reality, not the representation of reality. Figuration is, therefore, both the most linguistic moment of all language and the impossibility of language.

In this sense, the importance of Kierkegaard's work cannot be restricted entirely to the realm of direct commentary, even in as profoundly Kierkegaardian a reading as Adorno's. Kierkegaard's work crosses the formal boundaries between genres. Of interest here are those authors whose interest in Kierkegaard might offer some useful account of transformations within their own work. For it is within literature that language meets its own end and the limit of its own possibility. We begin, therefore, with the poetry of Rainer Maria Rilke, whose work, perhaps beyond that of any other, engages in language the very limit of existence itself.

Rainer Maria Rilke began reading Kierkegaard in the winter of 1903–1904 and learned Danish for the sole purpose of reading Kierkegaard and Jens Peter Jacobsen in the Danish original. Though sparse and often cryptic, references to Kierkegaard are to be found throughout Rilke's letters. However, explicit citations of works by Kierkegaard are rare. For example, in a letter to his wife, Clara Rilke (September 16, 1907), Rilke refers to Kierkegaard's "The Care of Poverty," recalling the time they spent reading Kierkegaard together in Paris. More common are more general citations of Kierkegaard. For example, to Marie von Thurn und Taxis, Rilke writes: "Now I am reading Kierkegaard, it is magnificent, real magnificence, never has he moved me so" (August 30, 1910). In a letter to Lou Andreas-Salomé, he refers to Kierkegaard's "melancholy" *(Schwermut)* (February 7, 1912). And in one to Katharine Kippenberg he refers to "the terribly great Kierkegaard" (February 11, 1915). Most significant for our purposes here are the numerous references to Kierkegaard's essay "At a Graveside" in letters from the summer and fall of 1915, just after the first publication of the text in German translation, to his friends Editha Klipstein (July 27, 1915), Ilse Erdmann (August 18, 1915), and Sodonie Nádherný von Borotin (August 2 and 19, 1915).[1]

Rilke is also said to have been familiar with several of Kierkegaard's most important philosophical texts as well, including *Stages on Life's Way* and *Either/Or*. Thus, Rilke's familiarity with Kierkegaard was by no means limited, covering both important pseudonymous philosophical texts, many of the theological discourses, and commentaries and interpretations of Kierkegaard's work. Most important to Rilke appears to have been the commentary on Kierkegaard by Georg Brandes as well as the work of his friend, Rudolf Kassner, whose essay on Kierkegaard, "Sören Kierkegaard—Aphorismen" (Søren Kierkegaard—Aphorisms), Rilke praised as "the best that has been written about Kierkegaard, aside from Brandes' earlier excellent study."[2]

All this is to say, in short, that Rilke read Kierkegaard. If this interest in Kierkegaard is to be found of any significance for Rilke's work, however, it must be shown to impact that work more substantially. If the importance of Kierkegaard for Rilke concerned the "productivity" of a nonconceptualizable excess in language, how might the understanding of this excess appear in Rilke's work if it appears neither as direct commentary nor as the translation or incorporation of an idea into his work?

The invocation in Rilke's letters of Kierkegaard's "At a Graveside" (Ved en Grav), one of the few essays to which Rilke explicitly refers, proves a useful point of departure. For Kierkegaard—and, as I shall demonstate, for Rilke as well—the problem of death is without question a problem for language. "Death," Kierkegaard writes in this essay, "has no representation *[Forestilling]* and is not concerned with representations."[3] Kierkegaard articulates the specific problem presented by death as one of coming to terms with what does not as such appear and cannot as such be presented. There is simply nothing to represent, nothing to know. Because death is neither image nor idea, any attempt to present it, to explicate it and make it familiar by subsuming it within a given conceptual framework, would be to ignore its finite specificity. Death is simply the absolute limit to any possible representation. On the other hand, its unpresentability does not prohibit representations; death simply does not concern itself with them. Death is not somehow in search of a representation it would otherwise lack.

If death absolutely resists any attempt to represent it, as one would represent any other thing or any other idea, and if it nonetheless "exists" inso far as it is inevitable and unavoidable, it inevitably encounters language as the language of representations as its unsublatable limit. Even in its irreducibility to any linguistic representation, however, death still cannot be excluded. Its presentation, therefore, must in some sense be figurative, insofar as it can be present only in or as something else; yet, in each of its occurrences, insofar as the presentation of death is necessarily other than death, its representation as representation can no longer be the representation of death. Figuration in this context cannot be understood as the promise to transcend finite limitation and to represent the unknown as something in principle knowable and familiar.[4] Rather, the limitation death presents to all language poses a specific problem to any figuration conceived as such a promise. Any attempt to establish the figurative representation of that which is always only the finite limitation to representability necessarily undermines the very figurative gesture itself. Thus, in figuratively attempting to overcome finite limitations by subsuming them within an order of infinite and future reconciliation, the figure itself introduces a finitude that it is unable to overcome or control. The eternal and infinite redemption of figuration is categorically denied. Any promised redemption within a figurative conception inevitably founders on this inability to overcome its own finitude. The promise of figuration is absolutely unable to fulfill itself; the promise can only fail. And yet, neither Kierkegaard nor Rilke ever claimed that there can be no figuration, that there can be only a language of literal representations in which all figuration will be exposed as lies. On the contrary, precisely because of the failed promise of figuration in its encounter with death, figures of death themselves become figures of figurality: pure figuration. Thus, the figuration of "death" can be only the presentation of an always limited and limiting figurability. Death, in this sense, is decisive. To encounter death in language is to encounter the very limit of language. One cannot not encounter the finite limitation of language, and, accordingly, one cannot avoid its figurality. Figural language is not a promise; it is an imperative. Precisely what this means for Rilke, however, remains to be seen.

Though death appears virtually throughout Rilke's work, the difficulty with which death presents language is most succinctly taken up in an unpublished poem of 1915, written concurrently with his citations of Kierkegaard's essay. The poem reads:

Der Tod

Da steht der Tod, ein bläulicher Absud
in einer Tasse ohne Untersatz.
Ein wunderlicher Platz für eine Tasse:
steht auf dem Rücken einer Hand. Ganz gut
erkennt man noch an dem glasierten Schwung
den Bruch des Henkels. Staubig. Und: "*Hoff-nung*"
an ihrem Bug in aufgebrauchter Schrift.

Das hat der Trinker, den der Trank betrifft,
bei einem fernen Frühstück ab-gelesen.

Was sind denn das für Wesen,
die man zuletzt wegschrecken muß mit Gift?

Blieben sie sonst? Sind sie denn hier vernarrt
in dieses Essen voller Hindernis?
Man muß ihnen die harte Gegenwart
ausnehmen, wie ein künstliches Gebiß.

Dann lallen sie. Gelall, Gelall . . . . . .
. . . .

O Sternenfall,
von einer Brücke einmal eingesehn—:
Dich nicht vergessen. Stehn!

Death

Here stands death, a bluish distillate,
in a cup without support.
A wondrous place for a cup:
stands on the back of a hand. Quite clearly
one still recognizes on the glazed arch
the handle's break. Dusty. And: "*Ho-pe*"
on its bow in worn-out script.

The drinker, whom the drink befalls,
registered that at a far-off breakfast.

What sorts of beings, then, are those
who must ultimately be scared off with poison?

Would they otherwise remain? Are they engrossed here
with this eating of hindrance?
They must have the hard present
removed, like artificial teeth.
Then they babble. Babble, babble . . . . . .
. . . .

O falling star,
once seen from a bridge —:
Not to forget you: to stand!

(Rainer Maria Rilke, *Werke in Drei Bänden* II, 103–104)

Neither the thematization nor the representation of death, this poem is rather about language and, in particular, the language of death. To insist, however, that death is neither thematizable nor representable does not mean that death does not somehow make an appearance. What is presented is not so much the figuration *of* death as it is figuration *by* death. Thus, the poem does not trace the presentation of representations, each of which would stand symbolically for death, but rather it articulates the finite delimitation requisite for any representation whatsoever.

The poem begins simply with a declarative assertion: "Da steht der Tod . . ." (Here stands death. . .): There it is, death. The gesture is first and foremost demonstrative, simply indicating and situating something apparently already there and giving it a name. There is, first of all, nothing but the demonstrative gesture—"Da steht" (Here stands), or simply, "Da" (Here)—and only then can what is named in this gesture be figuratively described. This requires still a perhaps more precise reading. "Da steht" can also mean "Da steht geschrieben" (It stands written). "Da steht der Tod": It is written, the word "*death*." Or: It, death, is written. To encounter language at this limit would be to read, to read the inscription of "death"—to read, that is, what cannot be read, what is necessarily unavailable as such to any reading. Thus, this poem is concerned with the specificity of the verb *stehen* (to stand). What does it mean *to stand*? What stands? How is it registered? And to what effect?

The poem begins, in this way, not with the presentation of death itself (it cannot), but with the presentation of language. "Death" is perhaps to be taken quite literally; it might simply be the word "death," as it is written. It might be the literal manifestation of the word itself, being-written as such, simultaneously designating reading as the possibility of relating to death, making language the topos in which the encounter with death takes place. Only secondarily does this gesture become the occasion for a metaphorical identification or attribution. "Da steht der Tod, ein bläulicher Absud ..." (Here stands death, a bluish distillate). Only after the caesura does there appear a metaphorical correspondence between "death" and "a bluish distillate."[5] That is, there is an irreducible separation between the naming of death and its metaphorical appearance. Death is both a word and, as a word, also something other than a word in its phenomenal presentation: "bläulicher Absud"—blueish extract or "decoction."[6] "Bluish distillate" is first a metaphor for death, even taking up blue as the traditional color for death. But "bluish distillate" is not *blauer Sud* (blue brew)—and *Sud* is a far more common word in German than the rare and anachronistic *Absud*. Not exactly substantiation in any direct or immediate sense of making something substantive, whatever "substance" is presented here is given only insofar as it is taken away. "Bluish" is not *blue*; it is perhaps not even a color. "Absud" (distillate) is not so much a thing as it is an occurrence or event. "Absud" is "decoction": condensation by way of removal ("Ab–" means "away–").

"Bluish distillate" is only the first in a series of images that, in the absence of a restorative principle of figuration, present not death's figuration, but, in figurability itself, death's finite delimitation. At the same time, "bluish distillate" is only the first in a series of images of death's disintegration or of death as disintegration. Therefore, Rilke is concerned here not with the representation of death per se, but with the presentation of what would contain death. Rilke is concerned, first of all, with the cup *(Tasse)* in which "death" "stands" and with the singularity of its appearance. "Da steht der Tod, ein bläulicher Absud/in einer Tasse ohne Untersatz" (Here stands death, a bluish distillate,/in a cup without support). No sooner is it presented than it begins falling away. "Ohne Untersatz": It has no support, neither material nor logical. "Ein wunderlicher Platz für eine Tasse:/steht auf dem Rücken einer Hand" (A wondrous place for a cup:/stands on the back of a hand). "Wunderlich" (wondrous) in this context would first have to be understood simply as "sonderbar" (unusual or curious), but also—and, to a certain extent, this applies to the unusual word "Absud" (distillate) as well—as indication and historicization of language's decay. *Wunderlich* has not always meant only "unique" or "unusual"; it also used to mean what wunderbar now means: "wonderful" or "of wonder," and so on.[7] Yet, it is still not enough to trace the peculiarities of Rilke's diction here. We have to follow the grammar of this poem as well. The sentences in this first stanza are broken up: verbs are omitted—"Ein wunderlicher Platz für eine Tasse" (a wondrous place for a cup); subjects are left out—"steht auf dem Rücken einer Hand" (stands on the back of a hand) or cryptically reduced to a single word—"Staubig" (Dusty) or "Und" (And). We are witnessing the breaking up of language, its falling apart.

But wait; we have already gone too far. We must not imagine that this language of falling apart is a language already fallen apart, already past its end. Rather, language is itself this ending without yielding to some unknown beyond. Language is still language; and, in spite of its apparent desperation at this moment, it is still meaningful. Furthermore, it is no accident that the one sentence apparently robbed of all content is reduced—decocted—to the single conjunction "Und" (And). This falling apart still retains a certain kind of legibility: "Ganz gut/erkennt man noch an dem glasierten Schwung/den Bruch des Henkels" (Quite clearly/one still recognizes on the glazed arch/the handle's break). But what one still grasps here is its ungraspability; one cannot get hold of it other than by "recognizing" what, however broken itself, is still to be read: "Und: '*Hoff-nung*'/an ihrem Bug in aufgebrauchter Schrift" (And: "*Ho-pe*"/on its bow in worn-out script). The separation of word and meaning is presented here literally as the separation and division in the word itself is presented as its material ruination. What Rilke's poem exemplifies on this occasion is that reading involves something altogether different from the translation of a word back into its ideal meaning.

If death is to be read at all, it is legible only in its effects. Its effects, however, are neither singular in themselves nor reducible to a single meaning as death. There is no going back. Not even "distillate" is translatable back into death as the singular guarantor of its meaning, not even metaphorically. "Bluish distillate" is and remains "bluish distillate," with or without any equation with death. Rather, death in "Here stands death" becomes "bluish distillate" in all the senses of its material and grammatical disintegration. Death produces ruins. Figuration itself would inevitably be ruination. Ruination would in turn be the operative principle of language, and figuration the language of deformation and distortion. In the absence of any accountable ideal, one is rather confronted with the very finitude of language itself as the finitude that is death: "Das hat der Trinker, den der Trank betrifft,/bei einem fernen Frühstück ab-gelesen" (The drinker, whom the drink befalls, registered that at a far-off breakfast). The reading of the presentation of the written inscription is itself also broken, divided—or, rather, it itself also breaks and divides. The proximate relation of the ruination of language as "'*Hoff-nung*'" ("*Ho-pe*") to the presentation of death as extraction in *Ab-sud* becomes the possibility, or the impossibility, of the experience of language as such: language, then, as *ab-lesen* (to register or read off, or, more literally, read away). Reading becomes the literal ruination of language in the reading *(lesen)* away *(ab)* of an "aufgebrauchter Schrift" (worn out script). It literally wears away and uses up inscription. Death, as that which stands written, recedes from reading (is never itself graspable) and recedes by reading (is always thus being worn away). Reading away does not amount to the loss of meaning as its disappearance. Rather, reading as reading away is the disfigurative act whereby language itself might become meaningful—that is, where language itself is not merely understood as representative of an already established meaning, but, in its distorting turns, becomes productive of meaning.

To encounter death is to read its inscription, its continual wearing away, decoction, and deformation. There is no alternative. Yet to read "death" is not to refer back to a prior meaning as death. To read in inscription any prior meaning as its only meaning would precisely be to avoid death by avoiding its finitude, thus obscuring its deformations. Death, however, cannot be avoided. This is precisely what makes its finitude absolute. Death's end turns all language in its phenomenal appearance, whether as speech or inscription, into distortion. To avoid death would simply be to fail to recognize this necessity. Nothing would appear; yet in this nonappearance, there would still be death.

Just as death itself cannot be restricted to any singular figurative presentation, there might be more than one way to meet death, more than one way to die: "Was sind denn das für Wesen,/die man zuletzt wegschrecken muß mit Gift?" (What sorts of beings, then, are those,/who must ultimately be scared off with poison?) One way or another, however, death still arrives, and its inevitability still inflects language. Notice, first, just how compactly Rilke's text works: the line endings "Schrift" (script, or writing more generally), "betrifft" (befall), and "ab-gelesen" (registered or read away) become inverted in the following two lines, which end with "Wesen" (essence) and "Gift" (poison). Thus, "Gift" is presented as an alternative to "Schrift"—a certain potentiality of "Schrift" without delineating its singular possibility. Following the unrhymed verse of the first stanza, the regular *abba* rhyme scheme of the next four lines lends the transition from "Schrift" to "Gift" a sense of inevitability, even where the logical relationships appear all but certain.

The question posed here is this: What sorts of beings are those who *cannot* confront death, who cannot read it or take it in—take in, that is, its wearing away? "Blieben sie sonst?" (Would they otherwise remain?) Would they simply continue and persist in some arbitrary or undetermined fashion? Is it impossible for them to disappear or become anything else, to "become" in the emphatic sense upon which both Kierkegaard and Rilke insist? "Sind sie denn hier vernarrt/in dieses Essen voller Hindernis?" (Are they engrossed here with this eating of hindrance?) But "hindrance" of what? What is hindered here, and what hinders? Death, evidently, does not; rather, it is death that one would attempt to avoid. In fact, nothing is obstructed by this "hindrance" at all, except perhaps those who might try to rely upon it, to retain it so that it might retain them, where the desired retention of "presence" becomes a kind of vain and hopeless grasping at straws. Of those who would thus exclude death, it is said:

> Man muß ihnen die harte Gegenwart
> ausnehmen, wie ein künstliches Gebiß.
> Dann lallen sie. Gelall . . . . . .
> . . . .
>
> They must have the hard present
> removed, like artificial teeth.
> Then they babble. Babble, babble . . . . . .
> . . . .

From "vernarrt" (engrossed) and "Gegenwart" (present) to "Hindernis" (hindrance) and "Gebiß" ("teeth" or "denture"), it seems that presence itself, "the hard present," is precisely the obstruction that separates one off from death. "The hard present" here is conceived as exclusionary—the presence with which one would be exclusively "engrossed," even if this presence then were to acquire a sense of artificiality, "like artificial teeth."

One might even suggest that such absolute reliance upon presence can be conceived only as artifice, so long as its perception is sustained only in the avoidance of the necessity that death presents. Apparently freed of delimitation by death, speech is reduced to an inarticulate mumble or "babble" (Gelall) or to the mere nothing and absence indicated by ellipses. Yet this, too, is ultimately part of death's (il)legibility. This stuttering and mumbling, and the silence of the ellipses is perhaps death's purest presentation. Death obliterates; it is ob-literation itself in the most literal sense as the erasure or striking out of the letter or of what is written.

The poem does not end here, however, as if to suggest that death's finitude would be without consequence or that its obliteration would amount to the disappearance of language. The utter silence falling upon "babble" becomes another beginning. Without any mediating connection, the absolute obliteration in the ellipses gives way to one more image, one more of death's figurations. The possibility of silence and the inarticulate sound of "babble" are not simply forgotten, but carried over into another distortion:

> O Sternenfall,
> von einer Brücke einmal eingesehn—:
> Dich nicht vergessen. Stehn!

> O falling star,
> once seen from a bridge—:
> Not to forget you: to stand![8]

Not forgotten, "Gelall" is caught up in the falling figure of the star: "Sternenfall," simultaneously suspending in a single image both the "*stehen*" *(Stern)* of the inscription as "death" and the "falling" of speech into "Gelall" *(Fall)*: standing in falling; standing written in being read away. Reading "death" here does not end exactly in perceiving or understanding it. One has not completed one's task by restoring to the word or image its supposedly proper meaning. In the absence of any such resolution, the task of reading begins precisely where it breaks off: "—:/Not to forget you: to stand!" The breaking off of the now apostrophized image—an image no longer simply presented as an image of death, but one now addressed, whereas all others had apparently been merely descriptive—occurs prematurely, prior to its grammatical or conceptual completion, leaving behind nothing but the apostrophe and giving way to the command: "Dich nicht vergessen" (Not to forget you). Yet this command is not precisely an imperative in the sense that an imperative would always be explicitly addressed to another identifiable subject. There is no grammatical subject here. The verb is not conjugated at all, but is left simply in the infinitive.[9] "Not to forget you" can perhaps be understood only as a reflexive imperative, a command issued to no one but the speaker himself, where, however, no subject, not even the speaker, can appear. It is the command of language to itself in its very occurrence. "Not to forget you," a command from language to itself regarding death's figurability, becomes in the final instance simply: "To stand!" But what, we still must ask, can this imperative mean in a poem where standing is necessarily bound to fall?

"Death," written on November 9, 1915, occured at a pivotal point with respect to Rilke's work, one at which he concerned himself with death in various ways. There are two letters devoted to the discussion of death: one written on October 9, one month before this poem was written, and one written on November 8, the day before Rilke wrote the poem, both of which I will address in a moment. At the same time Rilke was also writing several poems concerned explicitly with death, including perhaps most important, the fourth of the *Duino Elegies,* which was written on November 22 and 23. Here, too, the encounter with death appears as one of necessity, though in perhaps less emphatic terms than those of "Death." Yet here, too, the discussion of death inevitably arrives at the difficulty of its representation or its description. The elegy concludes with the lines:

> Aber dies: den Tod,
> den ganzen Tod, noch *vor* dem Leben so
> sanft zu enthalten und nicht bös zu sein,
> ist unbeschreiblich.
>
> But this: death,
> the whole of death, still *before* life,
> so gently to contain, and not to be angry,
> is indescribable.
>
> (*Werke in Drei Bänden* I, 455–56)

This death has something in common with the death standing in the previous poem. One might, therefore, suggest an even stronger reading of the final word, "unbeschreiblich" (indescribable), and take it as more than simply descriptive. One might suggest that this necessary inclusion of death "*before* life," both spatially and temporally, renders death more than merely indescribable or without description, that "unbeschreiblich" (indescribable) might rather undo description, requiring that, whatever description *(Beschreibung)* there might be of life, its prior inclusion of death carries with it its own destruction, its own silent prefix "un–." What, in other words, does it mean to include within life, even before life, a death that cannot be presented in life? If death is nothing, and certainly nothing for description, what happens to description when it must also include this nothing? "Description" would, in this sense, neither describe nor even figure its object so much as it would have to transform it.

In this sense, death would become foundational for the whole issue of transformation that is central to the *Duino Elegies* and other of Rilke's poems. Here in the fourth elegy, for example, figurality takes up the relation between "Engel" (angel) and "Puppe" (doll):

> Engel und Puppe: dann ist endlich Schauspiel.
> Dann kommt zusammen, was wir immerfort
> entzweien, indem wir da sind. Dann entsteht
> aus unsern Jahreszeiten erst den Umkreis
> des ganzen Wandelns. Über uns hinüber
> spielt dann der Engel.
>
> Angel and doll: then is finally theater.
> Then comes together what we continually
> divide by being there. Then emerges
> from our seasons first the circuit
> of the entire transformation. Away above us
> the angel then plays.
>
> (*Werke in Drei Bänden* I, 455)

"Angel and doll," it is clear, never exactly come together: "Über uns hunüber/spielt dann der Engel" (Away above us/the angel then plays.) The very fact of our existence seems inevitably to obstruct any principle of figuration directed toward the ideal unification and reconciliation of a concrete finitude with conceptual universality. The point, however, is not to do away with figuration altogether, but to put it to another use—or, rather, in accepting its inherent inability to overcome finitude and contingency, to understand that it works in a way different from reconciliation.[10] Nonetheless, the parallel structures following the colon after "Angel and doll" do indicate something about what "coming together" in this context means. "Dann/entsteht aus unsern Jahreszeiten erst den Umkreis/des ganzen Wandelns" (Then emerges/from our seasons first the circuit/of the entire transformation). For Rilke, the only possibility of transition or transformation is attributed to the discrepancy in which existence holds unification apart. It is here that he situates death's imperative affirmation.

In the letter to Ilse Erdmann of October 9, 1915, in which Rilke cited Kierkegaard's essay on death, although death's finitude is certainly corporeal, appearing initially as "bodily pain," the efficacy and particularity of death indicate, rather, the body's "duality of thing and self." In the same way that "theater" first appears with "angel" and "doll," the indissociability of "thing and self" here suggests that neither "thing" (Ding) nor "self" (Ich), neither body nor soul, would be conceivable without the other. Rather than rendering a clear separation between what is corporeal and therefore unintelligible and the nonmateriality and pure intelligibility of spirit, or what Rilke calls "soul" (Seele), the indissociable duality evident in corporeal pain points up both the necessarily material quality of the intelligible and, vice versa, the intelligible quality of material things. Irreducible to one another and irreducible also to any concept that would in any way annul their opposition, Rilke describes pain simply as "an intensity experience": "I can only perceive it as an intensity experience, as we certainly have long known the intense *[Das Intensive]* from it before we, momentarily, rediscover it in joy, in rapture, in concentrated work." The pleasure, however, is not exactly the point. Its repetition is. What concerns Rilke here is the "momentary" rediscovery of this intensity "in concentrated work" *(in verdichteter Arbeit)*—in, one might suggest, poetry *(Dichtung)*. Death, the very source of all intensity in life, must preexist each of its rediscoveries.

There is, however, one moment, Rilke suspects, when this corporeal intensity is perhaps not so welcome: "In dying, on the other hand, corporeal pain must often be a nasty irritation, since it is certainly the most here *[das Hiesigste]*, invalid, so to speak, with respect to the infinite *[dem Allgemeinen gegenüber]* toward which the dying one is directed (*Briefe* vol. 2, 47). Pain's intensity remains attached to the "here" (Hiesige) as the "most here" *(das Hiesigste)*, its most proper expression in the inseparability and incommensurability of "thing and self," whereas to die would mean to move into the "universal," removing "thing" from "self," and eliminating the corporeal in order to preserve a pure and ideal "spirit." Death, however, is not the same as dying. Corporeal pain appears to disrupt the desired transition and transformation from "the here" to "the infinite," from the finite and particular to the universal, infinite, and eternal. "The here" is, however, precisely what Rilke's poems, particularly those of this period, are most concerned with. One need only recall the *Duino Elegies:* "Being here is magnificent" *(Hiersein ist herrlich)* (elegy 7); "<u>Here</u> is the time of the <u>sayable</u>, here is its home" (<u>Hier</u> ist des <u>Säglichen</u> Zeit, <u>hier</u> seine Heimat) (elegy 9); and so on. Furthermore, it is precisely "the here" that determines any possibility of "self" as always and unavoidably bound to the "material." Is this then simply to be abandoned in the face of a perhaps more desirable universality? Or is something else at work? Both here and in the poems, desirable though this universality may be, it is never attained as such—not even as promised in death. The transition to the universal apparently sought in dying is always interrupted by death.

Rather than to be done away with or negated, Rilke suggests that "the here" ought somehow to be appropriated: ". . . but to assimilate earthly means, in order to attain a certain completion of our relationships to the earth, to be here unsayably, indescribably, breathlessly *[unsäglich, unbeschreiblich, atemlos hier zu sein]*: would that not be the only way for us finally to be conceived as more than merely earthly?" (*Briefe* vol. 2, 47). Not directly to appropriate things themselves of the earth, the one way to become "more than merely earthly" is to become "earthly" in a different sense. Rilke insists that one must appropriate "earthly means *[Mittel]*" in order to achieve completely one's "relationships *[Beziehungen]* to the earth." The "earthly" becomes, in its appropriation, a kind of tool or means, rather than an end in itself, which determines the possibility of one's relation to the earth. Indeed, the only possibility of being related to the earth, it seems, would consist of having the "means" of the earth as opposed to the things themselves, which, we might suppose, would rather be obstructions. Furthermore, for Rilke, not surprisingly, the only possibility of "being here" is explicitly linguistic, though not exactly representational: "to be here unsayably, indescribably, breathlessly." "Unsayably" *(Unsäglich)* and "indescribably" *(unbeschreiblich)*, rather, define a particular way of relatedness to the earth, which, while exceeding the bounds of a strictly representational discourse, are not themselves alinguistic.

The singularity of one's own "completion" as "more than" simply earthly requires the incorporation and appropriation of the here and now ultimately as the appropriation of one's own finitude as one's own measure. Rilke continues (note again the particularly strong use of the prefix "un–"): "I believe we have to experience immeasurability *[Unermeßlichkeit]* in our inability *[Unfähigkeit]* to apportion even the measurable" (*Briefe* vol. 2, 47). Yet Rilke first indicates a discrepancy. One's own finitude is not simply available directly or immediately as experience. One experiences immeasurability through one's own inability to measure or mark off even the measurable. The appropriateness to us of the immeasurable, Rilke claims, is precisely what death would indicate. One cannot measure what death terminates, yet death is the only measure or limit appropriate to us: "That is why Kierkegaard encloses us in the earnestness of death without further attributing to us either a specific time-limit *[Frist]* or eternal future" (*Briefe* vol. 2, 47). The possibility of "being here" with which Rilke is trying to come to terms is not teleologically directed toward an ideal universality. What Kierkegaard reminds us of, and reminds Rilke of at this point, is precisely this: there is neither determinate delay (*Frist*, as a period of time given for the "completion" of one's life) nor an eternal future (which would overcome all the boundaries and uncertainties inexplicably delineating the possibility of experience as being-here). Death literally encloses life and makes life itself finite.

The "earnestness of death" *(Dødens Alvoren)*, Kierkegaard explains, is not just about the denial of a certain concept of the eternal. The discussion of "death's earnestness" to which Rilke refers in his letter appears in the third of Kierkegaard's *Three Discourses on Imagined Occasions* (1846) under the title "At a Graveside." Death is simply the end—"all is over," as he asserts at the very beginning—and there remains simply "nothing" ("At a Graveside," 71). "To die" does not constitute the translation from being alive to being dead. Life and death cannot be modulated in this way, as if life and death were merely part of the same continuum in which being dead simply follows upon being alive as its continuation in another form; death is not ontologically analogous to living. Death ends life without promising any continued existence. The "earnestness of death" is not about what death is; it concerns, rather, the way this particular absence intervenes. It concerns what Kierkegaard calls "death's decision" *(Dødens Afgjørelse)*: both the unavoidable yet indeterminable end to life as the absolute demarcation of its finitude and the appropriation of this limit as finitude into life as the always decisive and dividing possibility of life itself. This limit, as I shall demonstrate, always has two edges, two ways of cutting: its certainty and its uncertainty. What grants death's decision its "earnestness" is that it is absolute (it is absolutely certain, and its end does away with absolutely everything) and absolutely unpredictable at the same time. That death will come is certain. When it will come is not.

Death, Kierkegaard insists, can be neither avoided nor deferred. In opposition to Epicurus's assertion that death ought not to be feared, "because 'when it is, I am not, and when I am, it is not,'" Kierkegaard explains that this is simply a deception and "jest"—a way of appearing to separate death from life without actually effecting any such separation. Thus, in jest, "the cunning contemplator places himself on the outside...; it is still only a jest if he merely contemplates death and not himself in death, if he thinks of it as the human condition but not his own. The jest is that this unyielding power cannot, as it were, get at its victim, that there is a contradiction, that death, as it were, tricks itself" (Kierkegaard, "At a Graveside," 73–74). It is not enough to think that, in ending life, death simply follows upon life, occurs afterward, remaining insignificant prior to its occurrence. Death is not an event among others; it is not experienced as others are. Rather, death's inevitable possibility must always be present in every moment, because death may arrive at any moment without warning and without delay. Death, in this sense, requires "earnestness." "Earnestness," Kierkegaard explains, "is thinking death and doing what death is unable to do—namely that you are and death also is" ("At a Graveside," 75). This is its aporetic impossibility: to say that, with the thought of death, "I am and death also is" is also to say "I am and I also am not." The "thought of death" means thinking death as the absolute limit and end to all thought and in thinking what thought itself cannot think—involving both thinking the limit to thought, but simultaneously in thinking this limit, opening thought up to its own end, its own destruction. There can be no thought, no understanding, without death. Every thought that does not include its own inevitable end and destruction has not understood anything at all, but, remaining as it would within the status quo of given understandings and representations, is merely the vain attempt to ward off death. The difficulty is that death is not simply to be thought in the abstract; rather, the "earnestness" of death requires thinking the finitude and particularity of one's own death—more specifically, "witnessing one's own death," attesting to it—and this, moreover, not simply occasionally, but at every moment, always: now.

Kierkegaard defines "death's decision" broadly in three respects. "Concerning death's decision," he writes, "the first thing that must be said is that it is *decisive [afgjørende]*." And, in typically Kierkegaardian fashion, he then comments upon his own formulation: "The repetition of the word is significant, and the repetition itself recalls how sparing of words *[ordknap]* death is." Death's decision is decisive, and this is the only word *(ord)* that describes this decision; there is no other. Kierkegaard must take "death's decision" literally. It literally does *(gjører)* away *(af)* with everything, puts an end to everything, and brings everything to a halt. And yet, the effect of this end is not one of dispersal, but of collection or definition in a specific sense:

> When death comes, the word is: Up to here, not one step further; then it is concluded, not a letter is added; the meaning is at an end and not one more sound is to be heard—all is over. If it is impossible to unite all the sayings of the countless living into one saying about life, all the dead are united in one saying, in one single saying to the living: Stand still. If it is impossible

> to unite all the sayings of the countless living in one survey about the endeavors of their lives, all the dead are united in one, in a single saying: Now all is over. ("At a Graveside," 78–79)

The voices of death are gathered together in order to issue one and only one command. Kierkegaard's claim is conditional and, as such, affirmative. In each case, the impossibility of uniting all the statements about life and the living is conditionally related to the univocal command of the dead. Were there no such unification in death, there would be no multivocal speech in life. Death itself means nothing at all. Yet it always stands in relation to life, issuing the command that the multifarious voices of life necessarily heed. "Stand still!" is thus death's command that puts an end to life, cuts it short without transferring or translating it into something else. Death's decision—like the discussions of "decisive significance" elsewhere in Kierkegaard's work—concerns the possibility of the production of meaning in an explicitly linguistic sense. Death does not complete, summarize, or otherwise explain anything that came before; it adds neither "letter" nor "sound." Language itself must remain incomplete, its end always premature, though the very possibility that it means something requires that it simultaneously include the decision of its own end. "Stand still!" in death's command means inevitably and unavoidably to face death. "Stand still!" as death's own command, is thus the constitutive possibility of meaning as such.

Second, absolute and certain though it may be, death remains "*undefinable [ubestemmelig]*." That is, it eliminates all possibility of distinction. Death appears to make all equal. Young or old, rich or poor, master or slave, "they lie, grave by grave, and tolerate one another . . ." ("At a Graveside," 85). And yet, Kierkegaard insists, those who have died have not simply been equated with one another; "the difference is undetectable."[11] Its indeterminability is conceivable neither as "equality" (i.e., the certainty of death is the same to all and makes all equal) nor as "inequality" (i.e., death meets each one separately, and follows no normative principle). Both of these claims are equally true for Kierkegaard. The point is this: "By this, nothing is said, but this is the way it must be when the question is about an enigma. Death does indeed make all equal, but if this equality is in nothing, in annihilation *[Tilintetgjørelse]*, then equality itself is indeterminable. . . ; the difference is undetectable" ("At a Graveside," 85). Kierkegaard is not concerned simply about an indeterminate play of certainty and uncertainty, never able to decide at which point one would finally supersede the other, the result of which would always be the same inconsequential indeterminacy.

(A, the author of *Either/Or*, the quintessential presentation of the "aesthetic personality" for Kierkegaard, might simply say, for example, Either death is certain, or it is uncertain. Either way, you will regret it.[12]) "Death's decision," he writes, "is like an empty space and like a silence in which nothing is heard, or it is toned down like a silence that is not disturbed." Death's decision is absolute; its indeterminability lies not in the inconsequential either/or of the aesthetic, but in the absolute "or" of destruction: "in nothing, in annihilation" ("At a Graveside," 85).[13]

The destruction effected by this indeterminacy cannot simply be abandoned as merely aesthetic, but becomes the imperative of putting death's decision into practice: "The ordinary view of death only confuses thought, just as wanting to experience in general does. The certainty of death is its earnestness; its uncertainty is the instruction, the practice of earnestness *[Indøvelsen af Alvoren]*" ("At a Graveside," 94). The work of earnestness in death's decision can never be concluded. Any possible determination or predication is always simultaneously undermined by its uncertainty. Not simply "nothing," death's decision is the absolute annihilation of any possible determinable distinction or certainty. The moment at which difference would become perceptible would be the moment of its destruction. The "practice of earnestness," as the continual confrontation in the "thought of death" with the absolutely destructive uncertainty that is death's finitude, inevitably destabilizes any "ordinary view," any "common understanding," or any understanding held in common. This is even true for death's "earnestness" itself, of which there can be no guarantee. It is never earnest enough, never seriously earnest. Just as in Rilke's notion of "concentrated work" *(verdichtete Arbeit)* there was no suggestion that the work would ever come to a conclusion—as if the duality of "thing and self" already precluded such a happy resolution—the uncertainty of death is precisely the infinite source of all possible "instruction": its uncertainty is the indissociable preclusion of any (guaranteed) conclusion. "Practice," as the encounter with inevitable annihilation, becomes the only possible ground for any possible certainty.

"Finally," Kierkegaard says—and this is the third respect in which he defines death's decision—"it must be said of death's decision that it is *inexplicable [uforklarlig]*. That is, whether or not people find an explanation, death itself explains nothing." Even with the occurrence of death as the absolute and insurmountable end to life, it neither means anything in itself, nor does it cause the life that preceded it to acquire some new meaning. "Whether or not people find an explanation," it remains "inexplicable" insofar as no guarantee of a proper or truthful meaning is ever itself available. Death can never coincide or agree with any explanation to which it might give rise. Nor, Kierkegaard further claims, is it available in any metaphorical presentation as "'night,'" "'sleep,'" "bluish distillate," and so on: "Whether it comes as the greatest benefaction or the greatest misfortune, whether it is hailed with jubilation or with desperate opposition, death knows nothing about that, because it is inexplicable. Death is the transition; it knows nothing about the circumstances, nothing at all" ("At a Graveside," 96–97).

Nonetheless, Kierkegaard insists that this "inexplicableness" cannot, indeed must not, stand alone: "See, this inexplicableness certainly needs *[trænger jo vel til]* an explanation. But the earnestness lies in just this, that the explanation does not explain death but discloses *[aabenbarer]* how the explainer is in his innermost being" ("At a Graveside," 97, trans. modified). Explanation cannot explain what it claims to explain. Rather than representing death or making it somehow understandable, the explanation in turn displays only itself and the "need" for explanation. Suggesting that any hasty or thoughtless explanation, in unwittingly disclosing the explainer's "innermost being," necessarily forces "the explainer [to testify] against himself," Kierkegaard commends a certain "reticence" with regard to explanation. Indeed, he warns us: "[D]eath, just because it is nothing, is not some sort of strange inscription that every passerby is supposed to try to read or a curiosity that everyone must have seen and have an opinion about" ("At a Graveside," 97). "Just because it is nothing," death is not simply accessible to and assimilable into each and every reading, each and every attempted interpretation, insofar as the "nothing" that it is would thereby be replaced with either meaning or intention. Any translation or explanation thus produced would leave death untouched, just as inexplicable as it had always been. The question Kierkegaard poses concerns not whether one can read death, but rather what one reads when one reads the nothing that is death. Its failure itself to amount to explanation does not preclude the possibility—or even perhaps the necessity—of explanation in the face of death.

Indeed, for Kierkegaard explanation seems to stand outside the annihilation with which death necessarily confronts life. Although death's inexplicability gives rise to explanation, Kierkegaard suggests that there is in turn something about the explanation itself that secures it from the destruction that death inevitably brings: "What is decisive about the explanation, what prevents the nothingness of death from annihilating the explanation, is that it acquires retroactive power *[tilbagevirkende Kraft]* and actuality in the life of the living person; then death becomes a teacher to him and does not traitorously assist him to a confession that denounces the explainer as a fool" ("At a Graveside," 97). What secures explanation for Kierkegaard is not the possibility of a figurative understanding directed toward an inevitably fictitious future. Rather, Kierkegaard tries to invert this relationship and directs the efficacy of explanation toward what preceded it. Explanation's decision would have to be equivalent to death's own decision in order for it to escape the absolute destruction with which death presents everything else. Or they would have to be the same. But is this security somehow a security against death? Is it nothing more than a "trick," an attempt to exclude death?

The explanation "acquires retroactive power" not in order to oppose death and to become forever secure, free of death's destruction, but rather because of death. Its "retroactive power" would itself have to be destructive. Unable to represent death, explanation thus is shown to function in a manner opposed to representation; explanation as death is rather antifiguration, oriented destructively "backwards," prohibiting any figural reconciliation of explanation with what it claims to illuminate. In this way, and only in this way, explanation "acquires actuality in the life of the living person." It encloses life, surrounds it at every moment.

However, Kierkegaard becomes suspicious of every explanation, ultimately even his own. He insists that no explanation can ever be certain of its own viability. No explanation is ever explanation enough. No matter what the explanation claims, the moment the explanation is held to be truthful representation, either figuratively or literally, it can no longer account for its own truthfulness. Of the numerous "explanations" of death, he writes:

> Then, too, the explanation has used other descriptive *[betegnende]* names and has called death a transition, a transformation, a suffering, a struggle, the last struggle, a punishment, the wages of sin. Each one of these explanations contains a whole life-view. What an earnest challenge to the explainer! It is easy to recite them all by rote, easy to explain death when it costs no effort to refuse to understand that the discourse is about the acquiring of retroactive power in life through the explanation. ("At a Graveside," 99)

All explanations of death are equally true, but to hold any explanation of death as descriptively true in its own terms amounts to the refusal of its "retroactive power."

Yet, Kierkegaard never denies that even in their representational capacity, explanations continue to serve a function: "Why does anyone want to transform death into a mockery of himself? Death has no need of an explanation and certainly has never requested any thinker to be of assistance. But the living need *[trænger til]* the explanation—and why? In order to live accordingly *[derefter]*" ("At a Graveside," 99). The question remains, however, in spite of every explanation of death, in spite of the very need for explanations of death: can one ever "live accordingly"? Can one, in other words, mean what one says when one speaks of death? "Alas," Kierkegaard writes, "yet it is so easy, so very easy, to acquire a true opinion, and yet it is so difficult, so very difficult, to have an opinion and to have it in truth." This is perhaps the one question that can never be answered, revealing a necessary discrepancy between any representation whatsoever and the possibility of its truth. Death's uncertainty is always at liberty, at any moment, to intervene, and its intervention necessarily suspends every possibility of meaning what one says. There can be no truthful explanation of death, and one cannot live precisely in accordance with any explanation of death, however necessary. So what is it that one "needs" when one needs the explanation of death "in order to live accordingly"? With what does one live in accordance? At no point does Kierkegaard believe one "needs" prescriptive regulation. Indeed, death's uncertainty undercuts every regulatory impulse. The "need" for explanation can be nothing other than the need "to need," to live in accordance with the impossibility of all accord. All explanation, in and of itself, is emptied out by this very necessity. "Therefore," Kierkegaard concludes, "the discourse will refrain from any explanation. Just as death is the last of all, so this will be the last thing said about it: It is inexplicable" ("At a Graveside," 100).

Each of the three qualities attributed to "death's decision" gives way to an imperative. The "decisiveness" of death's decision becomes the command: "Stand still!" Its "undefinability," by eliminating the certainty of representational distinctions, turns into the imperative of "practice" and repetition. Finally, the "inexplicability" of death's decision itself becomes the need for explication and, in turn, displays the very need "to need," or the imperative of necessity and the empty command: "Obey!" In each instance, death's "decision" is registered in an explicitly linguistic realm, always undermining or superseding any regulative claim that language functions exclusively in a representational fashion or that language is able to control the rules of its own expressivity. In each case, death's decision refuses to allow any explanation to be simultaneously true and true in its own terms, or it prohibits any representation from coinciding with what it claims to represent.

Meaning, therefore, cannot be conceived as "figurative" in the sense that any word, statement, or explanation would be accounted for in an ideal, universal, and external meaning, redeemed in an always future temporality. Death's decision, Kierkegaard insists, prohibits meaning from being supplementarily completed ex post facto. The "earnestness" of death's decision, he informs us, "does not waste much time in guessing riddles; it does not sit sunk in contemplation, does not rewrite expressions, does not think about the ingeniousness of imagery, does not discuss *[afhandler]*, but acts *[handler]*" ("At a Graveside," 82–83). Death describes nothing; it is not a figure. Although, if all linguistic meaning is still in some sense figural, figuration cannot be accounted for as the completion and fulfillment of linguistic expression. Such linguistic fulfillment is obliterated in the same moment it would be presented. Thus, Kierkegaard claims that "death in earnest gives life force as nothing else does" ("At a Graveside," 83). With death as the "force" in life and the thought of death as the force of understanding, the relation to death becomes the force of meaning and the condition of figurality itself. Figural inscription inevitably gives way to an imperative of transformation that is unfathomable in terms of description alone. The explanation does not disclose any meaning; it can never mean (only) what it says.

Thus, death's decision, in somewhat more formal terms, effects the irrevocable separation of aesthetics from ethics. In volume II of *Either/Or,* the text devoted to the articulation of the necessary incommensurability of ethics with aesthetics, Kierkegaard's Judge William offers the by now familiar definitions of aesthetics and ethics: "[T]he aesthetic in a person is that by which he spontaneously and immediately is what he is; the ethical is that by which he becomes what he becomes. The person who lives in and by and from and for the aesthetic that is in him, that person lives aesthetically" (Kierkegaard, *Either/Or* II, 178). The author, however, refrains here from offering an equally succinct definition of a comparable ethical life. The point is simply that aesthetics is determined by and restricted to what is given and immediately available, thus excluding the possibility of becoming anything at all. Rilke's "Archaic Torso of Apollo," which, concluding the presentation of a figurative transformation with an imperative—"You must change your life."—might be taken as the figurative impulse of the ethical imperative in Kierkegaard's sense of "Choose yourself." Transformation becomes the imperative of every figural presentation. This would be the first step toward an ethical praxis of figuration insofar as, for Kierkegaard, transformation necessarily distinguishes ethics from aesthetics.

Archaïscher Torso Apollos

Wir kannten nicht sein unerhörtes Haupt,
darin die Augenäpfel reiften. Aber
sein Torso glüht noch wie ein Kandelaber,
in dem sein Schauen, nur zurückgeschraubt,

sich hält und glänzt. Sonst könnte nicht der Bug
der Brust dich blenden, und im leisen Drehen
der Lenden könnte nicht ein Lächeln gehen
zu jener Mitte, die die Zeugung trug.

Sonst stünde dieser Stein entstellt und kurz
unter der Schultern durchsichtigem Sturz
und flimmerte nicht so wie Raubtierfelle;

und bräche nicht aus allen seinen Rändern
aus wie ein Stern: denn da ist keine Stelle,
die dich nicht sieht. Du mußt dein Leben ändern.

Archaic Torso of Apollo

We did not know the unheard-of head
where his eyes ripened. But
his torso still glows like a candelabrum,
where his gaze, now turned back,

contains itself and shines. Otherwise, the curve
of the breast could not blind you, and in the faint turn
of the limbs, a smile could not go
to that middle that bore creation.

Otherwise, this stone would stand, fragmented and disfigured,
under the shoulders' transparent collapse,
and would not glimmer like a predator's hide,

And would not break through all of its borders
like a star: for there is no place
that does not see you. You must change your life.

(*Werke in Drei Bänden* I, 313)

The concluding command appears to come from nowhere and to have nothing at all to do with all that precedes it. In an otherwise solely descriptive poem—the description of one aesthetic moment, the perception of an ancient statue—the sudden emergence of the command at the end breaks off the previous descriptive figuration. As in *anacoluthon*, one mode of speech disrupts another, indicating the irreconcilability of one with the other and yet still formally insisting upon the continuity from one to the other, necessarily relating the one to the other. The imperative is still part of the whole poem; indeed, it completes the poem and makes it whole, both formally and conceptually. Formally, this poem is a perfect sonnet, admitting a completion that the later poem "Death," for example, does not. Conceptually, by dint of its conclusive position, sealing off the poem at its formal end, this imperative could be said to provide the formative principle upon which the entire poem is founded. "You must change your life" is apparently derived from the transformation upon which the poem insists from the very beginning: from an absent sight ("We did not know his unheard of head/where his eyes ripened") to a pure seeing that is no longer literally reducible to any organ for sight ("for there is no place/that does not see you"). The finite and fragmented statue continues to be held as productive. Without eyes and without a head, the statue continues to see. The transformation is both descriptive and rhetorical. Every potential transformation in the subjunctive—"Sonst könnte nicht ... blenden ... Sonst stünde ... Und flimmerte ... Und bräche ..." (Otherwise, ... could not blind ... would stand ... would not glimmer ... would not break through ...")—is traced back to the indicative assertion carrying over from the first stanza to the next: "But/its torso still glowed like a candelabrum,/ where his gaze, now turned back,/contains itself and shines." Sight, now turned in upon itself, directed inward rather than toward the outside world, turns the entire statue in its truncated form into the now radiant instance of seeing—and, in turn, the radiantly compelling author of the (ethical) command: "You must!"

The same image, that of sight turned inward in a body no longer capable of sight, also appears in an earlier sonnet, Rilke's "Morgue," from the first volume of the *New Poems* (1907).[14] Describing the corpses laid out in the morgue, the poem ends with this observation:

> Die Bärte stehen, noch ein wenig härter,
> doch ordentlicher im Geschmack der Wärter,
>
> nur um die Gaffenden nicht anzuwidern.
> Die Augen haben hinter ihren Lidern
> sich umgewandt und schauen jetzt hinein.
>
> The beards stand, a little harder,
> but more orderly in the taste of the warders,
>
> only to avoid repulsing the onlookers.
> The eyes behind their lids have
> turned themselves around and look now within.
>
> (*Werke in Drei Bänden* I, 259)

"Morgue," furthermore, includes a more direct indication of death's disruptive finitude than the later Apollo poem can apparently tolerate (although, as the imperative itself indicates, it is nonetheless there as well). Describing the corpses on tables—"Da liegen sie bereit, als ob es gälte,/ nachträglich eine Handlung zu erfinden ..." (Here they lie prepared, as if one could/belatedly concoct a story ...)—the speaker claims: "denn das ist alles noch wie ohne Schluß" (for that is still all as if without conclusion). The corpses in and of themselves permit no belated explication. But this line depends upon the understanding of "wie" (as if). There is, no doubt, an end; it just cannot mean what anyone else would attribute to it.

In this respect, the two sonnets are not quite the same. Having resolved the problem of death in "Morgue" by turning sight inward, cutting off the connection between the corpses and "the onlookers," in the Apollo poem the same reversal of sight, itself still an indication of an irrevocable finitude, refuses to rest within the aesthetic limits of finitude alone. The statue becomes the origin and source of a sight that continues beyond its limits in the image of a star: "And would not break through all of its borders/like a star...." The aesthetic object itself transcends its own boundaries. The indicative assertion that the eyes must continue to exist in the torso itself, however demolished through time, makes all subjunctive hypotheses in turn indicative. It must be the case that the statue still sees. Otherwise nothing that the speaker perceives of the statue would exist at all and the transformation that the poem wrought could not have come about. Indeed, if none of this were true, there could be no imperative; if sight did not break "through all of its borders," the imperative "You must change your life" would never be heard.

Or would this imperative be heard? In what sense is it heard? From what does it emanate, and to whom is it addressed? How is it addressed? Is not the "Aber" *(But)* of the second line, which becomes a "Kandelaber" (candelabrum) in the third and ultimately a "Stern" *(star)* at the end—is not this disjunctive conjunction already indication enough of a finitude that the poem can either never (entirely) overcome or that it cannot entirely abandon or obliterate in order to make way for and ultimately bring about the transformation commanded at the poem's conclusion? In other words, even in the end, there remains an absolute difference between the finite material form of this thing, undeniably fragmented, and its transformation into an idealized whole. The command, however, is not the ethical imperative to become the universal ideal; the "Aber" does not overcome the fragmented form with which the poem began. The command issues precisely from this impossibility—from the failure of any ethical ideal, insofar as it would be conceived as universal, to overcome the irrevocable finitude that it would have to transcend but cannot. The command leaves and binds the speaker at the same place in which he found himself in Rilke's "Morgue": "for that is still all as if without conclusion." It is the imperative not to overcome finitude and become something else, something perhaps more ideal, but rather ultimately to take up this finitude, to change, but not by becoming another, in the same sense that Kierkegaard's Judge William describes the imperative of becoming: you must choose yourself. It is the imperative of finitude.

"But what is it, then, that I choose," Judge William asks in *Either/Or*, "do I choose this or that? No, for I choose absolutely, and I choose absolutely precisely by having chosen not to choose this or that" (*Either/Or*, II, 214). "This or that," insofar as they exist as possible choices, are always separate from and external to the one making the choice. The speaker in Rilke's "Apollo," for example, does not choose to become Apollo, but is rather turned back upon himself. The absolute choice can be only to choose oneself absolutely. That is, it is simply to choose oneself, "for I myself am the absolute." Judge William explains: "I choose the absolute that chooses me; I posit the absolute that posits me—for if I do not keep in mind that this second expression is just as absolute, then my category of choosing is untrue, because it is precisely the identity of both. What I choose, I do not posit, for if it were not posited I could not choose it, and yet if I did not posit it by choosing it then I would not choose it" (*Either/Or*, II, 213). The author insists upon a dialectic of choosing and positing, which can never be resolved without giving way to the indecision of the aesthetic. One cannot choose oneself as "either this or that" without simply choosing oneself as already given. At the same time, however, one cannot choose what is not somehow already available. To choose oneself is to divide oneself infinitely. One cannot choose the self that one is, but can only choose oneself as another.[15]

One must, in Judge William's argument, posit oneself as another in order to choose oneself in choosing it. Yet the moment this other exists as posited—exists, that is, as "either this or that"—then to choose it would no longer be to choose absolutely. On this point he is clear, if still paradoxical: to choose oneself is simultaneously to posit the self, whereas to posit oneself would not necessarily be to choose. Accordingly, one chooses oneself by choosing to choose, not by choosing some other thing or one thing as another. At the same time, the absolute choice is not a choice at all. Either it is held in infinite suspension, only to choose oneself without ever oneself being chosen—that is, without ever being able to conclude the choice. Or one does not choose oneself, but gives way to necessity: "I choose the absolute *that chooses me;* I posit the absolute *that posits me.*" One chooses to be chosen. The choice founders, in the one instance, on the irrevocable finitude of what is to be chosen and, in the other, on the renunciation of its own freedom or autonomy.

Yet this is precisely the point. One is not free to become absolutely anything at all. To become anything at all is only to become bound in aesthetic determination and is, thus, neither freedom nor choice (in the same way that meaning in language is never arbitrary; words cannot mean whatever one wants to make them mean). This would amount to becoming only "in a figurative *[uegentlig]* sense," limited precisely in the sense that it remains forever "inactual" *(u-egentlig)* and entirely inconsequential, thus indecisive. To become "in a figurative sense" would be only to become one thing or another from any number of possibilities without eliminating any of the other possibilities in the choice. One could always choose another; it would not really matter. "In other words," says Kierkegaard through Judge William, "the person who lives aesthetically sees only possibilities everywhere; for him these make up the content of future time, whereas the person who lives ethically sees tasks *[Opgave]* everywhere" (*Either/Or,* II, 251). As far as Judge William is concerned, there can be only one "task": oneself. One has only oneself in one's own finite particularity as one's only and necessary task. One must take responsibility for all that one is: "The individual, then, becomes conscious as this specific individual with these capacities, these inclinations, these drives, these passions, influenced by this specific milieu, as this specific product of a specific environment. But as he becomes aware of all this, he takes upon himself responsibility for it all *[overtager han den Altsammen under sit Ansvar]*" (*Either/Or,* II, 251). One has only oneself in one's own finite determination as one's own and only task, to which one is not simply given over as a matter of fate. Judge William continually insists that one can choose oneself only in freedom. One must, however, choose. The choice, he explains, "does not want to make the individual into someone else but into the individual himself; it does not want to destroy *[tilintetgjøre]* the esthetic but to transfigure *[forklare]* it" (*Either/Or,* II, 253).[16]

Judge William conceives of this "transfiguration" as a "transformation" *(Forwandling)*: "The task the ethical individual sets for himself is to transform *[forwandle]* himself into the universal" (*Either/Or,* II, 261). The difficulty for this author now is to articulate a possible mode of transformation and transfiguration. If, as he insists, "the ethical is the universal and thus the abstract" (*Either/Or,* II, 255), how is it possible to transform the finite and particular into the ethical without necessarily doing away with finitude itself? He first suggests a figurative relationship between these two possibilities, suggesting that the singular might "express" the universal:

> The person who views life ethically sees the universal, and the person who lives ethically expresses the universal in his life. He makes himself the universal human being, not by taking off [affpre] his concretion, for then he becomes merely nothing, but by putting it on [ifpre] and interpenetrating [gjennemtrænger] it with the universal. The universal human being is not a phantom [Phantom], but every human being is the universal human being—that is, every human being is shown the way by which he becomes [bliver] the universal human being. (*Either/Or,* II, 256, trans. modified)

The finite particularity of phenomenal presentation, however, does not indicate, refer to, or otherwise present a nonphenomenal, ideal universality. The figure would seem to fall apart, unable to unite the finite and the universal that figurative representation apparently promises. By dint of its very finitude, phenomenality refuses to disappear into ideality. If there is to be transformation at all, it must work the other way around. If "ethical life" is to be possible at all, it cannot, in Judge William's terms, require that each individual absolve his or her individuality for the sake of some universal ideal. Rather, "every human being is the universal human being"; that is, each individual must, in his or her particularity, be "the universal human being." Thus, the "expression" of the universal in "ethical life" is not the expression of something other than particularity. It is "the way" of particularity.

Now, however, Judge William warns: "The person who lives aesthetically is an accidental *[tilfœltige]* human being . . ." (*Either/Or,* II, 256). The difference between living "aesthetically" and living "ethically" concerns the difference between a life governed merely by chance and one directed by choice. To live ethically, one must choose. One must give oneself to oneself as one's own universal obligation. If the individual is the universal, it cannot be the universal in general. One individual cannot be "the universal" for another. Only in this way can one have oneself as one's own "duty" *(Pligt)* in its most particular sense—that is, as Judge William defines "duty," as the simultaneity of universality and individuality. "Duty" cannot be accounted for in the abstract relation to an ethical universality as the relation to something necessarily "external." On the contrary, it requires the inherent relationship of oneself to oneself—to oneself as one's own obligation. The author explains this through the ordinary use of the word "duty":

> I never say of a man: He is doing duty or duties; but I say: He is doing *his* duty; I say: I am doing *my* duty, you do *yours*. This shows that the individual is simultaneously the universal and the particular. Duty is the universal; it is required of me. Consequently, if I am not the universal, I cannot do the duty either. On the other hand, my duty is the particular, something for me alone, and yet it is duty and consequently the universal. Here personality appears in its highest validity. It is not lawless; neither does it itself establish its law, for the determination *[Bestemmelse]* of duty continues but the personality takes the form of the unity of the universal and the particular. That this is so is clear; it can be made understandable to a child—for I can do the duty and yet not do *my* duty, and I can do *my* duty and yet not do the duty. (*Either/Or*, II, 263, trans. modified)

One's duty must be one's own; it belongs to no other and can belong only to oneself alone. Because this is the case, to do one's duty, apparently, does not guarantee that one does "the duty." That is, whether one does one's duty or not, duty itself may or may not remain. One can never be secure in the claim that one has done one's duty and therefore be done with it, put it behind oneself and rest assured that this accomplishment will remain accomplished and not have to be repeated. Duty always remains. There is nothing about doing one's duty that amounts to its being done. There is no direct and immediate relation between "my duty" and "the duty" as universal. One can do only one's own duty, not that of another—even a transcendant other. "The universal," then, can be only one's obligation to do one's own duty, not the universal of an absolute duty.

In Rilke's Apollo poem, "You must change your life" is the expression of precisely such a duty. Addressed to each and every reader as a finite individual, it gives universality with finitude itself—as the obligation of each individual to each individual, which both emerges from and breaks off the poem's figurative reconstitution of the statue's missing and "unheard-of" head not by creating the head again, but by giving over its power of sight to the already fragmented and broken statue itself. This, moreover, is not merely situated within the statue as a kind of container, but, in being substantiated in the statue, also breaks through its finite limits. As Judge William points out, however, the shift from aesthetic "accident" to ethical "duty" is more than simply a change in reference, as if what appears as particularity might be preserved now as universality. No, the difference between "accident" and "duty" must be more destructive than this: "The ethical is the universal and thus the abstract. That is why in its perfect abstraction the ethical is always interdictory *[forbydende]*. Thus the ethical appears as law. As soon as the ethical is prescriptive *[befalende]*, it already has something of the aesthetic" (*Either/Or*, II, 255). The ethical forbids; it does not command. The command "Do this; this is the ethical," is not ethical at all, no matter what it may prescribe. Perhaps the only possibility of ethics is the necessity of the injuction: "No!"

However, within the context of *Either/Or*, Kierkegaard still shies away from this destructiveness. One of the fragments excluded from the "Diapsalmata" of A's papers in the first volume reads: "Either/or is the talisman with which one can destroy *[tilintetgjøre]* the whole world."[17] Neither exclusively aesthetic nor ethical, this destruction rather marks the irreconcilable difference between ethics and aesthetics. The "transformation" or "transfiguration" of the aesthetic through ethics is perhaps impossible so long as that transformation remains limited to the still aesthetically determined material. The fractured indeterminacy of the aesthetic marks not simply its dislocation from the ethical. More important, it inaugurates the imperative of another conception of the ethical. Thus, perhaps, it is in the fractured fracturing of the aesthetic that ethics becomes most ethical by risking becoming most destructive and most reckless. That is, any conception of the ethical that cannot address the possibility of its own destruction (in both senses: the possibility that it might destroy and be destroyed—by itself) can be conceived only as ideology and, in that sense, as the precise opposite of the ethical. Ethics must become its own material. Only with the later consideration of death does Kierkegaard begin to accept the necessity of a total destruction as the unavoidable accompaniment to ethical choice.

Almost one month following Rilke's citation of Kierkegaard and on the day before writing the poem with which we began this discussion, Rilke again wrote about death, this time in a letter to Lotte Hepner. Here, as in his novel *The Notebooks of Malte Laurids Brigge*, Rilke poses the following question: "This: how is it possible to live when after all the elements of this life are utterly incomprehensible *[völlig unfaßlich]* to us? If we are continuously inadequate in love, uncertain in decision and impotent in the face of death *[im Lieben unzulänglich, im Entschließen unsicher und dem Tode gegenüber unfähig]*, how is it possible to exist?" (Rilke, *Briefe* vol. 2, 52). This is, in some sense, the Kierkegaardian question par excellence, which is taken up broadly in Rilke as the self-questioning attempt to present one's own *Dasein* (existence). This is not just a rhetorical gesture. Another way to get at this would be to understand *Dasein* for Rilke as itself a kind of experiment or test—*Daseinsversuch*—as a way of getting hold of, if not determining, one's own *Dasein*. The three "elements" of life—"love"

(Liebe), "decision" *(Entschließen)*, and "death" *(Tod)*—are related, and it is no accident that Rilke says here "in love," "in decision," but "in the face of death" *(dem Tode gegenüber)*. The relation to death is always oppositional and inflects the possibility of the other two, "*Lieben*" and "*Entschließen.*"

Later in the same letter, Rilke is even more precise about this opposition, wondering how one might "prepare oneself for" *(sich vorbereiten auf)* this encounter, or even this "experience" *(Erleben)*: "But ... how do we manage to be properly prepared for that experiencing of life which at some time or other, in human relations, in our work, in suffering, seizes upon us and for which we must not be vague *[ungefähr]* because it is itself so precise *[genau]*, so precise that we can only meet in opposition *[Gegensatz]*, never in chance *[Zufall]*" (*Briefe* vol. 2, 57). Not "we can only meet *it* in opposition," but "we can only meet in opposition." Meeting itself is possible only oppositionally. The oppositional relation to death in its "earnestness" is the exact opposite of arbitrary chance. Yet this one necessity seems also—perhaps necessarily—to lie beyond the bounds of possible cognition and outside the possibility of experience. Immediately prior to this claim about the necessity of preparing oneself for the experience of death, Rilke writes: "But we cannot speak of experience; it is a secret, not one that locks itself away, not one that demands to be hidden; it is the secret that is sure of itself, that stands open like a temple, whose entrances are famed as an entry, singing between pillars larger than life, that they are the portals" (*Briefe* vol. 2, 56–57). Neither concealing nor disclosing itself, this secret presents itself. It is perhaps nothing but presentation, disclosing nothing but its own inability to disclose anything else.

Thus, for Rilke the discussion of death is inevitably bound up in the discussion of mystery. Death and the divine remain together for him insofar as they remain absolutely unknowable and lie beyond the limits of perception and possible experience. Our "confusion," Rilke says, might simply be related to a kind of backward orientation, whereby we might approach the gods only from behind, "separated from their sublimely radiant visage through nothing but themselves, quite near to the expression we long for, only just standing behind it" (*Briefe* vol. 2, 53). The point, however, concerning the relation to the god or gods (Rilke consciously uses both the singular and plural) is the possibility of turning toward and relating oneself to something imperceptible, nonempirical, and unpresentable. Yet it is not entirely clear that this situation could be rectified by a simple inversion whereby we would effectively move in front of the gods rather than remaining behind them. What would it mean to stand face to face before the gods? Would one then no longer be obstructed by the gods themselves? Or is the point rather that one is unavoidably separated from the gods by the gods and, in the same measure, separated from death by death? Thus, he writes simply: "But assume the meta-physical *[Über-Sinnliches].*" Appropriate it or, more precisely, incorporate it. But what is to be assumed and incorporated is not thereby made sensible.

What follows now can perhaps be called Rilke's theogony or, since this is about death rather than about the gods, Rilke's thanatogony: the explication of an originary relation to death by way of a genealogy of death:

> Let us agree that since the earliest beginnings man has shaped gods in whom here and there were contained only the dead and threatening and destructive and frightful, violence, anger, superpersonal stupor, tied up as it were into a tight knot of malice: the foreign, if you like, but, already to some extent implied in this foreign, the admission that one was aware of it, endured it, yes, acknowledged it for the sake of a certain, secret relationship and connection: *one was also this*, only that so far we have not known what to do with this side of our own experience; they were too big, too dangerous, too multi-faceted, they grew beyond us to an exaggerated significance *[Übermaß von Bedeutung]*; . . . (*Briefe* vol. 2, 53–54)

The gods, under the rubric of their "foreignness," designate something about "us." In spite of every acknowledged threat, there remains a certain identification: "*one was also this.*" But in the same gesture, one would simultaneously have to acknowledge that one would not simply be oneself alone. Or that being oneself entails more than a direct self-identification; it means having to accept oneself as in part fundamentally incomprehensible. Rilke is concerned with a certain partition vis-à-vis the relation to the foreign that would simultaneously be both the exclusion and the acknowledged inclusion of what is unassimilable and always also destructive. What makes the foreign here unassimilable and therefore also dangerous is not simply the sense, for example, of its inclusion of "death" as destruction. It is, moreover, its conception as "excess," both as a kind of uncontrollable multiplicity and as the linguistically conceived "*Übermaß von Bedeutung,*" an excess of meaning. It is the excess *(Über)* that exceeds the very measure *(Maß)* of meaning.

The mistake one makes, according to Rilke, is that one forgets. One forgets one's relation to the "foreign" the moment one takes the representation of the foreign as its only possible signification, thus forgetting its oppositional but participatory relation to oneself. This is the case for "death" as well as the "gods": "And so you see, it was no different with death. Experienced, and yet in its reality not to be experienced by us, always knowing better than us and yet never rightly admitted by us, distorting and exceeding the meaning of life from the very beginning; it too, so that it should not continually interrupt us in the search for this meaning, was dismissed, pushed out ... (*Briefe* vol. 2, 54–55). Unacceptable, and inadmissable into a desired "meaning of life," death is simply excluded under the presupposition that its presence would amount to some sort of constant irritation and constant interruption, and accordingly the efficacy of interruption is also denied as the only possible and therefore necessary foundation of existence. The exclusion of death becomes foundational and constitutes a fundamental mistake, "*Grundfehler*," in considering the possibility of any *Daseinsversuch*. It becomes a kind of "babbling" or mumbling in one's existence, as if one's life were governed solely by immediate chance, as if "one just lived along, as it came, on real profits and wrong additions, and in the total result there was bound in the end to reappear a fundamental error that very condition upon the assumption of which this whole experiment in existence was set up; that is, while from every accepted meaning God and death seemed to have been eliminated (as something not here-and-now, but later, elsewhere and different) ..." (*Briefe* vol. 2, 55). What is missing, that is, with the exclusion of god and death from every common linguistic meaning, is the possibility of one's own self-determination in life.

Rilke's discussion is presented simply as if a choice could in fact be made, as if one could simply decide by oneself either to incorporate death or not and thereby could either formulate a truthful "meaning of life" or not. Rilke, however, never claims that such a choice would be available. The "fundamental error" attributed to the mistaken *Daseinsversuch* is attributed not to a bad decision, but to "a world imprisoned in itself, which forgot that it, however it set itself up, was ultimately surpassed *[endgültig übertroffen]*" (*Briefe* vol. 2, 56). There is no choice. It simply had been forgotten that death already and ultimately exceeds life. The question of the "meaning of life" is necessarily left open. Rilke neither suggests that what is achieved in the exclusion of death would be thinkable as "meaningful" *(sinnvoll)*, nor does he claim that its incorporation would guarantee its "meaning" *(Sinn)*. All meaning and knowledge is already exceeded and preceded by death, surrounded by it. It cannot be excluded. Yet knowledge or experience of death itself is always precluded—"Experienced, and yet in its reality not to be experienced by us." Simultaneously experienced and excluded from the possibility of our experience, effecting and eluding any desired "meaning of Life" *(Sinn des Lebens)*, death's power is a distorting power, "distorting *[kränkend]* and exceeding *[überholend]* the meaning of life from the very beginning." Its continual interruption *(be-ständige Unterbrechung)* is mortifying *(kränkend)* and transformative *(über-holend)*[18] from the very beginning, before the beginning.

Rilke returned to the consideration of death some years later in a letter of January 6, 1923, to Countess Margot Sizzo-Noris-Crouy on the occasion of her mother's death. Beginning with the refusal of "consolation," he describes the imperative of the oppositional confrontation with death. The avoidance of death in "consolation" *(Trost)* is simply "diversion" *(Ablenkung)* or, worse yet, "dissipation" *(Zerstreuung)*. "All consolation is turbid" *(Aller Trost ist trübe)* (*Briefe*, 380), he exclaims: it lacks clarity. More than that: it makes one unclear oneself. Rilke's opposition to "consolation" is not set in opposition to death in general. Rather, he is concerned with the specificity of death (the counterpart to the specificity, as he said before, with which one must confront death). Rilke condemns the Christian representation of death as "beyond" not simply because, as he indicated earlier, it represents the "danger" of the separation of death from life or of the dead from the living. Not only does it lose the dead in some unreachable, eternal beyond: "but we too, drawing ourselves away in longing and away from here, become less definite, less earthly: which for the present, so long as we are *here* and related to tree, flower and earthly kingdom, we do have, in a purest sense, to remain, even still to become!" (*Briefe* vol. 2, 379).

"Consolation," in its inevitable "dissipation," only precludes the possibility of determining oneself through death's (material) specificity, thus also precluding "becoming" as the only and necessary task of life, a task inextricably bound to the "*here* . . . related to tree, flower and earthly kingdom." One's relation to death is conceivable as a relation only through its absolute specificity and singularity. Death is always the death of someone in particular:[19] "Not wanting to console ourselves for such a loss should be our instinct, rather it should become our deep painful curiosity wholly to explore it, the singularity, the uniqueness of this particular loss, to learn its effect within life, yes, we should cultivate the noble avarice of enriching our inner world by this very loss, its meaning and its weight" (*Briefe* vol. 2, 378). Without the dead, we would be lost; we would not "become" ourselves. Yet, the appropriation of death is not "becoming" in the sense of becoming something or someone else, but in the sense of its infinite deferral. Death's decision, in this sense, is always the incorporation of a limit: the possibility of demarcation and measure. As such, the incorporation of death is always the appropriation of more than one thing; here it is the simultaneous appropriation of its "meaning" and its "weight"—"thing and self." The "weight" and "meaning" of the dead thus becomes the possibility of our own weight. It is our weightiness itself—our own, as Rilke says, "*Schwersein*" (*Briefe* vol. 2, 381).

In the death of the other, the loss disappears to me, literally, "so to speak," into me: "Thus has died, what has died for me, so to speak, into my own heart." Incorporation, however, involves one's own inevitable yet indeterminable reformation. This, Rilke says, is our "task" and our "burden" *(Aufgabe)*: "of taking into our possession afresh, differently and finally, what now in the being lost is stressed with hopelessness: this then is unending accomplishment *[unendliche Leistung]*. . . ." The work is never over; the taking in of death is the infinite reformation, "newly" ("neu") and "differently" ("anders"), of its finite specificity, its effects the infinite work of mourning. As hopeful and promising as this may sound, the dead are never claimed, never fully appropriated. The infinite work of mourning continues without end. Its effects, however, are nonetheless registered *(abgelesen)* and registered in language as the possibility, "so to speak," of speech: "Where would this always secret effect be held more secure than in us? Where can we come closer to it, where more purely celebrate it, when obey it better, than when it appears bound to our own voices, as if our heart had learned a new language, a new song, a new strength!" (*Briefe* vol. 2, 380). When I speak, death speaks as well. In speaking death (not in speaking about death), one's voice is always again new—yet always and again new only to the extent that one hears and "obeys" *(gehorcht)*. And one obeys because one cannot do otherwise; one obeys because one must. Death's voice always silently accompanies my own. Yet, and this is crucial for Rilke, its silent accompaniment is not the effect of speaking. (It is not, for example, the dying away of speech.) Rather, it must be originary. Death's silence always makes speech new, and in making it new, makes speech possible.

Yet for Rilke the possibility of "obeying" here, as in Kierkegaard's conception of "duty," requires that one obey what must remain silent and cannot be known; one must obey what cannot as such be obeyed. Death is not a command that one could successfully perform or carry out. The mysteries thus consist of death: "Nothing, I am certain, was ever contained in 'initiations' other than the imparting of a 'key' which allowed the word 'death' to be read without negation . . ." (*Briefe* vol. 2, 381). This "key," however, cannot be given. If the possibility of reading "death" without negation is communicated at all, it must lie within its communication as communication, not in the delivery of a certain message. This is not the "key" for a symbolic translation that would leave behind its negation, its annihilating power as insubstantial or immaterial. As opposed to "life," death's communication (as imparting and decision) is its affirmation: "life always says simultaneously: yes and no." That is, life alone cannot decide, cannot form the basis of distinctions, differentiations, and so on, and thus always negates any possible transformation. Rilke continues: "It, death (I implore you to believe!) is the actual yea-sayer *[Ja-Sager]*. It says only: Yes. Before eternity" (*Briefe* vol. 2, 382).[20]

Death's "Yes" carries the force of the imperative. This "Yes" is not so much response as it is beginning, a decisive cut and opening. Its "yes" is absolute, as opposed to the "yes/no" of life. This "yes" is the originary affirmation that makes the "yes/no" of life possible. Before all eternity and opposed to all eternity, death's command obligates all language to its finitude. Thus, in situating the end in the beginning, death's command is both destructive and transformative. Its end is always beginning. "Here stands death"—death stands because it must, but it stands only and repeatedly in its falling away, in its extraction—from "bluish distillate" to "falling star." As transformability itself, death does not change something into something else by way of metaphorical transposition or figurative determination. Death's affirmation becomes the force or condition of figurality not because it guarantees that something will be changed into and presented as some other thing, but because death's destructive uncertainty—whether acknowledged or not—inevitably distorts and ungrounds. Death's uncertainty continually erodes any posited (aesthetic) certainty.[21] Reading death in Rilke's "Death" is reading as reading away, reading what falls away under its aesthetic dimension. One's relation to death always eludes the security of the ethical imperative of simultaneously choosing and positing oneself. Death's imperative, on the other hand, is the absolute injunction toward the ethical imperative. Without any positable self to be chosen, there remains only the decision not to forget and to choose:

O falling star,
once seen from a bridge—:
Not to forget you: to stand!

"'Stand still'": "Yes."

4

The Other Proposition: *Philosophical Fragments* and the Grammar of Life

Death, we might still say, constitutes but one aspect of existence. It demarcates life, and its infinite effects are present everywhere in life: it makes all of life, in each of its effects, strictly finite. This infinite finitizing of life in existence, however, is infinite in all but one aspect: death does not negate life. There is life, and because life exists, death does also. And if existence itself is the one thing that remains unaffected by the perpetual presence of death, existence alone, it seems, would be the one thing, apart from death, held with absolute certainty. I exist. This I know with all and absolute certainty. The self-certainty of my own existence forms the very foundation of knowledge as such. What I know, I know with the certainty of existence itself. And yet, it is precisely this certainty, my own self-assured certainty of my own existence, that will continually draw all that I know—and my very existence itself—into uncertainty. To know that I exist is, with death, to know also that I might not exist. Life itself is confined and circumscribed by the inevitable possibility of death. That is, death is of a different order than life or existence, but there would be no existence without it. Accordingly, because precisely the absence of death demarcates the very finitude of life's existence, life is more than it is: it is at once itself and its end in death.

Yet, for Kierkegaard, certainly, to focus exclusively on death as the sole demarcation of life's finitude, making death the single and only possibility of life, would be perverse. Death is not the sole demarcation of life's finitude. We might even say that there must be something more originary than death. Because life comes to an end, there must also be a beginning. There must also be, to speak within the same metaphor, birth. This is true for all of existence. Existence is not eternal. Whatever exists must somehow have entered into existence. Death, then, is possible only because it is made possible by the coming into existence of existence as such. The actuality of coming into existence opens up the possibility of coming to an end. By being itself the possibility of nonexistence, the possibility inaugurated in existence is the possibility of the impossible. The possibility of impossibility in death must already have been made possible in existence. Because there is existence, it is possible not to exist. This is so, Kierkegaard suggests, because the possibility of possibility that is existence is the absolute change of coming into existence—the "change," according to Kierkegaard, from nothing to something. Whatever exists must not have existed. There is, accordingly, a hole in the heart of existence. For this nonbeing that is before all existence cannot be undone by the actuality of existence. Nonbeing and being are not separate attributes of some other thing. They are, together, the very substance of existence. In this way, Kierkegaard's understanding of existence is always doubled. This doubling of existence will always remain irreducible and, hence, paradoxical.

The problem of "coming into existence" describes the crucial problematic of Kierkegaard's *Philosophical Fragments,* which was published in 1844 under the pseudonym "Johannes Climacus." In spite of the apparent self-certainty of existence, Climacus insists that we still do not know what existence is. The thought begins implicitly with a question: If existence is something, then it must be different from nonexistence, and if existence occurs only in time, then whatever exists must have undergone the change from nonexistence to existence. So, what is this change? And what does it mean for existence? It is, first of all, what Climacus calls an "absolute" change, as opposed to a qualitative one: the absolute change from not being to being. There can be no process, neither system nor mechanism—that might assimilate nonbeing into being. Such a change would only turn "non-being" and "being" into mere attributes of one continuous "existence." If a change occurs in coming into existence, whatever enters into existence can no longer be the same as what preceded it. In this case, the question of coming into existence would appear irrelevant, for what would have come into existence would no longer be the same thing, and this new existence would still present the same question. The question would not have been answered, but merely deferred. "But if it comes into existence, unchanged," Climacus asks, "what, then, is the change of coming into existence?" (Kierkegaard, *Philosophical Fragments,* 73). What comes into existence cannot already exist, yet in coming into existence it must absolutely be changed. "This change, then is not in essence *[Væsen]* but in being *[Væren]* and is from not existing to existing." There must be an absolute separation between the being that comes into existence and that which does not. "But this nonbeing that is abandoned by that which comes into existence," Climacus insists, "must also exist" (*Philosophical Fragments,* 73). As soon as there is being, there must also be nonbeing. Being as absolutely other than nonbeing can neither negate nor assimilate nonbeing in any way.[1]

The change of "coming into existence" is the change from "possibility" to "actuality." "Possibility and actuality"—as the difference between nonexistence and existence—"are not different in essence but in being." In this case, Climacus continues, "the possible ... turns out to be nothing the moment it becomes actual, for possibility is *annihilated* by actuality" (*Philosophical Fragments,* 74). And, as opposed to Hegel, Climacus insists that actuality as the annihilation of possibility is not unified in "necessity."[2] That is, actuality simply annihilates this possibility, without turning it into something else. They remain "absolutely different," and therefore, the existence of possibility is always its existence as "annihilated." That is to say, possibility does not disappear, but in "actuality," possibility is always the existence of the possibility of annihilation.[3] If coming into existence, because of its actuality, is always irrefutable and cannot be undone, it is not made irrefutable because of any "necessity." On the contrary, Climacus insists, the very fact of its actuality does not in any way alter the fact of its coming into existence. But this is a different kind of assertion or a different kind of fact. "All coming into existence," he writes, "occurs in freedom, not by way of necessity" (*Philosophical Fragments,* 75). Actuality, in this way, seems to give only the appearance of necessity, without being created out of necessity. The seeming appearance of "necessity," in this instance, has rather more to do with the absolute irrefutability of actuality: "What has happened has happened and cannot be undone" (*Philosophical Fragments,* 76). So, if the change of coming into existence is the change from possibility to actuality and this change is irreversible, it is not irreversible because it is somehow necessary. Rather, it is what cannot be undone in the very freedom of coming into existence itself.

Accordingly, what is, is forever plagued by its own uncertainty—the uncertainty of its own coming into being, the reminder that whatever now is, previously was not. Existence itself is, moreover, the very reminder that what is does not have to be. Existence is always the actuality of possibility, not the necessity of actuality. The fact of existence in no way alters this uncertainty and may, in actuality, be its ground: "But that it occurred is, in turn, precisely its uncertainty, which will perpetually prevent the apprehension from taking the past as if it had been that way from eternity. Only in this contradiction between certainty and uncertainty, the *discremen* [distinguishing mark] of something that has come into existence and thus also part of the past, is the past understood" (*Philosophical Fragments,* 79). The difficulty is one for the understanding, beyond immediate perception. The actuality of existence, in spite of its apparent unalterability, its apparent constancy, is, by having come into existence, indication that it has not always been, has not always existed. Although what exists, having come into existence, exists as unalterable, its very unalterability ungrounds the sense-certainty of immediate perception by bringing into existence the nothing that (it) also is. In spite of its perception, existence is not eternal.

Nor, Climacus adds, is existence "necessary" (*Philosophical Fragments,* 80). That is to say, the perception of history that would translate the unalterability of the historical into its assumed necessity does not amount to its understanding: "If what is apprehended is changed in the apprehension, then the apprehension is changed into a misunderstanding. Knowledge of the present does not confer necessity upon it; foreknowledge of the future does not confer necessity upon it (Boethius); knowledge of the past does not confer necessity upon it—for all apprehension, like all knowing, has nothing from which to give" (*Philosophical Fragments,* 79–80). So, what is it, we might ask, to give? Necessity is already in existence, not a quality of existence—or not all of it. If there is necessity, it must be "conferred upon" existence. Neither knowledge nor perception alone can confer this necessity. If it is conferred, it must come from elsewhere; it must be given in some other way. The very perception that existence itself is not all that exists calls this question forth. Yet "necessity" itself—under the assumption that something still needs to be "conferred upon" the perception, that perception is not complete in itself, not certain of itself—is but the consequence of the gift. It is not necessary, but there must also be something. If there is a gift, it too, like existence itself, must come from nowhere, without immanent cause. In this sense, being more than it is, existence, having come into existence, always gives something other than existence.

Yet this giving of existence—the gift that is existence—is never as such available; it is not itself perceptible. This does not mean, however, that it is not somehow part of perception. Simply, it cannot be perceived directly:

> So much for the apprehension of the past. It is presumed, however, that there is knowledge of the past—how is this knowledge acquired? Because the historical intrinsically has the illusiveness *[Svigagtighed]* of coming into existence, it cannot be sensed directly and immediately. The immediate impression of a natural phenomenon or of an event is not the impression of the historical, for the coming into existence cannot be sensed immediately—but only the presence. But the presence of the historical has the coming into existence within itself.... (*Philosophical Fragments,* 81)

Knowledge of history, however, cannot confer eternal universality upon the historical. In spite of the very unalterability of the past, this too is never free of its own finite contingency—is never free of the fact of its own existence, of its own coming into existence, even in the past. The very particularity, specificity, and singularity—indeed, because one does not exist in general, one cannot come into existence in general; this is always only singular—infinitely defers every possibility of universality.

What is known or perceived is, thus, always different from what is. This difficulty, as formulated already prior to Kierkegaard/Climacus's *Philosophical Fragments,* might be said to begin with the apparently rudimentary argument against the understanding of "life" offered by "philosophy." That is, it begins when philosophy (or rather, a philosopher) makes "life" the object of its (or his or her) understanding. Given the supposedly conceptual order of understanding and given the very existence of any philosopher who would attempt to form such an understanding, the very objectification of "life" in this process produces nothing other than the distortion of its object, the distortion of life. How, Kierkegaard asks, is it possible for "the philosopher" to forget or to avoid the inevitability of his or her own existence?[4] What are the effects of this avoidance? At first sight, it seems as if the temporality of understanding must miss the temporality of life itself. Understanding does not live in the same way that life does. "It is perfectly true," Kierkegaard wrote in a journal entry of 1843, "what philosophy says, that life must be understood backwards *[baglænds]*." If the conceptual understanding offered by "philosophy" tends toward universalization, then the appearance as universalization for the understanding is the same as its retrogressive appearance. That is, it can appear only with a kind of retrogressive fixity, as something already complete within itself. This is, as Kierkegaard says, "backwards." Now, as if to suggest that the difficulty is not exhausted in this one specification—as if to suggest that there must be some other possibility for the understanding outside of its universalized, or "backwards" appearance—in the journal entry Kierkegaard continues with another proposition: "But then one forgets the other proposition, that it must be lived forwards *[forlænds]*. The more one thinks through this proposition, the more one concludes that life in temporality never becomes correctly understandable, simply because at no moment can I find the necessary rest from which to take in the situation: backwards" (Kierkegaard, *Journals and Papers* I, 450, trans. modified).[5]

At no point does Kierkegaard, even in such a schematic articulation as this journal entry, suggest that the difficulty would be overcome by simply supplying the "correct" understanding that would assimilate the two opposed temporalities into their ideal or proper understanding. There is always the problem of "rest" *(Ruh)*: the ideal point from which the suspension of my actuality makes understanding in its apparently retrogressive temporality possible. "Rest" exists only outside of existence.[6] "Rest" is precisely what temporality as such must miss. The true conversion of life and its understanding appears only as the rest and suspension of temporality as such. In other words, it cannot exist at all. And yet, that rest is always somehow there, even in its unavailability. It is there when I live my life forward and it is there when I understand my life backward. It is there in the difference between the two, between the one "proposition" and the other.

Returning to the problem of cognition in the *Philosophical Fragments*, Climacus insists that what is lost to the understanding is irrecuperable by any act of remembrance, through any recollection. This is in opposition to more idealist or metaphysical conceptions of the truth in life as "recollection," both Socratic *anamnesis* and Hegelian *Erinnerung*. The presentation of any understanding for Kierkegaard concerns, rather, the appearance of something that cannot as such appear. The very existence of the philosopher necessarily disrupts—and thereby, paradoxically, grounds—any possible understanding. Can "life," however, continually be placed outside of understanding? On the contrary, recollection is assumed to be the very essence of knowledge. In its most schematic expression, Socrates insists that one does not acquire knowledge or "learn" by discovering something new and previously unknown. Rather, if one is capable of knowing something in the first place, this can be only because one already possesses the condition for this knowledge. Indeed, one already possesses the knowledge itself, and needs but to recall that one does in fact know it.[7] Recollection in this sense is taken simply as the "demonstration for the immortality of the soul—retrogressively *[retrogradt]*, please note—or a demonstration for the pre-existence of the soul" (*Philosophical Fragments*, 9–10). If "truth" is necessarily "eternal," Socrates takes any suggestion that this "truth" can be known as "proof" that the soul, too, in its "truth," is equally eternal, that is, "immortal." In every case, then, no matter what I learn, I learn only what I already know. If learning is really nothing other than "recollection," this "recollection" itself indicates, rather than confirmation of my own existence, only that I have always existed already. My own actual existence is inevitably lost to the "pre–" of my pre-existing soul. At the end of the *Fragments,* after the more explicit discussion of the problem of "coming into existence," Climacus claims: "Socratically understood, the individual has existed before he came into existence and recollects himself; thus, recollection is pre-existence, not recollection of pre-existence" (*Philosophical Fragments,* 96). Whereas, in this presentation, Socrates would thus seem reassured by the suggestion that even death will not negate or destroy who he is and that his soul will always transcend the contingencies of his existence, Climacus hears only this: I cannot exist. Existence itself is already annihilated in recollection.

Somewhat later, in the *Concluding Unscientific Postscript to Philosophical Fragments* (1846), Climacus extends a similar argument against Hegelian speculation: "*Speculative thought* ignores existence; for speculation, 'to exist' becomes 'to have existed' (the past); existence is a vanishing and annulled element in the pure being of the eternal. Speculation as abstraction can never become contemporary with existence . . . and therefore cannot comprehend existence as existence, but only afterwards" (*Postscript,* 570–71). Existence is never itself the object of comprehension, and thus always stands apart from it. Insofar as "speculative thought" always involves the recollective recuperation of experience in order dialectically to constitute understanding, this understanding inevitably proceeds ex post facto, relegating the objects in understanding always only to an infinite past, no longer part of the present temporality of existence.[8] For Climacus, however, the actuality of existence cannot simply be erased.

Put another way, the understanding thus achieved in speculation can be only a distortion of understanding: "[E]verything said about mediation can be true and glorious but becomes untruth in the mouth of the existing person since he as an existing person is prevented from obtaining such a foothold outside existence that from it he can mediate that which by being in a process of becoming also precludes completion" (*Postscript,* 399). There is no rest. If the problem Climacus associates with Hegel and Hegelianism is that it constitutes a removal of existence, he then proposes a different task for philosophy: "The subjective thinker's task *[Obgave]* is to understand himself in existence. . . . He does not abstract from existence and from the contradiction, but he is in them, and yet he is supposed to think" (*Postscript,* 351). To understand oneself in existence is not the same as understanding oneself only in relation to it. The "subjective thinker" exists, is in existence, in all its contradictions, all its impossibilities and uncertainties. Is it possible, we might ask, however, to understand oneself in existence and to be in existence at the same time if the two orders stand in mutual contradiction? Or is this new "task" anything other than the very impossibility of philosophy itself?

The answer, if there is one, lies in the direction of philosophy's encounter with its potential impossibility. Whatever understanding is to take place in philosophy, it must involve the limit of understanding as such, the limit of its own possibility. If philosophy is to understand anything, it must begin to understand what it does not already, and perhaps cannot, understand. In the *Philosophical Fragments*, Climacus thus poses what he calls a "Socratic" question: "To what extent can the truth be learned" (*Philosophical Fragments,* 9)? That is, if the recollection of "truth" is nothing other than its distortion, since recollection itself marks the impossibility of existence, will it ever be possible, beginning with what already exists, to arrive at understanding as the appearance of something new? To exist is to be in time, and there is nothing that is not in time that exists. If, then, "truth" is eternal and, thus, not in time, can I still possess it? What, exactly, would it mean that I, in time, might possess something that eludes or even annuls every demarcation of time? "All knowledge," Climacus claims in the *Postscript*, "is an annulment, a removal from existence" (*Postscript*, 348). However, he claims not that there is no knowledge, but rather that what knowledge is, is always apart from existence. It does not exist in the same way that I do. In *Practice in Christianity*, Anti-Climacus similarly claims: "The past is not actuality—for me" (Kierkegaard, *Practice in Christianity,* 63–74). Recollection, then, as the recuperation of an always preexisting eternal truth, can only fail—for me. It can appear only as the withdrawal from the world of time in which I necessarily exist:

> The temporal point of departure is a nothing, because in the same moment I discover that I have known the truth from eternity without knowing it, in the same instant that moment is hidden in the eternal, assimilated into it in such a way that I, so to speak, still cannot find it even if I were to look for it because there is no Here and no There, but only an *ubique et nusquam* [everywhere and nowhere]. (*Philosophical Fragments,* 12–13).

Everything disappears. And yet, "recollection" would seem to promise the very method that would allow nothing to disappear. Accordingly, recollection, which must somehow take place in the present, cannot, at the same time, be of the present. The moment recollection succeeds is also the moment it disappears from presence. Once there is existence, there is time, and once there is time, there must be something more than recollection, which recollection cannot recall. If recollection appears, that is, it appears as some other thing.

It is impossible, however, for Climacus to decide about the validity of recollection's "truth." At no point does he claim with absolute certainty either that there is no recollection or that the truth that one would recollect is not eternal. This is perhaps the one thing he cannot decide. With regard to "the eternal," as he claims in the *Postscript*, "I do not decide. . . , time does not allow me to do this, simply because I am in time" (*Postscript*, 411). The nowhere that is everywhere of the eternal is not for me. Or, rather, it is not subject to my decision. And yet, in spite of its apparent unavailability, it must also exist. If this is the case, then it too—against all logic—must come into existence. It must abandon its eternity: "If the situation is to be different, then the moment in time must have such decisive significance *[afgjørende Betydning]* that for no moment will I be able to forget it, neither in time nor in eternity, because the eternal, previously nonexistent, came into existence in that moment" (*Philosophical Fragments*, 13). The failure of recollection is not abandoned as the failure to know, the ineluctable shortcoming of all learning, even if this truth cannot exist within the same temporality that I do. It must, however, enter into existence and must become temporal in some way—or it cannot appear. We assume, then, that we do learn; even Socrates believed as much. His explanation, however, as Climacus reminds us, left room for doubt: "The Socratic line of thought annulled the disjunction, since it appeared that basically every human being possesses the truth" (*Philosophical Fragments*, 13).

There can be no continuous transition from unknown to known. What is more, the unknown can only exceed and surpass all cognition.[9] The unknown, necessarily and wholly other than any form of knowing, remains forever unequal to any knowing and resists all assimilation. Knowledge cannot follow and supplant nonknowledge. Even if one could somehow be reminded of the truth that one must already know, there would be no prior truth of which one could be reminded. This is not to say that there is nothing to be "recollected." It is just that what is recollected is not truth; it can only be "untruth." More than this, the learner in recalling this untruth, recalls the untruth that he already is. "He is, then, untruth" (*Philosophical Fragments*, 13). Existence itself seems somehow to stand in the way. One's own existence seems to contradict the possibility that the knowledge one would possess might also exist. The two existences seem mutually exclusive. Either one exists oneself, turning anything one would know into "untruth," or "truth" exists, the very eternity of which always negates the possibility of one's own existence. There must be another way, Climacus suggests, one perhaps no less contradictory or paradoxical. The difficulty, he insists, is not to possess the truth, but rather to possess it in truth. "Truth" is not itself a qualification of knowledge; it is a way of knowing.

If one is to learn something of "truth," this truth cannot already be present. It must arrive from elsewhere. Yet, if it comes into existence as fully other than existence, how can one, in existence, perceive it? How can it be known? Can it be known? To what extent can it be learned? Indeed, the very absence of security in this regard seems to suggest to Climacus that there must be something more—that there must be something that, when added to the equation, will explain what knowledge must be, and do so in a way that will not cancel me out. If knowledge participates in "the eternal," and I in my existence am forever separated from the eternal and am still to perceive it, I must first, Climacus suggests, be given the condition for its perception: "Now, if the learner is to obtain the truth, the teacher must bring it to him, but not only that. Along with it he must provide him with the condition for understanding it" (*Philosophical Fragments,* 14). Having the condition, he says, must be like being able to ask a question, because "the condition and the question contain the conditioned and the answer." I cannot already possess the condition, because if I did I would be able to produce the truth for myself. The very fact that I know it must then be indication enough that the teacher has also given its condition.

Already one can sense a certain desperation in Climacus's argument. Each addition continually proves itself insufficient for one and the same reason. The learner cannot alone recollect the truth. In this case, recollection would dissolve into tautology. The learner would already be the truth. Therefore, there must be a teacher, someone else, who would, possessing the truth himself, give it, to the learner, that he too might have it. Yet, if it could simply be given directly from one to another, and if it would be the same for one and for the other, then, again, no truth would be given; nothing would transpire. The learner would already be capable of the truth that he would then possess by himself. That is, if the truth is received, its condition must already be present. Accordingly, if the learner cannot recollect his own truth—which would not be truth, but untruth—and if the teacher cannot directly give the truth—which, again, would be only untruth—then the teacher must give more than the truth. The teacher must give the truth together with the condition for understanding it. So what, then, is the condition? And, within this figural framework, is there anything to prevent it, too, from being consumed and exhausted in tautology—from exposing learning as nothing other than impossible? "Ultimately," Climacus says, "all instruction depends upon the presence of the condition; if it is lacking, then a teacher is capable of nothing, because in the other case *[i andet Fald]*, the teacher, before beginning to teach, must recreate *[omskabe]*, not reform *[omdanne]*, the learner" (*Philosophical Fragments*, 14, trans. modified).[10] The only sufficient condition for the possibility of learning appears to be the radical alteration of the learner himself—an alteration conceived as "re-creation," an alteration akin to creation, without itself being originary in the same sense. What, we might ask, is this "re-creation," if it is not conceived as the mere change of one thing into something else? If learning is not to lapse into the tautology of "recollection," it must constitute the appearance of something absolutely new, that is, the "coming into existence" of something that did not already and would not otherwise exist. Re-creation, then, can be conceived only as creation creating itself. And this, cannot take place unless there is also nothing. How, then, can learning ever begin?

But the one who not only gives the learner the truth but provides the condition, Climacus insists, "is not a teacher" (*Philosophical Fragments*, 14). Learning does take place, but not by recollection alone. One must be taught. Yet, what one learns is not the same as what is taught. One cannot directly acquire and thereby "learn" the truth the teacher teaches. Ultimately, the teacher must be subject to the same limitations as anything else in existence. The teacher, too, must exist. If one cannot re-create oneself, neither can the teacher. Naturally, Climacus insists, "no human being is capable of doing this; if it is to take place, it must be done by the god himself." Ergo: "The teacher, then, is the god, who gives the condition and gives the truth" (*Philosophical Fragments*, 14–15). "The teacher," then, is not a human being. And the gift of this teacher—the "condition" that this "god" gives—can be construed only as the disruption of every possible exchange. The "gift" is not a gift.

This abyssal impossibility will continually exhaust and consume every figurative presentation, even Climacus's own. "The god," "the teacher," "the learner," "the condition"—the very articulation of any logical and, thus, temporal relation—continually and incessantly lapses into its very disarticulation. Yet, these figures are never as such abandoned. The very critique of recollection, as Climacus presents it, continually fails to overcome the conception of recollection, and appears itself to lapse into the same tautology that constitutes the failure of recollection. Critique, then, is not enough: Climacus must invent a new vocabulary. If the figuration of critique is not yet enough to circumvent recollection's exhaustive tautology, and if that tautology consumes critique precisely at the level of its presentation—the level, that is, of the word—what other way is there to avert recollection's consumption than to intervene on the same level and eschew in advance the possibility that the word might recall any thing or any concept?

The results here are surprising, for Climacus does not invent new words (in this, he is similar to Adorno), but redeploys others whose recollections continually appear out of place—appear to be, that is, at once required by and opposed to the very terms of his critique. Thus, the moment his own figurative presentation encounters its fundamental impossibility, Climacus resolves: "The teacher, then, is the god himself, who acting as the occasion, prompts the learner to be reminded that he is untruth and is that through one's own fault. But this state—to be untruth and to be that through one's own fault—what can we call it? Let us call it *sin*" (*Philosophical Fragments,* 15). From this point on, Climacus's text is literally riddled with similar moments of naming. "The god" also receives a new name: "Let us call him a *savior*.... Let us call him a *deliverer* ... a *reconciler*" (*Philosophical Fragments,* 17). Yet, in this way we discover further that "the god" is not "the god," but simply a name for something else, something otherwise perhaps unnameable: "Therefore, let us call this unknown *the god.* It is only a name we give to it" (*Philosophical Fragments,* 39). Thus, "the god" *(Guden)* is not "God" *(Gud).*[11] Climacus's text is not about belief in the report of the appearance of the god as proof of the existence of god. Rather than substantiating any ideological notion of divinity, the effect of Climacus's exploration is to articulate possibilities of relating outside of the dogmatic designation of and adherence to any specific notion of god. In spite of all appearances to the contrary, the *Philosophical Fragments* is not a description of Christianity, and the god in human form is not Christ. Yet, at the same time one cannot help but notice that this language is anything other than arbitrary. It is no accident that Climacus invokes an explicitly theological discourse. The words Climacus chooses continually recall this discourse, even if his text cannot be subsumed within it. And this recollection, like all recollection, continues to be disquieting.

Climacus, like every other, is condemned to speak a language that can never fully belong to him. Throughout the *Philosophical Fragments*, Climacus is aware of his inability to speak with a voice that is authentic and original—authentic and original in the sense that one is oneself the sole "author" of what one says, that what one says as an author can be only one's own and not properly that of another. The performative renaming and re-calling of the concepts through which his argument is articulated is symptomatic of a broader difficulty. Beyond these recollections, each of Climacus's chapters is interrupted, cut off in the end, by the objections of an imagined listener, introduced by some version of the formulaic expression "But perhaps someone will say ..." (*Philosophical Fragments,* 21). Each time, the objection remains essentially the same: Your words, Climacus, are not your own. They must be stolen; this text can be nothing more than an act of plagiarism. "'You are the most ludicrous of all project cranks,'" Climacus's imagined interlocutor contends, "'for even if someone comes up with a foolish scheme, there is always the truth that he is the one who came up with it.'" What sort of "truth" is this, however? Does the attribution of "original" authorship amount to the "truth" of its assertions? Or rather, as this objector imagines, even if the contents remain untrue, there is at least the more fundamental "truth" that the one speaking is their originator, that he and no other is speaking. But, Climacus wonders, is even this true? He consents: "Maybe so. I hide my face in shame" (*Philosophical Fragments,* 21). His admission of guilt or culpability in this matter, however, brings him no closer to resolution: "I am just as close to having invented it as any other person. Therefore, you are not angry with me because I falsely attribute to myself something that belongs to another human being, but you are angry with me because I falsely attribute to myself something that belongs to no human being, and you are just as angry when I mendaciously want to attribute the invention to you" (*Philosophical Fragments,* 21–22).

Authorship, in spite of any apparent originality, is never itself originary. Put simply, language always preexists each of its occurrences. Because of this, speech and language must remain forever unequal, and, moreover, speaking itself will never render the language an originary possession. One does not possess language, just as truth itself is never a possession. Thus, the "truth" of language, can be attributed to no human being—or, in Climacus's words, neither "you" nor "me." If words cannot belong to Climacus—and he freely admits that they cannot—to whom, do they belong? To whom can they ever belong if they cannot belong to a "human being"?[12] What, then, is one's relation to language if one does not possess it?

Unable to author his own argument, Climacus can only take what is given by others. His own discourse consists of words borrowed without direct or proper citation from a host of others. "Those phrases do not belong to you," his detractor insists, "but are very familiar and everyone knows to whom they belong." His listener even recites them for us on occasion. It is precisely their familiarity that might be said to preclude any attribution of proper authorship, proper originality. Their familiarity and commonality is what prohibits them from being the sole possession of any human being. This Climacus finds somehow reassuring: "Ah, my dear fellow, what you say does not pain me as you perhaps think it does; no, it pleases me immensely, for I admit that I trembled when I wrote them down. I could not recognize myself, could not imagine that I, who as a rule am so diffident and fearful, dared to write anything like that" (*Philosophical Fragments,* 53). All that is perhaps recognizable in the words is that they cannot be his own. Although Climacus's listener believes to have refuted Climacus's argument by catching him with "the stolen goods," Climacus himself remains untouched by the claimed refutation. At no point does he claim "ownership" of them. Indeed, he knows nothing else than that they cannot be his own—or those of any other human being. Moreover, the impossibility of "ownership" in this regard, in the broader context of the inevitable separation of speech from language, indicates as well the inevitable failure of any utterance to refer back to any totality of which it might be conceived to be a part.[13] It is, in this sense, the very fact that the words Climacus uses belong of course to others that continually disrupts and prohibits their subsumption to any (other) unified whole. There is not, nor can there be, any totality free of its own disruption and suspension.

All that appears in this moment, then, is the suspension of understanding. For Climacus insists that even he has "not completely understood it" (*Philosophical Fragments,* 69). Nor will he ever—not completely. The point is that at no moment would such completion or totalization of the understanding be available as such, for him or any other. And this, as his listener himself must recognize, is precisely because of the way in which "authority" intervenes or of what "authority" recalls and/or is re-called. Again he admonishes Climacus for theft: "[Y]ou always mix in some little phrase that is not your own, and that disturbs because of the recollection *[Erindring]* it prompts" (*Philosophical Fragments,* 105). For this listener, the disturbance seems to have to do only with knowing the origin of each of Climacus's inadvertent citations. Again, Climacus does not dispute the correctness of the listener's objection; yet again, his own thought remains untouched by it. The question remains, even where authorship may to a certain extent be traced to others, if always only incompletely: What is it that recollection recalls (for Climacus never disputes that this is the case) when what recollection recalls is nothing other than the ultimate limit and failure of all recollection? When recollection ought to indicate nothing other than the truth and proper ownership of language—that one is oneself in language and that this language is one's own—it recollects nothing other than the disturbance of another.

If recollection is always primarily recollection in language and subject to the language of another—the unknown other, "the god"—and if recollection nonetheless takes place, what precisely is it that recollection recalls?

Or, likewise, what is the effect of recollection, if, being recollection it demarcates nothing other than its own impossibility? Beyond the mere refutation of any doctrine of recollection, however, Climacus is concerned with its limits. The totality of the preexisting "soul" as well as the totalization of speculative "self-consciousness" will always remain unavailable as such. Nevertheless, recollection in some form—even if just in the form of the unavoidable use of the words of another—does form the basis for thinking and understanding. If recollection, then, is the suspension and interruption of any possible understanding, can there be any understanding as such that would not end in the impossibility that is recollection? In other words, is it possible for there to exist understanding beyond the inevitability of its own impossibility, the impossibility that is its end? Is understanding anything other than the perpetual encounter with its own end? Climacus insists unequivocally: No. Moreover, understanding would not be understanding if it did not encounter its own end. Understanding for Climacus is nothing other than the "collision" in thought with its own end. And, if the goal of all thinking is to arrive at an understanding—finally to have understood some thing—thinking, too, must include its own aporetic impossibility: "But the ultimate potentiation of every passion is always to will its own downfall, and so it is the ultimate passion of the understanding to will the collision *[Anstødet]*, although in one way or another the collision must become its downfall. This, then, is the ultimate paradox of thought: to want to discover something that thought itself cannot think" (*Philosophical Fragments,* 37). That is to say that thinking is the failure of totalization. Moreover, there would be no thought and no understanding if totalization were ever to succeed. The very fact that there is thinking signifies nothing more than the fact that there is also something more than thought itself. To think, for Climacus, is to reach the end of thought, both as its limit and its own demise. Thought itself must be the paradox.[14] It must always exceed and surpass itself as the unknown that it is not. But this can happen—and it does happen—only if the unknown beyond thought and understanding actually exists. What understanding is, then, is the becoming apparent of the limit of thinking. This, however, can be only a beginning.

The limit *(Grændse)* to thought is never knowable as such. If what can be known is always presentable only as the content of thought—if it is thus always representable—there can appear nothing outside of thought that would also be knowable even as the unknown. This unknown must exceed, and in exceeding supersede, the very rule(s) of representability.[15] The word itself, the "unknown," already recalls the inevitable failure of recollection, of which representation consists. The threat to representability in this moment is, however, secondary. Primary for Climacus in this moment is that, insofar as thought itself is present, there is always something present that is not the same as thought and remains irreducible to thought: "The paradoxical passion of the understanding is, then, continually colliding with this unknown, which certainly does exist but is also unknown and to that extent does not exist. The understanding does not go beyond this . . ." (*Philosophical Fragments,* 44). Thought, thus, in the collision with the unknown that is understanding, is always doubled, but doubled as always simultaneously other than it already is:

> But it is the absolutely different in which there is no distinguishing mark *[Kjendetegn].* Defined as the absolutely different, it seems on the verge of being disclosed, but not so, because the understanding cannot even think the absolutely different; it cannot absolutely negate itself but uses itself for that purpose and consequently thinks the difference in itself, which it thinks by itself. It cannot absolutely transcend itself and therefore thinks as above itself only the sublimity that it thinks by itself. (*Philosophical Fragments,* 45)

"Transcendence" can appear only as a kind of fiction, for thinking is never anything other than thinking. And thinking can never surpass its own presence, its own existence. If it encounters or "collides with" its limit, it must do so already as the existence that it is. To view thinking as the only possible transcendence of finite existence into infinite understanding or "absolute knowledge," then, even this transcendence as thought cannot escape its own impossibility—an impossibility grounded in the unavoidable finitude that Climacus here generally accounts for in "coming into existence."

In this way, the end of thought can never be absent from thought. Just as what inevitably detours recollection's totalizing gesture is the fact that there must be someone in existence who recollects something not in existence in the same way, so, too, thinking must be thought: "This passion of thought is fundamentally present everywhere in thought, also in the single individual's thought insofar as he, thinking, is not merely himself" (*Philosophical Fragments,* 37). One is never oneself in thought. Even in self-consciousness, one can think oneself only as other than oneself in existence. Thus, knowledge brings uncertainty to an otherwise exclusive epistemological certitude by exposing within the certainty of cognition the unavoidable presence of an unknown that is absolutely irreducible to cognition: "But what is this unknown *[Ubekjendte]* against which the understanding in its paradoxical passion collides and which even disturbs one in self-knowledge?

It is the unknown. But it is not a human being *[Menneske]* ... (*Philosophical Fragments,* 39). Rather than suggesting that everything is in principle knowable with recollection, Climacus insists that everything is (also) unknown. Also, that is, in understanding, one is not "merely" oneself alone; there is always another. All thought is qualified by a fundamental and absolute difference within itself. "But," Climacus continues, "this difference cannot be grasped securely."[16] Any attempt by the understanding to come to terms with this difference results in something for which the understanding can no longer remain entirely accountable. This is true not only in this case, not only when difference is sought, but always.

Climacus nevertheless insists that the "paradoxical passion of thought" is to be understood—that is, not known, but "understood," he insists, "as a paradox" (*Philosophical Fragments,* 59). There must be, then, the possibility of a relationship between understanding and the paradox outside the delimitations of cognition. Climacus describes two such possibilities. One is that the relation is an "unhappy" one in which there is no "mutual understanding of their difference" (*Philosophical Fragments,* 49). This he calls "the offense," maintaining that it nonetheless provides an "indirect testing of the correctness of the paradox, for the offense is the erroneous accounting, is the conclusion of untruth, with which the paradox thrusts *[støder]* away" (*Philosophical Fragments,* 51). The erroneous accounting is nonetheless also accountable to the relationship between understanding and the unknown. Furthermore, the offense is always somehow responsible for the understanding, although it is not itself understanding: "The offended one does not speak according to himself but according to the paradox, just as someone caricaturing another does not originate anything himself but only copies the other awkwardly *[bagvendt]*" (*Philosophical Fragments,* 51, trans. modified). The unknown speaks, and, in speaking, it turns understanding into its own caricature or bad copy. It is not that the copying per se is questionable—indeed, speech can be nothing other than repetition—but that there is apparently no guarantee that speaking would produce anything but caricature, "bad copies" where no good copies might exist.[17] A caricature is simply one kind of copy, however "awkward"—or, more precisely, "turned the wrong way," or even "turned backwards" *(bagvendt).* Yet, is not this awkward caricature produced every time thinking thinks or understanding understands, whether apparent or not, whether it knows it or not? Does not this "caricature," this "awkwardness," by exceeding the limits of "proper" representation, also elude, already in advance, the (ethical) strictures of recollection? If speech is the coming into existence of the unknown, it is only in speech and language that its effects become apparent. Language itself is nothing other than "caricature" in this sense; it is nothing other than the coming into existence of the unknown. I will return to this thought.

Or—and this is the other possibility—the relationship between understanding and the unknown is the "happy" and "mutual understanding of their difference." The understanding of the "paradox" as a paradox describes the proper condition of the "follower." The situation here, however, is not entirely unlike that described as "offense."[18] Here, too, the understanding belongs to the unknown—and yet here, too, there must be something beyond understanding, something other than understanding:

> How, then, does the learner come to an understanding with this paradox, for we do not say that he is supposed to understand the paradox but is only to understand that this is the paradox. We have already shown how this occurs. It occurs when the understanding and the paradox happily encounter each other in the moment, when the understanding steps aside and the paradox gives itself, and the third something, the something in which this occurs (for it does not occur through the understanding, which is discharged, or through the paradox, which gives itself—consequently *in* something), is the happy passion to which we shall now give a name, although for us it is not a matter of the name. We shall call it *faith [Troen]*. (*Philosophical Fragments*, 59)

If one cannot understand the paradox, what exactly is the encounter with the paradox? It is, first of all, the end of understanding. And at this end, Climacus now finds something else—something other than the paradox even—for, after the understanding, if the paradox is still to be understood even as a paradox, this must happen "in something," which is nothing other than the effect of the paradox. The paradox itself produces what he now wants to call "faith." As is the case with the representation of "the god," "faith," too, is simply the necessary misappropriation of a name: "[F]or us," Climacus insists only in part facetiously, "it is not a matter of the name." No, "faith" is not faith, but something else. "Faith" is this "third" thing, which is produced by the paradox and which is perhaps nothing other than this effecting through the paradox, which, he says, "gives itself." Faith is then nothing other than the receiving of the gift of the paradox. The effect of paradox, then, must be the giving itself of the giving itself. It is, thus, not a thing. The question remains: What exactly does the paradox give in giving itself? Does it give, say, something where otherwise there would have been nothing? Is the gift of the paradox nothing other than the gift of giving, where the gift is always not a gift?

Climacus's paradox ultimately appears as the paradox of appearance. If "faith" is receptivity toward "the unknown" effected already by the paradoxical presence of the unknown, faith's reception grants, paradoxically, appearance to the same effect. The self-discrepancy of the existence of "the god" in human form is what we might call the appearance par excellence of the paradox. The appearance of the god-man is the paradox of every other paradox. This appearance as such, however, is not without its consequences: "But the servant form is not something put on but is actual, not a parastatic but an actual body, and the god, from the hour when by the omnipotent resolution of his omnipotent love he became a servant, he has himself become captive, so to speak in his resolution and is now obliged to continue (to go on talking loosely) whether he wants to or not" (*Philosophical Fragments,* 55). Climacus insists, however, that he is not arguing for the existence of the god. Existence is already the existence of and as the unknown. What the paradox gives, then, must have something to do with its expression. It is only insofar as it appears that it might "give" in the first place—even if that appearance can never amount to its immediate availability as such. Moreover, it is this very appearance which as appearance paradoxically causes the paradox to give. The paradox gives itself as soon as it appears. Because of this actuality, however, there is something else to which "the god"—in spite of any assumed omnipotence—is also subject. The very facticity of existence necessarily interrupts any exclusive control of "the eternal." This facticity itself is also an obligation. Everything, it would seem, originates in corporeal existence. Furthermore, it would seem that there is nothing other than its very presence, a presence that, as I have already shown, is not originary itself, but the very disruption of any origination, the disruption of any recollection of origin. Because there is existence, there must also be "the god." This presence, Climacus now insists, is itself "the teaching," as opposed to any doctrine or ideology. "The presence of the god in human form—indeed, in the lowly form of a servant—is precisely the teaching . . . " (*Philosophical Fragments,* 55). Yet what, exactly, does this "teaching" mean? What does it teach?

How, in other words, can one learn what cannot be known? What sort of knowledge is this? If the teaching here is to be understood as the giving itself of the giving of the paradox and the paradox must give itself in the moment it appears, what is "faith" if faith is the name for the possibility of receiving this gift that, in its perception, can never appear as knowledge of the gift or knowledge of the paradox? The question, now, is more than one of "faith" or "belief" *(Troen)* in something: Do you or do you not believe that this person is the incarnation of the god? There can be no evidence of the presence of the god in this human being that would distinguish this person from all others. There is no "distinguishing mark" *(Kjendetegn)* that would make this god knowable or familiar even as corporeal. There must, then, be something in the claim of one person, "I am the god," that will allow another to respond, "I believe that that person is the god." Or rather, there must be something about the assertion, "I believe that that person is the god," that will allow others to claim, "I, too, believe that that person is the god." The assumption of a direct and causal link between these statements seems at best absurd.

But wait, Climacus implicitly says. How is this evident absurdity to be understood? At first, the appearance of the god-man seems to denote an explicitly historical situation. The question of belief in relation to the human appearance of the god concerns first the "contemporary follower," who would have had the advantage of a firsthand account of this person, would have been able to experience—see, hear, touch, and so on—this person immediately. Does re-creation end when the relationship is no longer immediate? Can the historical appearance of the god in human form continue to produce re-creations in subsequent generations of followers who cannot have had firsthand experience of the god? Is immediacy, in fact, such an advantage? If "the god" in human form is indistinguishable from every other "human being"—when one does in fact perceive this god and believe this "human being" to be "the god"—is this solely because of the person's immediate presence? Is it the human form, the corporeal presence, that produces belief? Climacus's response, which should not come as a surprise, is: Yes. It is precisely because of the person's immediate appearance that the immediate perception of the person will be impossible. That the paradox appears—gives itself—every time there is appearance, is the very disjunction that directly undermines any possibility of direct knowledge. Appearance itself in this instance is always the appearance as some other thing; and accordingly as an unknown other, it is also the appearance of the other.

For Climacus, all "followers" will be what he calls "followers at second hand." Of the "contemporary follower," he claims: "But let us not forget that in regard to the birth of the god he will be in the very same situation as the follower at second hand ..." (*Philosophical Fragments*, 59). There is nothing about the sense-certainty of immediate perceptions in themselves that can give rise to anything other than strictly limited "historical knowledge." Understanding as "faith," even with the said certainty of an "eyewitness," must still be based on something other than immediate perception. Immediacy is the inevitable disruption of what Climacus calls "actual" contemporaneity, "so that the real contemporary is not that by virtue of immediate contemporaneity but by virtue of something else" (*Philosophical Fragments,* 67). From this he concludes: "*[E]rgo* the noncontemporary (in the sense of immediacy) must be able to be a contemporary by way of the something else *[det Andet]* by which the contemporary becomes an actual *[virkelige]* contemporary" (*Philosophical Fragments,* 67). This "something else" re-creates all followers as "followers at second hand" *(Discipelen paa anden Haand).* Re-creation depends upon this being "at second hand"—upon, that is, being at the hand of the other.[19]

"The god *has* been," Climacus declares. This is a "fact" like any other. What makes it a "fact for faith" is rather the "organ" of its perception. Therefore, the "fact for faith," which the human appearance of the god is, is the "historical fact" where the fact is understood to have "come into existence." This, however, is the "self-contradiction" of the historical fact. "Faith," Climacus explains, "pertains not to essence but to being" (*Philosophical Fragments,* 87). That is to say, "faith," as the perception of the "coming into existence" of the historical fact, is the perception of the very uncertainty of coming into existence. Faith, in this sense, is the perception of what cannot immediately be perceived: that it exists means that it did not always exist, nor did it ever have to exist. Faith, in all its uncertainty, is the perception of the nonbeing that precedes and pervades the fact of existence without either negating that existence or being negated by it: "Every time the believer makes this fact the fact of faith, makes it historical for himself, he respects the dialectical qualification of coming into existence" (*Philosophical Fragments,* 88).

What makes the fact a "fact for faith" is what we might preliminarily call the "grammar" of its perception—the way it is understood. Faith, Climacus explains, has two separate but indistinguishable functions: "Here faith is taken in its straightforward and common *[almindelig]* meaning as the relationship to the historical; but secondly, faith must be taken in the wholly eminent understanding, such that this word can appear but once, that is, many times, but only in one relationship *[Forhold]*" (*Philosophical Fragments,* 87). There is, on the one hand, a common meaning, a meaning held in common. This refers, according to Climacus, to the status of the "fact" in question as a necessarily historical fact. On the other (hand), the meaning of the "fact for faith" is regulated by its usage. This understanding restricts the meaning of the word to one still unspecified thing without restricting this meaning to a singular occurrence: "It is not a question here of its truth but of giving consent *[give Samtykke]* to the god's having come into existence, whereby the god's eternal essence is inflected *[flekteres]* into the dialectical qualifications of existence" (*Philosophical Fragments,* 87, trans.

modified). Faith is nothing more than the inflection, the turning of a single word into many occurrences. Yet, it is not as if faith itself has a "proper" meaning that would then appear in all inflections, but that inflections in faith inflect the unknown into all linguistic occurrences. Both meanings of "faith," then, occur simultaneously. Faith, in short, is the grammar of the unknown. But what does this mean? How might such a grammar function? In accordance with what rule? Does it function on its own? Without one's "consent"? What exactly does one give in "giving consent"? In what sense would this giving be anything other than a giving (up)? If faith is a grammar and this is a grammar of the unknown, what would prohibit the unknown as unknown from consuming even its own rule?

The difficulty is that the "fact for faith" is not an object of knowledge. It is neither perceptible nor determinable through knowledge at all. And yet, this "fact for faith" does not appear without a certain responsibility. In other words, it is not as if its separation from any possible knowing would absolve one of the responsibility to know and to confirm that this "fact" indeed is one—a fact, that is. The "fact for faith" is the fact of paradox. It is not merely a certain category of facts, one kind or genre among others, but is the inevitable qualification of any fact as fact. Every fact is inevitably suspended by its own facticity. Because of this, these facts inevitably refuse all regulation. To know them or to perceive and understand them is to refuse all normalization: "That fact, however, has no respect for domestication. . . , refuses to be naturalized. . . . That fact is only for faith" (*Philosophical Fragments,* 96). Thus, to know this fact is always to know something else, something outside and beyond the normative rule of cognition, thus suspending any such rule in advance. It is nonetheless to be "appropriated" (*Philosophical Fragments,* 98), even if this appropriation cannot be construed as domestication or naturalization. "The unknown" must be "appropriated" as unknown, without determination.

This "appropriation," however, is not without its consequences. Knowledge itself is one such consequence. Yet, what is knowledge, as a consequence of the refused naturalization of the unknown in the fact for faith, if knowledge must somehow be a consequence of that refusal? Climacus suggests:

> But, humanly speaking, consequences built upon a paradox are built upon the abyss, and the total content of the consequences, which is handed down *[overgives]* to the single individual only under the agreement *[Overenskomst]* that it is by virtue of a paradox, is not to be passed on like real estate [*urørligt Gods*—literally, "inviolable goods"], since the whole thing is in suspense *[er svævende]*. (*Philosophical Fragments,* 98)

In other words, can knowledge appear as anything other than the declaration of its own impossibility and the suspension of any determinate certainty?

Climacus distinguishes between three different categories of "facts": "historical," "eternal," and "absolute." The three categories are distinguished by the possibility of one's relation to them: "Every historical fact is only a relative fact, and therefore it is entirely appropriate for the relative power, time, to decide *[afgjør]* the relative fates of people with respect to contemporaneity" (*Philosophical Fragments*, 99). Knowledge of a "historical fact" would mark simply one's adherence to a given chronological temporal order. One's perception of the "historical fact" would be determined solely in terms of one's relative place in chronology. Climacus's objection here is not that time somehow determines the relation to objects in understanding, but that this determination by time would be singular and exclusive, thus prohibiting any possible understanding outside of or beyond a linear and continuous temporality. Time, that is, exclusively determines one's relation to a given event in the past with a deciding force that apparently is not yet "decisive significance." Time simply plays itself out, simultaneously deciding the condition of one's relation to the historical fact of the past in accordance with a strictly linear and irreversible progression. Thus, "time," even in its determination of the facticity of facts, is by no means the sole determination. The very communicability of facts, regardless of temporality, exhibits an excess beyond the confines of a linear temporality.

There must be, then, another time, another temporality. "Facts" must then be in some sense "eternal." "Eternal facts," which would be equally valid for all, irrespective of temporal occurrence, would appear to offer a kind of corrective to the inviolable decision carried out by chronological temporal progression. "Eternal," however, would be nothing less than the denial of an exclusively temporal determination. "Eternal facts" would somehow exist outside of time. Yet, could they then still be called "facts"? Or would their description as "eternal" somehow amount to an aberration, to a "less correct use of language" (*Philosophical Fragments*, 99), a kind of linguistic error that would lead one to believe that what exceeds temporality falls properly outside of time?

All "facts," then, are necessarily temporal, and any relation to them is necessarily historical, though their historical temporality cannot exhaust the possibility of their understanding. Re-creation depends not on the refusal of the efficacy of facts in time, but on the rearticulation of one's own relation to these facts with respect to time. The "fact for faith"—or, as

Climacus identifies this third category of fact here, the "absolute fact"—is still temporal, "for faith and the historical," he explains, "correspond *[svare til]* entirely to one another" (*Philosophical Fragments,* 99). In what way, however, do they "correspond" to one another? Whereas the historical fact unilaterally determines one's relation to it strictly by virtue of temporal proximity, one's relation to a fact as "absolute" is determined by something else as well:

> If that fact is an absolute fact, or, to define it even more exactly, if that fact is what we have set forth, then it is a contradiction for time to be able to apportion *[dele]* the relations of people to it—that is, apportion them in a decisive sense *[afgjørende Forstand]*, for whatever can be apportioned essentially by time is *eo ipso* not the absolute, because that would imply that the absolute itself is a *casus* in life, a status in relation to something else *[Andet]*, whereas the absolute, although declinable in all the *casibus* of life, is continually the same and in its continual relation to something else is continually *status absolutus.* (*Philosophical Fragments,* 99–100, trans. modified)

The "absolute fact" is not one fact among others, but the absolute is the inevitable consequence of every fact. Accordingly, its occurrence is not restricted to the temporal occurrences of facts within history. The temporality of this fact has nothing to do with one's relation to it such that its temporality would either determine or preclude all possible relations. Its significance is not restricted to and by its singular occurrence.

Whereas the "historical fact" properly "apportions" one's relation to it only with respect to the temporality of its occurrence, one's relation to the "absolute fact" is "apportioned" by something else. Thus, in terms of the "poetical test" of the *Philosophical Fragments,* as an earlier draft makes more explicit, all followers are always in the same position with respect to this fact: "It is not the case that the status of a contemporary is *status absolutus* and the status of one who comes later is *status constructus,* but that the status of faith is *status absolutus* for both the contemporary and the one who comes later."[20] And according to the published version, *status absolutus,* even for faith, makes possible one's apportionment with respect to a given fact, the "absolute fact." This fact is not restricted to a unique *casus,* but is, grammatically speaking, "declinable in all the *casibus* of life." What makes it significant, however, is not only that it is declinable in all the *casibus,* but rather, specifically, "something else." The absolute fact is not equated with the *status absolutus,* but "in relation to something else is continually *status absolutus.*" Its decisive and signifying function, grounded in its relation to this something else, grants it the "recreating power" of the *status absolutus.*

One is always "apportioned" by facts. The question is simply: How? In accordance with what grammar? Climacus's example here concerns the relation between the *status absolutus* and the *status constructus* unique to genitive case constructions in Hebrew grammar.[21] In the absence of case endings, Hebrew, in the case of the genitive, relies only upon the spatial and temporal relations of the words in immediate proximity in order to designate their respective grammatical functions. The question in the genitive case is one of governance and determination, where the appearance of one word is explicitly subjected to that of another. Here, the word in the *status absolutus*, effectively in the genitive case, further determines the word immediately preceding it, apart from its own case. For example, in a phrase such as "the word of the god," "the word" would appear in the *status constructus* and "the god" in the *status absolutus*. As *status absolutus*, the word governing the *status constructus* remains itself unchanged while effecting a change in the *status constructus*. The changes caused in the *status constructus*, to which Climacus refers, are neither syntactical nor logical, but are rather tonal and rhythmical.

More than the system of rules that govern the declensions and inflections of words for the production of intelligible speech, grammar here is related to what is actually understood. Grammar is neither strictly determinate nor finitely circumscribed, but given with the actuality of temporal alteration. What interests Climacus about the *status absolutus*, then, is its ability, in its grammatical function, to effect change in another word, regardless of any prior determinations of that word (it makes no difference, for example, whether it is in the nominative or accusative case) strictly through its proximate relation to that word. Now, in the specific use to which he puts this grammatical function, it becomes clear that it is not the *status absolutus* per se that interests him, but the sense in which it forms a connection between the specific linguistic occurrence and what he repeatedly refers to as "something else." The *status absolutus*, in short, declines this "something else" into "all the *casibus* of life." And yet, this declension can be posited as nothing more than an ideal. As Climacus later points out in the *Postscript*, the "something else," even as it is inflected in every other appearance, never appears as such: "[T]he subjective thinker will find it inexhaustible when his faith is to be declined in the manifold *casibus* of life" (*Postscript*, 351). The work of such a task will never be finished. It has no end.

Grammar for Climacus is not normative; his is rather a grammar of declension and inflection—a grammar, in short, of disruption and disjunction, the desultory grammar of falling. Life itself, then, is nothing but the endless series of *casibus*, and thus never exists itself as a prior referent. Its appearance itself inevitably suspends the possibility of referring back to any "life" as a pregiven unity (its appearance being the illusion of any such unity). Thus, life itself is inseparable from the understanding that produces it and that, in producing it, inscribes it as the possible object of the understanding in the first place. "Faith" is required for something peculiar to the grammar that makes the "fact for faith" meaningful for each and every follower, but not meaningful for each as the same thing: "Just as the historical becomes the occasion for the contemporary to become a follower—by receiving the condition, please note, from the god himself (for otherwise we speak Socratically)—so the report *[Efterretning]* of the contemporaries becomes the occasion for everyone coming later to become a follower—by receiving the condition, please note, from the god himself" (*Philosophical Fragments,* 100). In one instance, the case of the contemporary follower, the god is present in human form and provides by means of this corporeal presence the condition for "faith." This is as true for the contemporary as it is for the belated follower. Just as the corporeal presence of the god is the "teaching," so too is the report. The report is the god. This means nothing more than the fact that "the unknown," as "the god," is present in the report in the same way that it was in the body. It is this persistent presence of the unknown that makes the report meaningful in the first place, not by guaranteeing that it will have a definitive and directly communicable meaning, but by making any attempt at such definition impossible in advance. The unknown, in this sense, incessantly turns the report, as the historical appearance of the god-man, into a cipher—not the sign of the unknown, but rather the unknown and unknowable of the sign itself.

The paradoxical duality of the god-man makes the presence of this god-man a sign, as Climacus's counterpart, Anti-Climacus, explains in his *Practice in Christianity* (1850). That is, insofar as the god is present in the man, his existence is at once irreducible to either eternity or mere existence. There is always something more than presence, in turn making what is present the "sign" of something more. In this case, the problem directly has to do with the problem of Christianity. Here, Christ is "the teacher," and the teacher, as both Climacus and Anti-Climacus attest, is more important than the teaching claimed. "What," Anti-Climacus asks, "is meant by *a sign*"? He begins simply by explaining that the sign requires, first of all, a difference: "A sign is the denied immediacy or the *second* being that is *different* from the first being. This is not to say that the sign is not immediately something but that it is a sign, and it is not immediately that which it is as a sign or as a sign is not the immediate that it is" (*Practice in Christianity,*

124). Anti-Climacus defines signs not through what they offer or present, but through what they refuse. A sign is always doubled: it is both a sign and not a sign at the same time. It is both immediacy and nonimmediacy. Being itself is thus always doubled in the sign. There is both the sign and what is not the sign; there is what the sign is, and, at the same time, there is also that other being, the negative of the first, which (it) is because it is a sign. These two aspects of the sign refuse all reconciliation. Because it means something else, it cannot be what it is.

Yet, Anti-Climacus still insists that this is not enough. This duality of being in the sign still does not explain what is meant by a sign. A sign means what it does not because it is what it is. Anything can be a sign: "A navigation mark is a sign. Immediately it certainly is something, a post, a lamp, etc., but a sign it is not immediately; that it is a sign is something different from what it immediately is." It is always something different from what it immediately is, but it is not immediately something different from what it is; this something different is not immediately available—even in immediacy: "This underlies all the mystification by means of signs, for the sign is only for the one who knows that it is a sign and in the strictest sense only for the one who knows what it means; for everyone else the sign is that which it immediately is" (*Practice in Christianity*, 124). Even at its most mysterious, a sign is anything but "mystification." This does not mean, however, that what signs mean they mean unequivocally. On the contrary, every sign, in Anti-Climacus's definition, risks becoming what he calls a "sign of contradiction"—"a sign that contains a contradiction in its composition," a sign, we might suggest, that must mean two mutually exclusive things simultaneously—and, moreover, cannot mean one thing without the other. This is, he insists, a "contradiction" beyond the initial contradiction of first and second being. It is a contradiction that comes with the being of the second. And yet, contradiction here is never thoroughly contradictory. It never cancels itself out, thus erasing the sign altogether. "But the contradictory parts must not annul each other in such a way that the sign comes to mean nothing or in such a way that it becomes the opposite of a sign, an unconditional concealment," we are told (*Practice in Christianity*, 125). A sign is never transformed into something that it is not. It is always its own immediacy, and at the same time is always also the contradiction that it is, the self-contradiction that it is also another. These two discrepancies, two "disjunctions," are there as soon as the sign appears. And because the sign is this disjunction, it is a sign. That is, only because of its duplicitous disjoining, and not in spite of it, does the sign mean something, whether one knows it or not.

A sign, in spite of all its mystery—or perhaps even at its most mysterious—is the opposite of concealment. What a sign reveals, however, is not the same as what it means. A sign perhaps never exactly reveals its meaning. What one encounters in the face of the sign is nothing other than the secret of oneself:

> A contradiction placed squarely in front of a person—if one can get him to look at it—is a mirror; as he is forming a judgement, what dwells within him must be disclosed. It is a riddle, but as he is guessing the riddle, what dwells within him is disclosed by the way he guesses. The contradiction confronts him with a choice, and as he is choosing, together with what he chooses, he himself is disclosed. (*Practice in Christianity*, 127)

A sign is not a sign without contradiction. Because it is contradiction, the sign confronts the reader with a choice. In this choice, then, the reader, not the sign, discloses himself. Yet, at the same time, Anti-Climacus stops short of insisting that what is revealed would be immediately understandable, that we would then know who he is.

The sign, Anti-Climacus suggests, exists only in communication. A sign in communication is always a contradiction, and because it is self-contradiction, it renders all communication indirect. Communication is, first of all, a problem of existence, as it concerns the communication of something by someone in existence. In this sense, with respect to the one in existence, the communication, its utterance, requires what various Kierkegaardian pseudonyms have called "reduplication," the doubling of the communicator in communication. In summarizing the arguments of the other pseudonyms, Anti-Climacus writes that this "reduplication" can take place in one of two ways. In the case of the argument presented by Johannes Climacus in the *Postscript*, the "reduplication" appears as a "double reflection," in which case "the communicator" becomes "a nobody" with respect to the communication (*Practice in Christianity*, 133).[22] As opposed to the presumed analogy implied by the doubling of the speaker and the communication, Climacus rather insists on the impossibility of any such parallel relationship. Or, on the contrary, in absenting oneself from communication, the communication itself is rendered undecidable. The other sort of indirection is, however, not entirely opposed to the first. In this, "the communicator is present" in the communication. Communication in this instance, like all communication, concerns existence: "Any communication concerning existing requires a communicator; in other words, the communicator is the reduplication of the communication; to exist in what one understands is to reduplicate" (*Practice in Christianity*, 134).

However, it is impossible to communicate anything and not somehow exist in relation to the communication, even if only as "a nothing." The "reduplication" of communication is thus never the reduplication of the same thing. It is the reduplication of one existence in another. The separate existences of the communicator and the communication, however, remain mutually exclusive, even if potentially analogous. The existence of one is never the same as the existence of the other. The possibility of any confluence or congruity of existences in communication is already suspended in advance. The "existing person" can never exist in what he or she says or understands in the same way that he or she exists in life. Thus, what is presented in communication is always a contradiction: "Because of the communicator, the communication contains a contradiction, it becomes indirect communication; it confronts you with a choice: whether you will believe him or not" (*Practice in Christianity*, 134). Because the communicator exists, the unequal existence of communication is itself the contradiction. Even prior to the communication with another "existing person" (another expression of mutual incompatibility), the communication itself as linguistic expression—the expression of existence in the language in and of existence—is already self-contradictory. For this reason, Anti-Climacus insists, "there is no direct communication" (*Practice in Christianity*, 133). Communication is the impossibility of direct communication. Because any communication is already the presentation of a self-contradiction, the relation to what is communicated will never be direct, even in its most immediate perception.

"Communication is a choice," says Anti-Climacus (*Practice in Christianity*, 140). A choice, we might ask, of what? Anti-Climacus remains decidedly silent on this matter. Even his previous suggestion that the choice is one of "whether to believe him or not" is nothing other than a reiteration of the insistence of the choice itself. "Faith," he also informs us, "is a choice" (*Practice in Christianity*, 141). So, if faith is a choice and communication is a choice, one cannot result from the other. It is not because one already has decided "to believe" that one can then directly "believe" in the content of the communication. The choice already prohibits any such direct and causal sequence. On the contrary, faith and communication are the same choice; they are given in the same moment, and neither precedes the other. And the choice that is communication and faith is not absolved by choosing to believe the communication or choosing to communicate faith. This would no longer be a choice, as decision, and thus would no longer be either faith or communication. It is precisely to this notion of "communication" that Climacus turns at the end of the *Philosophical Fragments*.

"Communication" and "coming into existence" are thus related. The inevitable uncertainty of "coming into existence" is itself the very ground of the equally inevitable impossibility of direct communication. At the very least, communication exposes language as always more than it appears and thus equally the impossibility that its function will be exhausted in referentiality or conceptuality. If communication is to take place at all, it must be a strictly momentary occurrence; with no prior determination, each utterance in communication can give itself only with the (non)rule of its own (un)intelligibility. Communication, in each case, gives itself in breaking with itself—in giving itself, that is, with or as its own radical discontinuity. In this way, communication is already the very prohibition that its finite occurrence ever yield infinite universalization:

> Thus, if I say that this and this occurred, I speak historically; but if I say, "I believe and have believed that this happened, *although it is folly to the understanding and an offense to the human heart*," I have in the very same moment done everything to prevent anyone else from making up his mind in immediate continuity with me and to prohibit all partnership, because every single person must comport himself exactly the same way. (*Philosophical Fragments*, 102, trans. modified)

In the same way that Wittgenstein says that the statements "This pencil is five inches long" and "I feel that this pencil is five inches long" are subject to different grammars,[23] Climacus, too, insists on the particularity of grammar specific to the communication of belief. Both for Climacus and for Wittgenstein, grammar would refer at the very least to a conception of "use." Statements of fact and statements of belief are used in different circumstances to mean different things, and they mean different things in different ways. The "historical" statement is taken to be simply true and is handed down from one person to another, "like real estate," as an object of cognition. The historical fact would simply be known as true, and thus both be the same for all who would know it and, like the "truth" of recollection, would establish a relation of equivalence and continuity among those who know it. As far as the knowledge of the fact would be concerned, there would be no difference from one human being to another. In this sense, Anti-Climacus suggests in *Practice in Christianity*, that "what one knows about him," in the sense of the historical appearance of the god, "is different from what he is" (26). That is, the merely historical determination is inevitably insufficient as far as any understanding is concerned. The statement of belief, on the other hand, becomes communication only under the prohibition of continuity between one person and another. Yet, such a prohibition cannot appear as a certain legislative obligation, a call or command that one would heed, choosing either to obey or to transgress, thereby somehow absolving one of obligation, this having already been determined prior to any possible choice. Communication *(Med-delelse)* enacts a separation; it "thrusts the learner away." In order for understanding to be understanding at all, one must oneself bear responsibility for it.

The communicability of the report, in this sense, has to do with the way in which it is understood, not with the truth or falsity of its assertions. In the same way that the human body *is* "the teaching" of the god, the significance of the report has nothing to do with its intentional content. It is not what one says that communicates its significance to another, but the "authority" with which it is imparted:

> Whether he [the contemporary] actually had the faith that he testified he had is of no concern to one who comes later; it is of no benefit to him and makes no difference to him in coming to faith himself. Only the person who personally receives the condition from the god (which completely corresponds to the requirement that one relinquish the understanding and on the other hand is the only authority that corresponds to faith), only that person believes. (*Philosophical Fragments,* 102–3)

The "something else" of grammatical understanding simultaneously forms and undermines the "authority" of the understanding as that of communication.[24] This "authority" cannot guarantee what the communication means. Rather, it is opposed to any such security. Authority, in this sense, can be conceived only as nonauthority in the same way that grammar here is inevitably agrammatical. The text, like the body, is not representative of something else; its meaning does not give way to an ideal or metaphysical presence. Its faithful communication appears as absolute disjunction: "The believer, however, passes the report on in such a way that no one can accept it directly and immediately, for the words 'I believe it' (despite the understanding and my own inventive talents) are a very disquieting *aber* [but]" (*Philosophical Fragments,* 104). If this is to be understood at all, it can be understood only as the very relinquishing of the understanding itself.

However, this is not to say, by faith, that its object is "understood" somehow in a space outside of understanding and thus still nonetheless "understood." No, it is in the suspension and relinquishing of the understanding that understanding takes place. This is what learning means. This is why, Climacus insists, furthermore, as he has all along, that "faith is not a knowledge but an act of freedom" (*Philosophical Fragments,* 83). Faith is not an object; it is not a thing to be known or understood, however peculiar it may appear. It is an act and exists only in its action—exists, that is, only insofar as it transpires or takes place. This act of faith, however, is not free to take place in any way whatsoever. On the contrary, it can occur only insofar as it is given, and it is given only in communication. Faith, insofar as it is the paradoxical effect of the giving itself of the giving itself of the paradox in the relinquishing of the understanding, is the effect of communication's indirection. Faith, like communication, is "a choice." This choice, however, is never not a choice, never finally decided, whether one believes or not. It is present only as choice—not a choice between one thing or another, but the inevitable self-contradiction or self-suspension of the possibility of appearance in appearance itself. This choice is, however, never as such presentable, but is present only in the giving itself of the paradox. The choice is this act of giving. This act, as Climacus says further, is the inexpressible taking place of freedom—the freedom of coming into existence, which cannot be undone.

5

Abraham: Departures

When God commanded Abraham to go to Mount Moriah and sacrifice his son, Isaac, Abraham went without hesitation: "And Abraham rose up early in the morning, and saddled his ass, and took two of his young men with him, and Isaac his son, and clave the wood for the burnt offering, and rose up, and went unto the place of which God had told him" (Genesis, 22:3).[1] The journey took three days. On the third day, upon seeing the mountain in the distance, Abraham continued alone with Isaac, carrying only the wood, fire, and knife for the sacrifice, until they came to the place that God has designated. Here they stopped. Abraham built an altar, bound his son Isaac, and laid him down upon it. Abraham reached out and took the knife to slaughter his son. "And the angel of the Lord called unto him out of heaven, and said, Abraham, Abraham: and he said, Here am I." At the brink of sacrifice, God commanded Abraham not to harm his son. "And Abraham lifted up his eyes, and looked, and behold behind him a ram caught in a thicket by the horns." Abraham sacrificed the ram in place of Isaac and they returned together. "And Abraham called the name of that place Jehovah-jireh; as it is said to this day, In the mount of the Lord it shall be seen" (Genesis 22:11,13, 14).[2]

But what do we see here? A sacrifice? God? The ram? The mountain? Is there an identifiable object in the ordinary sense of the word? If something is seen, does it have to be just one thing? The question is not only about the object. Who exactly sees here? Abraham? Isaac? Do we see? And do we even know what we see? The answers to these questions are by no means certain. The difficulty appears at the moment one has to give an account of what has taken place. In this account conventionally taken as an originary narrative of sacrifice, it is impossible to say that Abraham has committed only one sort of sacrifice. Is this only the sacrifice of a ram by Abraham? Indeed, it seems the narrative would be of little interest if Abraham simply went out and sacrificed the ram. But in what sense can the narrative be understood as Abraham's sacrifice of Isaac if Isaac is never sacrificed, at least not literally? If Isaac is not sacrificed by Abraham, what takes place in the transition from Isaac to the ram? How can we possibly account for this sacrificial substitution? What happens here? What do we see?

Abraham and Isaac simply go out so that Isaac may be sacrificed in accordance with God's command. Yet, at the moment just before the sacrifice will irrevocably have been completed, Isaac is replaced by a ram suddenly and incongruously revealed in a thicket. Although Abraham's sacrifice is traditionally valued as the demonstration of his faith because he is doing what God commands simply because God commands it,[3] the failure in the end to commit this sacrifice as commanded leaves open the question whether faith can be presented in this manner at all. From another perspective, all that remains certain is that Abraham and Isaac go out and then return, neither gaining nor losing anything. Nothing out of the ordinary can be observed, nothing of the sacrifice. So in the end, the question still remains: What has taken place? How is it perceived? If it is "seen," what is accounted for in this presentation of sight, where even sight itself appears blind?

"I cannot see the leap," Kafka writes in a letter to Robert Klopstock from 1921 in oblique reference to Kierkegaard's discussion of Abraham and the remarkable "leap of faith" that Abraham must have made in order to be prepared to sacrifice his son, Isaac: "If he already had everything and yet still should be taken higher, then something, at least in appearance, had to be taken from him; that is logical *[folgerichtig]* and not a leap" (*Briefe*, 333). Here Kafka is concerned with what is often taken to be the central assertion of Kierkegaard's *Fear and Trembling*. Abraham, it is assumed, is the "father of faith," and his paternity in this regard is accounted for in his unhesitating preparedness to sacrifice his son, Isaac, only fortuitously to be spared this monumental loss at the last moment, when the ram is offered in Isaac's stead. Apparently, the only possible explanation of Abraham's ability to offer his son's life rests in his "faith" that this sacrifice is required of him by God. Abraham, Kierkegaard seems to suggest, was required to forego his ethical obligation to his son in service of his "higher" religious duty to God. This religious duty thus isolates Abraham, the individual, "above" the otherwise universal form of ethical obligation.[4]

Yet Kafka's observation on this point indicates a twofold limitation in this otherwise hierarchical schematization and conceptualization of Abraham's act—a limitation, furthermore, that is more in agreement with Kierkegaard's presentation of Abraham in *Fear and Trembling* than it is simply in critical opposition to it.[5] Does the "leap of faith" that is said to mark the unconceptualizable limit of ethics vis-à-vis "the religious" in fact exist? That is, can it be presented? Can it be perceived? Does this "leap" account for the conceptual discrepancy between ethics, defined in terms of the obligation of the individual to all others, and the religious, defined as the singular and individual obligation to "the absolute"—in this instance, to God? Is there—and this would be the second part of Kafka's objection—a perceptible discrepancy between the ethical and the religious such that one would have to suspend the conceptual order of the ethical in order to articulate the inescapable particularity of the religious order, which, by its very insistence upon an obligation to something absolutely unknowable, would resist the conceptual ordering of the ethical at every turn? Or, rather, is not the intention to present in Abraham a "faith" that would explain and account for his ability to sacrifice Isaac still fully in accordance with the "ethical" mode of understanding? Can the *justification* of Abraham's act as a religious act oppose the ethical at all? Does this justification as such offer anything more than consolation for an only apparent transgression of the ethical, whereby the negative moment of Abraham's ethical transgression is simply appropriated into the formulation of a "higher" obligation to God? In this case, instead of ethical duty, Abraham would fulfill a religious duty functionally no different from the ethical. To echo Kafka: "That is logical and not a leap." This "sacrifice" would mark no transgression; neither would it require an alternative conceptual explanation of the apparent discrepancy between the assumed ethical obligation and the religious command.

In other words, one cannot resolve the transition that seems to have taken place simply by shifting the conceptual framework from that of ethics to that of the religious. The sacrifice shows only that such a conceptual transition is not possible. The difficulty is that, as both Kafka and Kierkegaard point out, nothing is taken away from Abraham. In spite of all preparation, Abraham never sacrifices Isaac. He never has to. Abraham and Isaac go out to Mount Moriah to perform a sacrifice, nothing more. Every account of Abraham, then, is an attempt to come to terms with precisely this: nothing changes. And yet, each account is an attempt in one way or another to come to terms with the paradoxically ethical transgression that constitutes Abraham's act.[6] The two thoughts here are coextensive: the fundamental paradox of ethics coincides with the impossibility of any change, conversion, or transformation. What comes into question, then, is precisely the conceptual possibility of an accountable progression or transition—accountable because of its orientation toward a presumed or given, even if as yet unknown, end. As long as there can be a universalizable justification that would entirely explain and account for Abraham's sacrifice, there can be no question of a "leap of faith."

Kafka's resistance to the notion of a "leap of faith" as the necessary link in the explanation of Abraham's sacrifice is not an opposition to "faith" as such, but an opposition to its ability in this case to absolve Abraham of his ethical responsibility. More important, rather than dismissing the notion of faith altogether, it is precisely through the articulation and understanding of faith that Kafka begins to understand Kierkegaard's work.

Several years prior to the reflections on Abraham I have just referred to, Kafka had engaged in a more thorough and critical reading of Kierkegaard.[7] In 1917, after having been diagnosed with tuberculosis, Kafka took a leave of absence from his work in Prague and lived for several months with his sister and her husband on their farm in Zürau. His writing from this period (1917–18) consists virtually entirely of letters written to friends and family in Prague (including more general and extensive discussions of Kierkegaard, particularly in letters to Max Brod) and notes and aphorisms making up the third and fourth of his "Oktavheften" *(Octavo Notebooks)*. The most explicit and extensive commentary is reserved, not surprisingly, for *Fear and Trembling*. Kafka's notes on this text appear in the final pages of the fourth *Octavo Notebook*. He precedes his reflections on Abraham, however, with a discussion of "faith" *(Glaube)*:

> Every person is posed two questions of faith *[Glaubensfragen]*: first, on the believability *[Glaubenswürdigkeit]* of this life; second, on the believability of one's goal. Both questions are so firmly and immediately answered with "yes" through the fact of our life that it could become uncertain whether the questions were correctly understood. In any event, one must now work through to this first fundamental "yes," for still far under their surface, the answers, in the rush of the questions, are confused and evasive. (Kafka, "Oktavheften," 91)

For Kafka, faith has nothing to do with a belief in God or a belief in some transcendent unknown. The two possible grounds of faith, life and its goal, are taken to be so self-evident that the possibility of anything but an immediate affirmation of "faith" in them seems all but entirely out of the question. How can one not have "faith" in what without doubt exists? The fact of one's existence is taken to be the guarantee of faith in one's existence. The fact of life and its goal or purpose *(Ziel)* would appear, under immediate affirmation, to coincide. One lives, and in living, one is assumed to have an end, a purpose.[8] Yet the possibility of faith is presented only as a question—a question, however, that cannot simply be answered in the affirmative. Its affirmation immediately gives way to uncertainty. There appears to be a conflict between the question of faith and its affirmation, such that immediate affirmation can mean only that the question itself has been misunderstood.[9] One is left with no answer at all—or certainly with none as definitive and self-evident as the original affirmation would suggest. The point of the question perhaps does not lie in the possibility of definitive affirmation. This affirmation is never as such abandoned. It is, rather, simply suspended, given only insofar as it is yet to be achieved. Arrival—return—is by no means certain. All answers, beneath an only superficial sense of certainty, appear ungrounded, unfathomable, "confused and evasive."

Kafka repeats this thought in the next entry, though now in the form of a dialogue and with a perhaps somewhat different sense of clarity. He begins again with the concurrence of life and faith. Already here, what previously had been presented as affirmation of the coincidence and simultaneity of life and faith, if still somewhat premature, is not so much uncertain as it is inexhaustible, never exactly totalizable. The first voice begins: "'One cannot say that we lack faith *[Glaube]*. The simple fact of our life itself is inexhaustible in its faithfulness *[Glaubenswert]*.'" That is, we do not lack faith, because we can never reach its end. The possession of faith is directly related to the impossibility of exhausting the fact of life; the point at which the "faithfulness" of life could be equated with the fact of life is not as such available. Life itself can never disappear into the question of faith in it; life exists only as remainder.[10] The second voice, responding to the first, points out the apparent tautology of this argument: "'Would there be any faithfulness? One certainly cannot not-live.'" Clearly, if the fact of life itself is the (only) guarantor of faith, it would be impossible not to have faith, impossible not to arrive at its affirmation. But this is not exactly denied. The first voice now replies: "'Precisely in this "certainly cannot" lies the insane *[wahnsinnig]* power of faith; it takes shape in this negation'"

("Oktavheften", 91). The impossibility of not living does not translate into the affirmation of life and, hence, the affirmation of faith in life. Rather, the impossibility of not living constitutes the absolute negativity of faith, one that does not simply disappear in the face of its affirmation. Kafka makes two inseparable, though in some sense incompatible, assertions. On the one hand, the "power" of faith requires that it have form. If faith were merely amorphous, it could not be had, could not be possessed. On the other hand, the only form given to faith is negation; it is thus perhaps not form at all, but something more like the impossibility of form, which, however, is not not form.

"But," as Kierkegaard under the pseudonym Johannes de Silentio also insists with regard to the possession of faith, "this having, after all, is also a giving up" (*Fear and Trembling,* 47). Here he is writing about the reliance of "faith" upon what he calls "the absurd"—that is, the reliance of "faith" upon something that cannot be reduced to reason. The image of faith that appears for Kafka is not far from the thought of faith described in *Fear and Trembling.* Faith is possible for thought only through a particular movement of negation in which the possibility of thinking faith requires the negation of thought itself. If one has faith—and this is by no means certain—one can have it only "by virtue *[kraft]* of the absurd, by virtue of the fact that for God all things are possible" (*Fear and Trembling,* 46). This, however, does not mean that the task of faith is simply to believe that all things are possible. This would clearly be delusional; it would be "madness": "Fools and young people say that everything is possible for a human being. But that is a gross error. Spiritually speaking, everything is possible, but in the finite world there is much that is not possible" (*Fear and Trembling,* 44). This separation between the "finite" and the infinite, or "spiritual," is absolute. It is impossible to think that "spiritually thinking, everything is possible" without the counterinsistence that "in the finite world there is much that is not possible." At no point is this "not-possible" of the finite world dissolved into the pure and infinite possibility attributed to the spiritual. Hence, the only possible relation between the two is necessarily negative. De Silentio continues: "The knight [of faith], however, makes this impossibility possible by expressing it spiritually, but he expresses it spiritually by renouncing it" (*Fear and Trembling,* 44). The infinite possibility open to the spiritual never overcomes the impossibilities of the "finite world." They can only be "renounced."

As for Kafka, faith by the "power" *(kraft)* of "the absurd" is possible only as a kind of negative affirmation. As such, the problem of "faith" remains an epistemological one. "The absurd," even in its having by way of giving up, does not exist as another possibility proper to some more determinate knowing: "The absurd does not belong to the differences that lie within the proper domain of the understanding. It is not identical with the improbable, the unexpected, the unforeseen" (*Fear and Trembling*, 46). In a way similar to the differentiation between the infinite possibility of the spiritual and the impossibilities inherent in the finite world, "the absurd" articulates a distinction between the "proper domain of the understanding" and something that would remain incompatible with it. What is absurd is not absurd because it has not already been situated within the temporality of conceptual epistemology, even as the negative, the "un–," of probability and expectation. The absurd has no futurity in this sense; it does not exist within a purely linear temporality that, even as unexpected or unforeseen, would, upon its sudden appearance, require or allow it to be appropriated into the same temporality, the temporality of the same. In a somewhat stronger formulation, de Silentio already insists in the "Preface": "Even if someone were able to transpose the whole content of faith into conceptual form, it does not follow that he has comprehended faith, comprehended how he entered it or how it entered into him" (*Fear and Trembling*, 7). Faith is not a concept; it cannot be fit to conceptual form. It cannot, we might further suggest, be put into form at all.

If faith resists all knowing and all understanding, can one, in any sense, "have" faith? Can one know not simply "how," but, more important, *whether* "faith entered him or he entered it"? On this point, de Silentio could not be more clear: "I cannot make the movement of faith, I cannot shut my eyes and plunge confidently into the absurd; it is for me an impossibility, but I do not praise myself for that" (*Fear and Trembling*, 34). To imitate Abraham, to do as Abraham did, does not result in "faith." Nor can "faith" be appropriated, even with the assumed assurance of "the absurd." It is impossible "to think" Abraham's "faith": "Thinking about Abraham is another matter, however; then I am shattered. I am constantly aware of the prodigious paradox that is the content of Abraham's life, I am constantly repelled, and, despite all its passion, my thought cannot penetrate it, cannot get ahead by a hairsbreadth. I stretch every muscle to get a perspective, and at the very same instant I become paralyzed" (*Fear and Trembling*, 33). Yet, is this perhaps not already precisely the point of "faith"—paralysis? "Every time I want to make the movement, I almost faint; the very same moment I admire absolutely, I am seized with great anxiety. For what is it to tempt God? And yet this is the movement of faith ..." (*Fear and Trembling*, 48). "But this movement I cannot make.... I am able to swim in life, but I am too heavy for this mystical hovering *[Svæven]*" (*Fear and Trembling*, 50).

The point here is twofold: First, the paradox of "faith" remains paradoxical because it resists the temporal ordering that otherwise determines conceptual thought. And second, one cannot read what de Silentio wants to say in *Fear and Trembling* without simultaneously holding on to his resistance, without holding on to his failure to achieve the "faith" he can only describe, and describe as an impossibility for him.

At no point does de Silentio suggest that there would be a smooth transition from the ethical to the religious. The paradoxical opposition of the ethical and the religious already suspends the very possibility of transition. The ethical and the religious designate two conflictual, though equally valid, accounts of Abraham's sacrifice. "The ethical expression for what Abraham did," de Silentio writes, "is that he meant to murder Isaac; the religious expression is that he meant to sacrifice Isaac—but precisely in this contradiction is the anxiety that can make a person sleepless, and yet without this anxiety Abraham is not who he is" (*Fear and Trembling,* 30). Who Abraham is, then, depends precisely on the maintenance of the contradictory relationship between the ethical expression ("murder") and the religious expression ("sacrifice"). Abraham would not be Abraham if "murder" could become "sacrifice." This contradiction, if it is to be truly contradictory, cannot unfold into logical or temporal succession. The religious expression does not succeed and replace the ethical. The ethical persists and is in no way resolved in or dissolved into the security of a newly formed "religious" understanding that would subsequently and forevermore justify the sacrifice in terms of a "higher" ideal. Accordingly—and this is the profound difficulty of *Fear and Trembling*—the religious expression is nonetheless present in every ethical expression, already displacing every ethical formulation.

The religious, however, knows no expression. "Abraham cannot speak" (*Fear and Trembling,* 60). That is, the religious as such can never appear and can never be perceived. If it is to be perceived at all, it can appear only in the dislocations effected within the ethical. Yet—and here we are following Kafka—can displacements as such ever be perceived? Can we ever see such a leap? "The non-communicability of the paradox exists perhaps," Kafka remarks in the fourth *Octavo Notebook,* "but it doesn't express itself as such, for Abraham himself does not understand it" ("Oktavheften," 91). Is appearance ever perceived as already displaced? Can it be understood as anything but "proper" appearance?

The contradiction apparent in Abraham's act is as much conceptual as it is ethical, insofar as the ethics de Silentio invokes function solely in accordance with principles of conceptual formation. Although Abraham exhibits the fundamental paradox of the ethical (that any ethics is as much unethical as it is ethical), the paradoxical formulation of this difficulty continually situates the ethical itself, by virtue of its contradictory relation to religious faith, beyond the realm of conceptual understanding. The ethical, in spite of its conceptual formality, continually recedes before and eludes any desired recuperation in the understanding. Yet, what becomes apparent through Kafka's appropriation of Kierkegaard's Abraham through his insistence upon the impossibility of any transformative "leap" is not simply that the ethical lies beyond discourse and is unassimilable to it. Rather, "faith" thwarts the very dialectical movement that would consolidate the ethicality of ethics in the continual appropriation of its own negativity. That is, it is the possibility and ethicality of the movement itself that comes into question, not ethics. Abraham's religious intent "to sacrifice" Isaac seems conceivable only outside the strictures of ethical obligation, through what de Silentio calls the "teleological suspension of the ethical."

The question of a "beyond" of ethics is continually broached throughout the text. Specifically, it forms the central concern, taken up variously, in the three "Problemata" that make up the interpretive part of *Fear and Trembling*, in which de Silentio explores the implications of Abraham's sacrifice for the delimitation of the ethical. Taken in their spatial and chronological progression, the succession of the three "Problemata" appears to suggest that what is being asserted, under the continual implication of affirmation, is ultimately the overcoming of the ethical incommensurability inherent in this sacrifice through an alternative allegiance to God, "the absolute," the "inexpressible"—through, that is, "faith." The three "Problemata" read as follows:

I: "Is there a teleological suspension of the ethical?"
II: "Is there an absolute duty to God?"
III: "Was it ethically defensible for Abraham to conceal his undertaking from Sarah, from Elizier, and from Isaac?"

Yet each of the "Problemata" begins from precisely the same point of departure and presupposes nothing about positing a surmountable end to the ethical. Each of these sections begins with the assertion: "The ethical is the universal . . ." (*Fear and Trembling*, 54, 68, and 82).

"Problema I" takes up the question of ethical universality under the question of the possibility of a "teleological suspension of the ethical." Here, universality as the realm of the ethical is defined expressly by way of its orientation:

> The ethical as such is the universal, and as the universal it applies to everyone, which from another angle means that it applies at all times. It rests immanent in itself, has nothing outside itself that is its *télos* but is itself the *télos* for everything outside itself, and when the ethical has absorbed this into itself, it goes no further. The single individual, sensately and psychically qualified in immediacy, is the individual who has his *télos* in the universal, and it is the ethical task continually to express himself in this, to annul his singularity in order to become the universal. As soon as the single individual asserts himself in his singularity before the universal, he sins, and only by acknowledging this can he be reconciled again with the universal. (*Fear and Trembling*, 54)

Here already, the accounts of Abraham indicate a divergence from a purely ethical orientation. For example, Abraham, as de Silentio points out, is not identical with Agamemnon, the "tragic hero." When Agamemnon sacrifices Iphigenia, terrible though this may be, he does it for the sake of a "higher expression of the ethical"; he does it for the sake of the nation (*Fear and Trembling*, 59). Thus, de Silentio explains, "he scales down the ethical relation between ... daughter and father to a feeling that has its dialectic in relation to the ideas of moral conduct. Here there can be no question of a teleological suspension of the ethical itself." That is, the individual act in this case is called for, explained by, and directed toward the maintenance of an "idea": the ideal of the nation. The notion of "sin" is accordingly defined as the incompatibility of individual singularity with a universal teleology. "Sin," therefore, is unavoidable, and not only for Abraham: "Thus, even though the child does not sin, because it is not conscious of its existence as such, its existence, from the point of view of the idea, is nevertheless sin, and the ethical makes its claim upon it at all times" (*Fear and Trembling*, 62).[11]

The point here is as much the impossibility of dissolving singularity entirely into an ideal of ethical universality (presenting the individual as a limit of a universalizing conception of the ethical in the continued persistence of individuality beyond the universal ideal) as it is the failure of an articulation of singularity to avoid or negate ethical ideality. Thus, even in "acknowledging singularity before the universal," the ideal "reconciliation" never as such takes place; the "sin" of finite individuality is never negated. De Silentio continues:

> If this is the highest that can be said of man and his existence, then the ethical is of the same nature as a person's eternal salvation, which is his *télos* forevermore and at all times, since it would be a contradiction for this to be capable of being surrendered (that is, teleologically suspended), because as soon as this is suspended it is relinquished, whereas that which

> is suspended is not relinquished but is preserved in the higher, which is its *télos.* (*Fear and Trembling,* 54)

Under the ideal of reconciliation, de Silentio describes two kinds of "suspension." One constitutes the reconciliation of two conflictual obligations in a "higher" ideal (for example, Agamemnon in service of the nation). And in the other, which Abraham exemplifies, the teleological orientation of ethical obligation is given up entirely, though in no way is it entirely dissolved. Abraham's sacrifice serves no higher ideal; it serves no universal reconciliation: "Insofar as the universal was present, it was cryptically in Isaac, hidden, so to speak in Isaac's loins, and must cry out with Isaac's mouth: Do not do this, you are destroying everything" (*Fear and Trembling,* 59).

Insofar as the future of the nation of Israel is promised in Isaac (Genesis 15), to sacrifice this promise would be to sacrifice at once the promise of the future and the promise of a national ideal.[12] And Abraham does this without positing an alternative and potentially more desirable or admirable end (*télos* or *Ziel*). Nonetheless, de Silentio seems at times to suggest that this would be one understanding of Abraham's sacrifice: "Abraham's situation is different. By his act he transgressed the ethical altogether and had a higher *télos* outside it, in relation to which he suspended it." Yet the "*télos*" thus construed can no longer be understood, strictly speaking, with the teleological orientation that constitutes ethical understanding. In the first place, Abraham's sacrifice is not performed in accordance with a "higher" ideal. Since this is not the case, de Silentio asks: "Why, then, does Abraham do it? For God's sake and—the two are wholly identical—for his own sake" (*Fear and Trembling,* 59). Thus, de Silentio, too, as we have already seen in Kafka, eliminates the possiblity that Abraham's "faith" would be determined in relation to a transcendent unknown. He is himself already the only possible justification of his sacrifice.

But how are we to understand this singular justification? Abraham, as the "single individual"—that is, restricted to the "finite world"—stands necessarily outside any possible transcendent determination or orientation. Accordingly, in the second place, this standing "outside" ethical teleology affects the possibility of any teleologically oriented understanding. That is, understanding, by positing an alternative end, would still operate in accordance with the teleologically construed reconciliation in a "higher" ideal that defines the ethical. This teleology, in Abraham's case, is suspended. De Silentio asks: "Or should Abraham's receiving Isaac by a *marvel* be able to prove that Abraham was justified in relating himself as the single individual to the universal? If Abraham actually had sacrificed Isaac, would he therefore have been less justified" (*Fear and Trembling,* 63)? Rather than exploring possible answers to these questions in search of one answer that might prove correct and might successfully explain Abraham's predicament, de Silentio questions the very motivation for these questions. What, after all, would "justification" be if not the continual preponderance of the ethical ideal? Rather than resolution, de Silentio offers the following objection: "But we are curious about the result, just as we are curious about the way a book turns out. We do not want to know anything about the anxiety, the distress, the paradox" (*Fear and Trembling,* 63).

To understand this sacrifice by way of its result, the successful return of Isaac to Abraham, circumvents and avoids the central "paradox" exposed within it. The difficulty of understanding Abraham's sacrifice cannot be resolved by reminding oneself that, no matter what happens, Isaac, having never left, is nevertheless "returned" to Abraham in the end. Indeed, the fact that Abraham does not sacrifice Isaac continues to haunt every account of the sacrifice that would find here any "justification" for Abraham's intent to sacrifice his son. The teleological justification in Isaac's return fails to absolve Abraham of his intent to sacrifice—or rather, ethically speaking, "to murder"—Isaac. Again: "But I come back to Abraham. During the time before the result, either Abraham was a murderer every minute or we stand before a paradox that is higher than all mediations" (*Fear and Trembling,* 66).

But what sort of paradox would this be? At this moment, evidently, de Silentio does not mean what he had earlier described as the "prodigious paradox that is the content of Abraham's life"—the same paradox that we rehearsed earlier as the conflict between "murder" and "sacrifice"—the conflict, as exemplified by Abraham, between singularity and universality. No, this is a paradox "from another angle": this is not the paradox of "content" that Abraham was a murderer, but the paradox, prior to any result and never alleviated by any result, that Abraham, for all his singularity, was "every minute" a murderer. There is no way out; at every moment, Abraham, by dint of his singularity, inevitably came into conflict with the ethical. Without making any attempt to decide this either/or (indeed, we might imagine that any attempt to make such a decision would inevitably lapse into both/and), de Silentio simply concludes: "The story of Abraham contains, then, a teleological suspension of the ethical. As the single individual he became higher than the universal. This is the paradox, which cannot be mediated" (*Fear and Trembling,* 66).

Two paradoxes cannot be mediated. First, Abraham was a murderer. This is the unavoidable consequence of eliminating the possibility that Isaac's return could ever justify his sacrificial intention. Second, and nonetheless still in accordance with the first, Abraham, in opposing all ethical obligation, placed the individual "higher than the universal." This, however, is by no means construed as "justification"; nor does it negate the otherwise ethically valid notion of obligation. Situating the individual "higher" than the universal is not an "end"; it is perhaps only a beginning, a beginning without end, or rather a beginning that already suspends the possibility of ever attaining an end, the satisfactory end of explanation or justification.

Kafka puts this another way. He writes in the third *Octavo Notebook*: "There is a goal, but no way; what we call way is delay *[Zögern]*" ("Oktavheften," 61). That is, the teleological orientation toward any given or posited end in no way constitutes its accountability. From another angle, we might say, there is no destination, only "the way." The end and the means toward that end, the destination and its "way," are never given within the same trajectory, the same temporality, and thus remain forever irreconcilable. The one, however, does not negate or otherwise do away with the other. The possibility of an end is not presented as the impossibility of a way, nor, vice versa, is the possibility of the way presented as the impossibility of an end. The one is not given without the other. We might even suggest that it would be impossible to eliminate the validity and necessity of this sort of teleological orientation, just as de Silentio is unable to eliminate the ethical structure that necessarily informs any possibility of understanding Abraham.[13] The difficulty, however, is that even within this structure, the end and its way never meet. The goal is given without the possibility of arrival. Yet, in being given, it is already the way. The way, however, with respect to the given destination, is given only as separation from any destination—a separation that at the same time temporalizes the relation to this destination always only as delay or hesitation *(Zögern)*. The way, even as directed toward a given end, is the way only insofar as it is not the end. The distance toward destination always exceeds the space of separation.[14] This insurmountable separation inevitably affects the possibility of any understanding temporally and teleologically oriented toward a given end.

Several years later, in 1922, Kafka thematized this break in a short text, posthumously entitled "Der Aufbruch" by Max Brod, which we might preliminarily translate as "The Break—Away" or, simply, as the translators of the English version have chosen, "Departure."[15] The text is exemplary, and I will cite it in full:

> I ordered my horse be brought from the stable. The servant did not understand me. I went myself into the stall, saddled my horse, and mounted it. In the distance I heard a trumpet sound; I asked him what that

> would mean. He knew nothing and had heard nothing. At the gate, he stopped me and asked: "Where are you going, Master?" "I don't know," I said, "only away from here, only away from here. Forever away from here, only in this way can I reach my destination *[Ziel]*." "Then you know your destination?" he asked. "Yes," I answered, "I said it already: 'Away from here,' that is my destination." "You have no provisions with you," he said. "I need none," I said, "the journey is so long that I must starve if I receive nothing along the way. No provision can save me. It is, fortunately, a truly colossal *[ungeheuer]* journey." (*Erzählungen*, 321; *Complete Stories*, 449)[16]

Like Abraham's excursions, the narrator's journey consists only of departure. Yet we are given everything but the departure itself. Like Kafka's "other Abrahams," this narrator appears ready *(bereit)* but incapable of departure, suspending the journey at the limit of its commencement and completion. The only possible account of this journey is presented without respect to an attainable goal, prior to any intended arrival at a goal. In this infinite separation, the conversion of departure and arrival, even in its proleptic expectation, can take place only as the unavoidable negation of any desired arrival; his only destination is "away."

Significant here, however, is not simply the necessary presentation of the destination already as its unavoidable negation, but this negative presentation, the presentation of the negative, which appears concurrent with the separation—but not necessarily the subversion—of all other hierarchies. The text begins with a crisis of communication, and the impossibility of communication crosses more than the merely linguistic relation; it crosses (out) both the social and conceptual relation between master and servant, *Herr* and *Knecht*. The end of communication, however, is not absolute, but constitutes only the suspension of a certain given and understood relation between these two figures. The servant does not understand the command to bring the horse from the stable, leaving the master, *Herr*, to retrieve it for himself as his own servant, *Knecht*. The servant does not perform the one task that his position requires of him; he does not serve. Nor does he explain anything. He neither hears nor knows of any trumpet call in the distance, thus severing the possibility of a certain relation to the world that would make something otherwise distant and unknown familiar and understood. Neither of these moments is pursued any further. Unlike the doctor in "Ein Landarzt" ("A Country Doctor"), for example, this *Herr* makes no effort to remedy or rectify an otherwise unacceptable situation.

This, however, does not prohibit communication in another form from taking place. The servant stops his master at the gate, at the border between inside and outside, interrupting him on his way only to ask one question: "Where are you going, Master?" The response is both positive and negative at the same time. The master both knows *(kennen)* and does not know *(wissen)* his destination; it is simultaneously familiar as "away from here" and unknown in any more positive or determinate sense. The possibility of destination is not simply negative. It is not not known, nor is it not not attainable: "It takes shape in this negation." This negation is not the same as opposition or contradiction. It is perhaps no longer containable within the dichotomous economy of oppositions insofar as it ungrounds any such economy in advance. Kafka relates the improbability of arriving at a posited destination to the impossibility of preparation for a journey never as such to be completed. No "provision" can save this *Herr*. Not simply a temporality of deferral, this "way" cannot be prepared for, cannot be anticipated or originated, but must continually be renewed without origin: "It is, fortunately, a truly colossal journey!" But why "fortunately"? What could possibly be so fortunate about such an undertaking, about inevitable starvation prior to any arrival?

Something of this "colossal" or "monstrous journey"—this static departure, neither leap nor fall—is conveyed in Kafka's "Forschungen eines Hundes" ("Investigations of a Dog"), which was written in the same notebook with "Der Aufbruch" ("The Departure") and "Ein Hungerkünstler" ("A Hunger Artist").[17] Here we are given an account of the life of a dog lived entirely in and through its investigations, which are acknowledged as hopeless from the very beginning. "Hopeless," that is, insofar as they promise no "success" in terms of universalizable "scientific" results. The investigations are nonetheless acknowledged from the very beginning as both necessary and yet impossible, forever without the promise of success or completion. The dog's life is chronicled through a series of hapless investigations that take place at the margins of the conceptual universalization that otherwise defines scientific inquiry, and the account points out the continual foundering of universality upon a particularity that necessarily precedes it. Already suspending the possibility of arriving at discovery in accordance with the logical rule of "science," it offers an account of what conceptual understanding itself necessarily precludes.

"How my life has changed," the text begins, "and yet how it has not changed fundamentally *[im Grunde]*!" (*Erzählungen*, 323; *Complete Stories*, 278). It already begins with a split. Under the assumption of a progressive narrative trajectory from beginning to end, this narrator seizes not the endless series of apparent progress, but the more fundamental and perhaps less graspable sense of stasis or suspension. That is, he takes both the progressive transformations of a life temporally and chronologically directed toward a certain, if unknowable, end together with its negation in the appearance in the end of the lack of any such transformation. Change without transformation, change within stasis, amounts to the removal of its trajectory or teleologically determined focus. It loses, one might say, its center.

When the text continues, the narrator tries to recall what must have led him to conduct his investigations in the first place, to give some account of the need for investigation and of what his investigations in particular are intended to accomplish or overcome:

> When I now think back and recall the times at which I was still a member of the canine community, sharing in all its preoccupations, a dog among dogs, I find upon closer observation that there has always been some discrepancy here, that a small fissure was present, causing me a faint discomfort in the midst of the most honorable communal presentations, yes, even occasionally in trusted circles, no, not occasionally, but very often, the mere sight of one of my cherished canine companions, the mere sight seen somehow in a new way, made me uncomfortable, shocked, helpless, even desperate. I tried to a certain extent to calm myself.... (*Erzählungen*, 323–24; *Complete Stories*, 278)

He begins with a certain discrepancy, a small incongruence—itself, however, as yet unknowable, even imperceptible. There is at once a palpable disturbance, causing an at least indirectly acknowledged agitation that is then to be stilled *(begütigt)*, without any understanding of its cause. What appears to cause the agitation, however, is nothing out of the ordinary. "Upon closer investigation," he finds it is caused by nothing other than the mere sight of another. "The mere sight," *der bloße Anblick*—apperception without anything else, without, one might suggest, any coordinating mediation—can appear only as pure novelty, "seen somehow in a new way": absolutely new, and thus, absolutely unfamiliar. "The mere sight," as only sight, neither gives way to nor contains something else, a secret yet to be disclosed, another presence, etc. It simply remains absolutely foreign.

It disturbs the very foundation of what would call itself community. At a point in this dog's life when he imagines that he felt most one with the community as a whole, even then there was already the disruption that would persistently unground that sense of community. Or rather, the discrepancy itself is originary *(seit jeher)*, and appears together with the fact of community; it has always been there. The two moments would appear to be irreconcilable. On the one hand, there is the community, which might be understood simply as a being together or a being in common and overcomes the particularity of individual experience or subsumes that particularity under a generalizable norm—a community, we might add, defined according to its ethical order. On the other hand, at the moment when the experience of this community might be said to be most general, something disrupts and interrupts the communicability of this generality: the absolute singularity of perception, perception and nothing else. The investigations now are an attempt to calm or quell the anxiety originating in the disruption of pure perception, the perception of the individuality that remains even after the commonality of community would appear to appropriate the individual into the generalizable ethical and social norms of the community. He undertakes his investigations, as he says later, "so that I might be left free again to regard the ordinary, calm, happy life of every day" (*Erzählungen*, 330; *Complete Stories*, 286). He wants only to see again—or perhaps to see something else not now available to him—and to free, perhaps, his perception of and for quotidian existence.

The narrator traces his investigations to their apparent source in an early experience. Suddenly and inexplicably, seven dancing dogs appear as if from nowhere: "There—as if I had conjured them up—out of some sort of darkness, to the accompaniment of terrible sounds such as I had never heard before, seven dogs stepped into the light" (*Erzählungen*, 326; *Complete Stories*, 280–81). At this point he is still a child, without any formal means of comprehending what he sees. Everything about their appearance remains inexplicable to him. And yet, what astonishes him is restricted not only to the utter absence of any sense of familiarity. He is astonished by their ability to perform without any apparent disturbance, without any loss of calm: "Truly, more than the artistry of the seven dogs—it was inconceivable to me, but also beyond my capabilities, thoroughly unattainable—what astonished me was their courage to present what they created fully and openly and their ability calmly to endure it without having it break their spines" (*Erzählungen*, 327; *Complete Stories*, 282).

Finding no acceptable convention, and unable alone to explain their behavior, the dog takes his case directly to the offenders themselves. Contrary to all norms and expectations, every attempted address is met with silence. Their failure to respond amounts to no less than the transgression of the law: "These dogs broke the law. Even for such great magicians, the law applied also to them; even as a child, I understood that quite specifically" (*Erzählungen*, 328; *Complete Stories*, 283). They break the law—the law which, in its ideal instantiation, must remain universal and applicable equally to all. What constitutes transgression in this instance is not merely the refusal to comply with the expectation of the universal applicability of the law. Failure to comply also amounts to the interruption of the universalizing capacity of the law. To refuse to speak, as de Silentio reminds us in *Fear and Trembling*, is to refuse to enter into the ethical relations of the community, to refuse to enter the universal. The dog continues: "They had good reason to remain silent, provided that they kept their silence out of shame. For how they behaved, because of the music I had not noticed it before, yes, they had dispensed with all shame, the wretched creatures were doing the very thing which is both most ridiculous and indecent, they went upright on their hind legs. Fie on them!" (*Erzählungen*, 328; *Complete Stories*). Left with no communicated explanation, the narrator is forced to seek other alternatives—explanations that offer some understanding of the peculiarity of this event while leaving the universality of the law intact. Perhaps he has simply misunderstood; perhaps he is making something—too much—out of nothing. Each explanation, in the absence of a universally objective account, shifts the burden of responsibility for this transgression from the offending dogs back to the observer/narrator. Who was he, for example, to question the behavior of his seniors: "Even if the law commands us to reply to everybody, is such a measly, good-for-nothing dog even worthy of the name *[überhaupt ein nennenswerter Jemand]*?" (*Erzählungen*, 329; *Complete Stories*, 285). Perhaps, even, it was he who somehow had constituted the transgression. Perhaps he should not have been there. Perhaps he only disturbed the privacy that would otherwise have freed these dogs to act against the law: "But they were alone, seven friends among friends . . . friends are certainly not the public and where there is no public, it cannot come from a small, curious street dog, but in this case: is it here not so as if nothing had taken place?" (*Erzählungen*, 329; *Complete Stories*, 285).

The goal, then, of each explanation is, retrospectively and belatedly, to make the singularity of the original disturbance disappear and to appropriate it into a universalizing account that would eliminate the specificity of its occurrence, as if nothing had happened.

"It is not completely so, but almost. . . ." Each explanation never entirely coincides with what it is expected to explain, grounded as it is in another temporality. The possibility of making sense of any occurrence is thus always only approximate: "All senseless appearances of our life, and the most senseless in particular, can be explained. Not completely, of course—that is the devilish joke—but enough to guard against embarrassing questions" (*Erzählungen*, 337; *Complete Stories*, 295). Every proposed explanation reaches the same conclusion—explanation enough, but never total explanation. There is always something left over, always a certain remainder that refuses to allow the transgression of the law's universality to disappear, to be brought back within the field of the law's universal applicability, to explain—away.

The alternative, then, is to insist that whatever happened is simply in no need of explanation, to declare simply that it was nothing out of the ordinary: "As I have said already: this whole episode contains nothing out of the ordinary; in the course of a long life one encounters many things which, taken out of context and seen through the eyes of a child, might well seem much more astonishing" (*Erzählungen*, 329; *Complete Stories*, 284–85). The dog attempts to relativize the occurrence, insisting that there is nothing more astonishing about this event than any other similarly removed from all context and viewed without any sort of conceptual framework. Indeed, almost any other event would certainly have been more astonishing had it, too, been similarly perceived—that is, had it, like the appearance of the seven dogs, been separated from all mediation. But they had not, and this one had. That is, there is nothing about this event itself that, in contrast to others, might account for its uniqueness—might exhibit a transgression that others would not. In this sense, it is not the fact that the dogs stood upright on their hind legs or refused to explain themselves that constitutes their particular transgression. The transgression occurs in another direction; it crosses another limit. Two contrary issues appear at once: the significance of the event requires explanation where no explanation can ever suffice, thus maintaining its radical singularity; yet, this radically singular and inexplicable event is nothing out of the ordinary and, thus, quotidian and somehow universal.

Still, when all else fails to account entirely for the perceived transgression, the dog makes one final attempt to eliminate—to void—its apparent exemplarity: "Besides, one can, of course—as the pertinent *[treffend]* phrase runs—'mis-speak' *[verreden]* it like everything else ..." (*Erzählungen*, 329; *Complete Stories*, 285). Precisely how "pertinent" the expression "verreden" is remains to be seen—meaning, as it can, anything from speaking too much to not speaking at all, from speaking ill of something to speaking in defense, or even, through speech, to drive something away.[18] Thus, what the narrator presents here is not the impossibility that "verreden" could ever be as "pertinent" as he might wish. Rather, it points out a discrepancy between the language of explication and the event for which it would offer an account.

When the narrator credits the dancing dogs with the founding of his investigations, he does so for a particular reason. It is not simply that the dogs' transgression needs to be explained or appropriated into conceptual order. Certainly, he admits, there would be explanation enough to account for what he has witnessed—at least enough to protect him from "embarrassing questions." Nor is it simply that no explanation can ever entirely explain or do away with the transgression. Rather, the transgression itself exhibits something about the relationship between individual singularity and the universality of the law—or something about the extent to which these categories, singularity versus universality, cannot simply be opposed. Whereas the preconception of the strictly universal aspect of the law would require prescriptive compliance with its (communicated) ideals, the dogs' transgression, in its very singularity and apparent opposition to universal norms, exhibits something else:

> But then I saw the musical dogs, and from that time on I held everything for possible, no prejudice limited my powers of apprehension, I followed the most senseless rumors, pursued *[verfolgte]* them as far as I could, the most senseless *[das Unsinnigste]* seemed to me in this senseless life more probable than the sensible *[das Sinnvolle]*, and particularly fruitful for my investigation. (*Erzählungen*, 336; *Complete Stories*, 294)

Everything is possible. In opposition to the prescriptive universalization of the law, the transgression indicates a limitless potential on the part of the strictly singular beyond any presupposed end to universal obligation. (This is similar to de Silentio's account of Abraham's sacrifice.) The difference between sense and nonsense is suspended—or rather, in a world where sense would mean mere conformity to an existing conceptual order, a given mode of explanation, only what eludes such conceptual prefiguration promises something other than pure stasis—eternity as the absence of time, the absence of future. The future, and the future of sense, exists only where it is not already given. As Kafka writes in the third *Octavo Notebook:* "To believe in progress is not to believe that progress has already taken place. That would not be belief *[Glauben]*" ("Oktavheften," 67).

Yet even this promise is not so certain as it might appear. The future meaning of *Sinn* remains out of reach. The dog's investigation never ceases:

> Just as at that time I did not cease loudly discussing that incident, which appears to me of much less significance today—discussing, dissecting it into its constitutive parts, gauging it against those present without any consideration for the society in which I found myself, always only concerned with the issue *[Sache]* which I found just as burdensome as everyone else, but which—that was the difference—for that very reason I wanted indefatigably to resolve through investigation so that I might be left free again to regard the ordinary, calm, happy life of every day. Just as I did then, if now with less childish means—but the difference is not very great—I worked in

> the time following *[Folgezeit]* and I cease no further today. (*Erzählungen,* 330; *Complete Stories,* 286)

His task is endless, investigation without end. Just as he worked then, he continues to work today—or, in Kafka's peculiar formulation, "he ceases no further today." Kafka's text itself even would be part of that investigation, fragmentary and without end.[19] The issue *(Sache)* is burdensome and amounts to the obstruction of habitual, daily life. Only in the infinite process of analytical separation does the narrator hope to free himself from the weight of the thing in order to return to the life that he must have left behind, in order to be free again to return to this daily living, free again to see. Although solution or resolution *(Auflösung)* may be the desired end of all investigation, it is equally clear—though perhaps still inexplicable—that this end can never be reached: "As far as I can see, I see no success" (*Erzählungen,* 339; *Complete Stories,* 298). The persistent absence of success gives way to another idea of the infinite.

Working against the very order of universal conceptualization, the dog's investigations stand apart from accepted scientific explanations. This, however, does not mean that he chooses to investigate what science refuses to examine. He admits that the main object of his investigation is also an object of scientific inquiry. What separates his investigations from those of science is a certain methodological orientation. Science requires the formal rule of method in order to evaluate the truth of its assertions. Under the systematic explication of particular occurrences, the rule of science seeks to derive objective and universal truth. Yet, insofar as it validates its own assertions solely in an ideal form, it quickly loses the capacity to comprehend them. The dog explains:

> I began to inquire into the source of nourishment for the canine community. That is, then, if you will, no simple question; it has occupied us since time immemorial; it is the primary object of our reflections; views, observations, and experiments in this area are numberless; it has become a science which, in its colossal scale, not only exceeds the cognitive power of the individual, but also extends beyond that of all the scholars together, a burden which cannot be borne except by the whole of the dog community, and even this only with difficulty and not quite in its totality, it continually breaks off in what we have long possessed, and must laboriously be supplemented, to say nothing of the difficulties and scarcely fulfillable expectations of my investigation. (*Erzählungen,* 330–31; *Complete Stories,* 286–87)

In the dog's conception, science falters on the very idea of the infinite upon which it would base the validity of its claims. Rather than assuring itself of its own truth, the universal form of scientific knowledge exceeds any potential conceptual understanding on two fronts: the desired ideal form of scientific knowledge exceeds both every individual capacity for understanding and every actual occurrence. Science exceeds itself. The two excesses are related. Every attempt to come to terms with it, to maintain or retain it in its universal totality, seems inevitably to fall short, leaving the ideal totality accessible, sustainable, only in part. And not only just in part; the ideal conceptuality of scientific understanding continually falls apart "in what we have long possessed," remaining always still in need of supplementation. Kafka is specific here: he says not that the conceptual understanding of science dissipates *into* nothing more than what the dogs already possess, but that it breaks apart already within what the dogs possess. He distinguishes between an only ideal understanding in the form of concepts *(Begriffe)* and a perhaps more originary understanding—if this can still be called understanding—that appears only as possession *(Besitz).*

Not only is the difficulty of science defined as ungraspable in its ideality, but its ideality remains incompatible with the actuality it is called upon to explain. What becomes clear here is that the dog holds science itself accountable to rules it could never admit. Although science seems assured in the epistemological presupposition of its systematic and ideal form—that is, the assumption that its rules are true irrespective of time and place, and thus free from all contingency—the dog is unable to leave the contingencies of temporal and topographical specificity behind: "Certainly, science gives the rules, but it is by no means easy to understand them only at a distance and in the roughest outline; and when one has actually grasped them the real difficulty still remains, namely to apply them to local conditions—here scarcely anyone can help, almost every hour gives new tasks and every new, minute portion of earth its particular ones ..." (*Erzählungen*, 340; *Complete Stories*, 299). The first difficulty is just to understand the rule of science in its general form. The real difficulty begins only then with its local application. Thus, science always lags behind every particular occurrence. For every application of scientific understanding to actual events, there exist innumerable others yet to be explained. There exists only delay between finite event and its universalizing account in which the particular occurrence always precedes the ideal explanation that succeeds it.

Yet, what comes into doubt in the wake of this discrepancy is not the validity of scientific form, but the status of finitude itself. The dog insists that one can in no way presuppose that there is an immediate and requisite relationship between finite particularity and its universalizing explanation. With hardly a break, the sentence begun in the previous paragraph continues: "no one can maintain that he has settled everything for good and that henceforth his life will go on, so to speak, of itself, not even I myself, though my needs shrink literally from day to day" (*Erzählungen,* 340; *Complete Stories,* 299). Without the simultaneous concurrence of a particular event with its ideal justification, the event itself—prior to any account—is always found lacking. This in no way suggests that the delay or lack occurring in the separation between actuality and its ideal account can ever be overcome. The infinite work needed to overcome this distance seems rather to have the opposite effect. To what end, then, science? "And all of these endless efforts—to what purpose? Merely to entomb oneself deeper and deeper in silence, it seems, so deep that one can never be dragged out of it again by anyone" (*Erzählungen,* 340; *Complete Stories,* 299). All this work, "efforts" *(Mühe)*—and here it is not entirely clear whether he is still speaking about science in general or about his own investigations in particular—results only in the impossibility of communication, in becoming completely closed off and entirely inaccessible to or rather *by* language.

What, however, would that mean? In what ways might one be either accessible or inaccessible to and by language? What sorts of presuppositions would this entail? And what does the possibility or impossibility of communication have to do with the form of scientific knowledge? If scientific truth is verifiable only insofar as it is expressed in ideal form, the form itself being then the goal of investigation, there must be some correlation between the truth of scientific observations and judgments and the possibility of its understanding. The form of scientific evaluation must have its epistemological counterpart in the understanding. Knowledge—and thus the ability to accept the observations of science as true—ought, then, to be in its form equally infinite and equally universalizable. Language itself, then, as the medium of these observations, ought, in its mediating capacity, itself to be universalizable. This apparently cannot be demonstrated. In a perversion of Socratic recollection, the dog claims that all dogs must already know all things. They simply remain incapable of expressing them:

> All knowledge, the totality of all questions and answers, is contained in the dogs. If only one could make this knowledge effective, if only one could bring it to the bright light of day, if only they did not know so infinitely more than they admit, than they admit to themselves. Even the most loquacious dog is more secretive than tend to be the places where there is the best to eat. One spies upon one's compatriot, one froths with desire, one even beats oneself with one's own tail, one asks, pleads, howls, bites and achieves—and achieves what one would achieve without any exertion whatsoever: amiable attention, friendly companionship, honest acceptance,

> ardent embraces, my howls mix with yours into one, everything is directed towards rapture, forgetting, finding, but the one thing that one wants to achieve most of all: admission of knowledge, that remains denied. (*Erzählungen*, 333; *Complete Stories*, 289–90)

No expression will ever give way to the totality of knowledge supposedly possessed by each and every dog. No matter what one does, no one (not even, we might imagine, Socrates) can ever seduce or otherwise lure the admission of this knowledge from another. It cannot as such be communicated, neither by the narrator nor by any one of his interlocutors, even the most talkative of them. That is, even the most talkative, in spite of all their speaking, in spite of language itself, remain in some sense "closed" *(verschlossen)*, unable to admit and express the knowledge they must in fact already possess.

The limitation here is apparently not a lack of capacity for knowledge on the part of the dogs; it seems to lie solely on the side of expression. Language cannot contain or refer to the universal that is the totality of all knowing. And yet, in spite of this denial, communication does not not take place. Every attempt to express this knowledge, to persuade others to express it, continues to arrive at the same result, continues to produce the same relationship among these dogs—"affectionate audience, friendly companionship, honest acceptance, warm embraces, my howls mix with yours into one, everything is directed towards rapture, forgetting, finding." The communication that takes place on this occasion is not the communication of an ideal; it is not the attempt to give expression to a knowledge that otherwise would remain elusive, in spite of every desire to produce this end. The voices are joined together ("my howls mix with yours into one") all for the purpose of ("everything is directed") not toward the expression of knowledge as such, but toward what he calls here "rapture, forgetting, finding." But what is "found" here is not the same as the knowledge the dog expected to discover; this still cannot be expressed. This "finding," inseparable from "rapture" and "forgetting," takes place precisely in the absence of any expressible knowledge.

The narrator, anticipating objections to his assertion, imagines the naive complaint:

> Now, someone might say: "You criticize your fellow dogs about their silence on crucial questions, you insist they must know more than they admit, more than they will allow to affect their lives, and this silence, whose reason and secret they naturally also hold silent, poisons life, makes it unbearable for you, you must either change it or have done with it; that may be, but

> you yourself are a dog, you also have the knowledge of dogs, well, say it, not only in the form of a question, but as an answer. If you say it out loud, who will resist you? The great choir of dogs will join in as if they were waiting for it. Then you will have truth, clarity, acknowledgment, as much as you want. The roof of this meager life, about which you say such terrible things, will open up, we will all, dog with dog, rise up into high freedom.... Now, then, why do you criticize the others for their silence while you yourself remain silent?" Easy: Because I am a dog. (*Erzählungen*, 333–34; *Complete Stories*, 290–91)

All he must do is say it, and then there will be no limit to the agreement of others. The promise of the expression of this knowledge is freedom—absolute and unrestricted freedom. If only they could speak. If only the knowledge could be spoken. The dogs do not speak because they cannot. They remain silent about the knowledge the dog-narrator wants them to express. But, rather than the result of a mere refusal to speak, to choose not to speak, their silence on this matter remains doubly hidden. They cannot speak, not simply because the knowledge they ought to acknowledge can find no expressible form, but because the secret and fundamental cause of this silence remains shrouded in a silence of its own. No mere expression can do away with this. The possibility of linguistic communication thus relies upon—requires—keeping secret about the secret of its own silence.

Both Kafka and Kierkegaard were faced with the same difficulty: how to speak about that which remains necessarily foreign to linguistic representation. Abraham, like all dogs, cannot speak; he cannot express the one thing that would make his sacrifice understandable to others. Can one, in fact, conceive of something in language that cannot be contained within the orders of representation and conceptuality and that accordingly is not available either to perception or to cognition? The answer—if there is one—lies not in the identification of some other thing, some other presence, reassuringly residing still outside and beyond conceptual discourse. Rather it lies in the undoing of the conceptual grounding of discourse as such or in the recognition that language, in spite of its necessarily temporal configuration, remains irreducible to conceptuality.

In short, neither Kierkegaard nor Kafka was concerned with a crisis in representation that would seek to discover already within existing forms of representation the expression of some concept or idea or some other thing apparently lacking preexisting representation. Rather, finding the form of linguistic expression as such already lacking, and without alternative means, expression itself is found irreducible to the existing order of representability. This process begins only with the identification of aporia—on the one hand, for Kierkegaard's de Silentio in the acknowledgment of a limiting and prescriptive understanding of the ethical, and on the other, for the narrator of Kafka's "Investigations," in the acknowledgment of conceptual discrepancy within the formally conceived scientific discourse. The task now is to articulate the necessity for an alternative understanding of speech and its prescriptions while still holding to and complying with the formal requirements of communication and, accordingly, ethical duty.

In de Silentio's account of Abraham in *Fear and Trembling*, Abraham's paradoxical transgression of the ethical is paralleled in, or perhaps even already anticipated and contained in, his inability to speak. De Silentio takes language itself to be a form of mediation such that any linguistic expression, any act of speech, is already and necessarily directed toward universalization: "As soon as I speak, I express the universal, and if I do not do so, no one can understand me" (*Fear and Trembling*, 60). The specificity of one's own individuality is thus inexpressible as such to another. That is, the universalization inherent in linguistic expression is at once the necessary compliance with conceptual formulation such that whatever is said can be understood and, simultaneously, the compliance within a necessarily communicative mode or model of linguistic expression such that what is said can be understood by another. Abraham's transgression of the ethical as the transgression of universal obligation can find no expression in language, because nothing he might say would concur with the expression of universalizable obligation. Abraham himself must fail to articulate it. "Abraham," says de Silentio, "cannot be mediated; in other words, he cannot speak.... Therefore, although Abraham arouses my admiration, he also appalls me" (*Fear and Trembling*, 60).

In the third and final "Problema" of *Fear and Trembling*, de Silentio begins, as he does in the two previous "Problemata," with an insistence upon the universality of the ethical:

> The ethical as such is the universal; as the universal it is in turn the disclosed *[det Aabenbare]*. The single individual, qualified as immediate, sensate, and psychical, is the hidden. Thus his ethical task is to work himself out of his hiddenness and to become disclosed in the universal. Every time he desires to remain in the hidden, he trespasses *[da forsynder han sig]* and is immersed in a spiritual trial from which he can emerge only by disclosing himself. (*Fear and Trembling*, 112)

"Ethics," he explains, "demands an infinite movement, it demands disclosure" (*Fear and Trembling*, 112–13). Ethics demands that Abraham speak, and the inability to speak is as much an ethical transgression as is Abraham's intent to sacrifice Isaac. That is, it "transgresses" ethical obligation as such and not just on occasion. But de Silentio does not name Abraham at this moment; he only speaks of the individual as distinguished from the universal. As opposed to universality, individuality itself is conceivable only as irreconcilable with universality. Ethical obligation, then, requires that individuality be rid of anything not expressible in conceptual form. The ethical goal of every individual, or the goal of every individual in the ethical, is understood as the negation of the immediacy and materiality of individuality in the concept. However, can individuality, in its material concretion, simply be negated? Is such a negation nothing other than a kind of forgetting, a refusal to acknowledge one's own material condition? That is, as Kierkegaard asks elsewhere, is this negation nothing other than "illusion"?[20] Can the individual as individual be mediated away? No. And: Yes.

Language is already taken to indicate the unavoidability of the ethical. That is, as de Silentio already suggests in his discussions of ethics, he is not simply interested in articulating the inherent limitations in language as a demand for something "higher" or beyond language itself. There is nothing beyond language that would overcome the infinite temporalization and universalization necessary for any communicable expression. He continues:

> Once again we stand at the same point. If there is no hiddenness rooted in the fact that the single individual as the single individual is higher than the universal, then Abraham's conduct cannot be defended, for he disregarded the intermediary ethical agents. But if there is such a hiddenness, then we face the paradox, which cannot be mediated, since it is based precisely on this: the single individual is higher than the universal, whereas the universal is in fact mediation. (*Fear and Trembling*, 82)

Either every "hiddenness" must be disclosed or Abraham cannot be "defended." But Abraham, in his exemplary status as the "single individual," refuses disclosure; he refuses to speak. The only possible "defense" of Abraham would appear to lie in a reorientation of the ethical altogether. Abraham cannot be "defended" as long as the ethical excludes in advance the possibility of a hiddenness already irreducible to linguistic expression. This is de Silentio's dilemma, the paradox that he can in no way resolve. That is, at one and the same time there is both the ethical demand for disclosure and the individual incommensurable with all disclosure: "Either the single individual as the single individual can stand in an absolute relation to the absolute, and consequently the ethical is not the highest, or Abraham is lost" (*Fear and Trembling*, 113). So Abraham is not lost. This would be the guiding supposition of the entire text. Yet Abraham can remain "who he is" only insofar as he cannot speak, cannot be "translated into the universal." To be sure, communication is not not universalization.

But, insofar as the interconnection of language and ethics takes place via the same principle of universalization, the limitation of ethical universality suggests a correlative limitation of language itself insofar as language freed from an obligatory universalization communicates something else, or communicates in another way.

The third "Problema" consists largely of various attempts to distinguish ethics from aesthetics, showing through a series of examples that ethics and aesthetics each pose conflicting and mutually exclusive demands. Each time de Silentio tries to show that the ethical demand for disclosure founders on the aesthetic demand for immediacy and hiddenness and, vice versa, that this hiddenness is always recuperable, redeemed, through ethical disclosure and mediation in universality. That is, in every case except Abraham's. Returning to Abraham at the end, de Silentio explains:

> But now to Abraham—how did he act? For I have not forgotten, and the reader will please remember, that I got involved in the previous discussion to make that subject an obstacle, not as if Abraham could thereby become more comprehensible, but in order that the incomprehensibility could become more desultory *[desultorisk]*, for, as I said before, I cannot understand Abraham—I can only admire *[beundre]* him. (*Fear and Trembling*, 112, translation modified)

Abraham's exemplary status is not limited to the articulation of the misrelation between ethics and aesthetics. De Silentio is not thereby trying to understand Abraham, and he offers no understanding of him. He finds no reconciliation or resolution that would make his sacrifice understandable and thereby return him to the norm of ethical universality. Rather, Abraham in this case serves another purpose. His radical singularity—exhibited, if still incomprehensibly, through his silence—rather serves to destabilize the very notion of comprehensibility. It secures a place for the incomprehensible not by hollowing out a space proper to it, but rather by freeing the fundamentally incomprehensible as the very disorientation of conceptual formation within its still ethically obligatory comprehensibility. The incomprehensibility that is Abraham is not explained away; it becomes more "desultory," eluding in advance the methodological orientation of language toward its ethically determined *télos* in universality.

As with the earlier appearance of *desultorisk* in the discussion of the fragment from *Either/Or*, the Danish editors of *Fear and Trembling* find it necessary to offer some explanation of Kierkegaard's use of this foreign term. They define it in this way: "springende [leaping]; faldende i adskilte stykker [falling in separate pieces]."[21] "*Desultory*," moreover, refers to a leaping or falling apart without rule, in the absence of any organizational principle. Its etymological root, no doubt familiar to Kierkegaard, is still more specific. *Desultory* is derived from the Latin *desilire*, "to leap down."[22] Abraham's desultory incomprehensibility thus stands apart from every methodology, working erratically from within to unground the principle of hierarchy. Even de Silentio's attempt via Abraham to inscribe a notion of the individual as "higher than the universal" does not escape. Abraham's incomprehensibility, which de Silentio never manages to overcome, turns the "leap of faith" away from its orientation toward something higher, presumably a "higher" ideal, turning it into a "leap down."

The return to Abraham in de Silentio's discussion at the end of *Fear and Trembling* inevitably returns to the problem of language. Abraham, desultor, ungrounds the ethicoteleological orientation of language toward universal comprehensibility in at least two ways. First there is the matter of his silence and the extent to which his inability to speak renders his sacrifice incomprehensible or fails to resolve his already incomprehensible sacrifice into comprehensibility, complete understanding. Second—and this is where Abraham's desultoriness becomes perhaps most erratic, most unpredictable and enigmatic—there is the difficulty that the silence of Abraham's incomprehensibility imposes upon language as such. The third "Problema" deals primarily with the first. Abraham remains incomprehensible because he does not speak:

> Abraham remains silent—but he *cannot* speak. Therein lies the distress and anxiety. Even though I go on talking night and day without interruption, if I cannot make myself understood when I speak, then I am not speaking. This is the case with Abraham. He can say everything, but one thing he cannot say, and if he cannot say that—that is, say it in such a way that the other understands it—then he is not speaking. The relief provided by speaking is that it translates me into the universal. (*Fear and Trembling*, 113)

Abraham cannot speak at all, not because the words fail him, but because there is still one thing that must remain unsaid. And as long as there is one thing that cannot be expressed, even although all others may be, he does not speak. He cannot make himself understood. All speaking is rendered meaningless: "Speak he cannot; he speaks no human language. And even if he understood all the languages of the world, even if those he loved also understood them, he still could not speak—he speaks a divine language, he speaks in tongues" (*Fear and Trembling*, 114).

Nothing Abraham might say is understandable as long as this one thing cannot be expressed, cannot be disclosed. Here the respective orders of ethical universality and the universalizing disclosure of speech work to exclude Abraham: "Abraham cannot speak, because he cannot say that which would explain everything *[det Alt Forklarende]* (that is, so it is understandable): That it is an ordeal such that, please note, the ethical is the temptation. Anyone placed in such a position is an emigrant *[Emigrant]* from the sphere of the universal" (*Fear and Trembling*, 115). Certainly he can say it *(det Alt Forklarende)*; he just cannot make it understood. It is in its totality perhaps not even understandable, available for the understanding. As long as he cannot say it, however, his sacrifice can never be construed as ethical. He is condemned to departure, to move away from universality and always only to move away.

Now this is Abraham's predicament—he cannot speak. But it is not de Silentio's, and it is not yours, at least not in the same way. De Silentio is not Abraham, and he does not not speak. He only wants to understand Abraham. In speaking about Abraham, however, what remains to be said? Certainly, as de Silentio himself admits, his goal is not to make the silence of Abraham comprehensible, even in its incomprehensibility. This question remains, however: In spite of de Silentio's insistence upon the requisite correlation of speech and ethics in terms of the same movement of mediation, does language remain in his account strictly universal? Or, rather, is the difficulty perhaps more that language is never entirely conceivable as exclusively and totally universal—that language, in spite of every ethical imperative, is never universal enough?

De Silentio tries to imagine what he would have done had he been in Abraham's situation. How would he have acted had he been called to sacrifice his son?

> I am quite sure that I would have been punctual and all prepared—more than likely, I would have arrived too early in order to get it over sooner. But I also know what else I would have done. The moment I mounted the horse, I would have said to myself: Now all is lost, God demands Isaac, I sacrifice him and along with him all my joy—yet God is love and continues to be that for me, for in the world of time God and I cannot talk with each other, we have no language in common. (*Fear and Trembling*, 35)

In thus resigning himself to his fate and reconciling himself to this inevitable sacrifice, de Silentio insists that he still would remain fixed within the universalizing order of the ethical. He ought, then, to find the relief this would have promised Abraham had he only been able to speak. That is, even within the universalizing demand of ethical disclosure, the possibility of disclosure that is language is restricted from another angle: "for in the world of time God and I have no language in common." And de Silentio's language can be nothing other than language in the world of time. There is no other—not even Abraham's speaking in tongues, Abraham's divine language.

So where does that leave Abraham with respect to de Silentio's account? Where does that leave de Silentio? Is the language that Abraham fails to make understandable the same language that de Silentio speaks? "Venerable Father Abraham! Centuries have passed since those days, but you have no need of a late lover who can tear your memory from the force of oblivion *[der kan udrive Dit Minde af Glemsels Vold]*, for every language calls you to mind *[thi ethverd Tungemaal minder dig]*—and yet you reward your lover more gloriously than anyone else" (*Fear and Trembling*, 23, trans. modified). If the structure of any language, as de Silentio suggests here, is recollective, what does language recall in recalling a silent and incomprehensible Abraham?[23] Abraham is first and foremost incomprehensible. Yet comprehensibility cannot be restored to him even in speaking about him. If all language requires universal disclosure—though the extent to which this is the case is far from certain—then to speak about Abraham ought to appropriate into and disclose within its universalizing form Abraham's fundamental incomprehensibility. This, however, is not the case. Abraham becomes an internal limit to the ethical imperative of disclosure. Thus, in recalling Abraham, every language does nothing other than recall its own fundamental incomprehensibility.

Where Kafka and Kierkegaard's de Silentio appear to part ways concerns the relationship between language and universality. For de Silentio, to speak is already to enter into the universal, insofar as language is disclosure and the communication of disclosure takes place only through a universalization of the disclosed. Insofar as universality is the precondition of communicability for de Silentio, what remains strictly incommunicable is singularity. Kafka, on the other hand, points out two moments of incommunicability: the singular and the universal.[24] Yet, as I have already pointed out with regard to *Fear and Trembling*, there is a difference between what is communicable and what is actually communicated. Even under the ideal of universal communicability, every language reaches its internal limit in terms of its requisite actuality. There is no language other than "in the world of time." God and I cannot speak with each other. For Kafka, there can be no proper connection between the world of time and that of the infinite. As he remarks in the third *Octavo Notebook:* "Every moment corresponds to something outside of time. A Beyond cannot follow the Here-and-now, for the Beyond is eternal and, thus, cannot come into contact with the Here-and-now in time" ("Oktavheften," 69). Yet Kafka does not say that there is nothing other than the world of time, the world of actuality. He says only that one cannot *follow* the other and that they therefore cannot stand in temporal relation. Their relation, if this still is one, is necessarily anachronistic. In this way, the irrdeucibility of language to the order of linear temporality opposes and unsettles the universalizing capacity of linguistic communication. The goal, however, is perhaps not to mitigate this difference, but to make it, as for de Silentio, more desultory, to make it tremble.

If the limiting problem of communicability lies in the unavoidability of its anachronism, then the problem of Abraham's "paradox" cannot be altered by his ability to speak about it; this would simply reproduce its inherent anachronicity. The paradox as such is not available—is not perceptible—within the necessarily universal conceptuality of communication, but this does not reduce the paradoxicality of each and every speaking:

> The uncommunicability of the paradox exists perhaps, but does not express itself as such, for Abraham himself does not understand it. Yet he neither needs nor ought to understand it, nor, then, even to interpret it for himself, but he may attempt to interpret it for others *[den andern gegenüber]*. Even the universal is, in this sense, not unequivocal, as is apparent in the case of Iphigenia, that oracles are never unequivocal. ("Oktavheften," 91)

Kafka thus objects to the assumption that if only Abraham were able to speak he would be rid of the paradox of his individuality, merely under the supposition that the capacity for communication is simultaneously its means of mediation. The paradox already exists prior to any communication. This, however, is not exactly the point for Kafka. Rather, insofar as paradox eludes in advance the ethical order of communicability, it cannot as such be expressed, nor, moreover, can it be perceived. What is perceived and what can be expressed is never presentable, strictly speaking, as paradox, since all paradox remains irreducible to the temporality with which communication and expression in their actuality comply. In this way, however, whatever is expressed in communication, unable to free itself entirely from the paradoxical anachronicity of its occurrence, can never be strictly unequivocal. All expression, even as universalization, always means more than one thing and means in more than one way. In this way, then, whether or not Abraham understands the paradox is irrelevant. He cannot. His "ethical" obligation with respect to others, however, is to interpret it *(deuten)*: to show by means of interpretation its ways of meaning.

A universal and unequivocal meaning is as such unattainable, and the possibility of a universalizing interpretation is necessarily foreclosed. This might be understood as the effect of Abraham's desultoriness: "Even my research has become disorganized," laments the dog-narrator of Kafka's "Investigations." This is perhaps inevitable. It is, after all, with the methodological discrepancy on the part of the universalizing pretensions of an ordered science that his investigations had begun. He recalls: "At that time, I was so strong that I did something unheard-of which contradicts all of our principles and which certainly would recall something uncanny to every eyewitness of the time. I discovered in science, which otherwise strives for limitless specialization, a peculiar simplification in one respect" (*Erzählungen*, 343; *Complete Stories*, 302). What is "unheard-of" here is precisely the calling into question of the ordered principles of scientific inquiry by pointing out that what ought to be uniform and unequivocal is in fact contradictory. To point out this fundamental discrepancy, however, cannot simply be dismissed as blatantly false. The dog's opposition to the principles of this rule-governed system is taken, rather, as a reminder of the "uncanny." Like the eternal recollection of Abraham in language, science too, even with its insistence upon method, continually recalls—if only in an indirect and unacknowledgeable fashion—the unruliness of its principles. The dog discovers this not in what had previously been dismissed by science, but in the very rules it continues to uphold and that continue to yield positive results. According to science, nourishment, for the most part *(in der Hauptsache)* comes from the earth. Under this presupposition *(Voraussetzung)*, it prescribes methods of "ground preparation" for its most effective production. "Now, of course, it is correct that the earth produces nourishment," says the dog, "of that there can be no doubt, but it is not as simple as it is typically presented, to the exclusion of every further investigation" (*Erzählungen*, 343; *Complete Stories*, 203). If "order" is to be preserved for science, its preservation seems to take place on the level of description. The very form of description, insofar as it excludes all further investigation once the desired results have been obtained, ought to prevent the possibility of "disorder" from entering into scientific discourse.

But does it? Concerned only with results, as with the end of a book, science sees no need for further or alternative experimentation, as if the description of positive results necessarily absolves every question of all its difficulties. The empirical rule of science, thus, as the dog explains, operates under the ludicrous slogan "'If you've got the food in your mouth, then you've answered all the questions for the time being'" (*Erzählungen*, 344; *Complete Stories*, 203). Results, and nothing else, appear significant. Nonetheless, even with its insistence on results, the narrator suspects that science, too, even as an already ordered discourse, must secretly continue to entertain a certain discomfort with its own discoveries, refusing to allow the successful achievement of results entirely to eliminate the need for further understanding. This is what the "simplification" would otherwise obscure, the unspeakable secret that "simplification" keeps. If, in fact, nourishment comes only from the ground, as the scientific description would have it, why does science continue to prescribe two methods of production—"ground preparation" and the equally indispensable performance of "speech, dance, and song"? The dog's question is this: If nourishment comes from the ground, why is the equally requisite performance of ceremonial songs directed upward?

The dog's experiments, thus, begin with the perception of a contradiction. "I began by emphasizing these contradictions." He performs a series of experiments intended definitively to decide which of the two contradictory methods is alone responsible for the production of nourishment. Instead of directing the song upward, he gives it only to the earth. "Later, I dug a hole for my snout and sang and declaimed into it so that only the ground might hear and no one else next to or above me" (*Erzählungen*, 344; *Complete Stories*, 304). His results, however, are anything but consistent. The contradiction cannot simply be separated in decision. Sometimes nothing is produced at all; sometimes nourishment comes only later, sometimes even more abundantly than before. No sooner does he detect "a trace which might lead further" than it dissolves again "into the indeterminate" (*Erzählungen*, 345; *Complete Stories*, 305). He can only conclude that his experimental methods are not yet adequate, not yet rigorous enough.

Assuming that there is some connection between the production of nourishment and its reception, as if the food were thereby conjured out of thin air, the dog next decides simply not to receive it, not to take it up. His method, thus, is decidedly negative. Achieving at first only limited and questionable results (he discovers that even this experiment had long since been abandoned by science as both too difficult, involving too great a sacrifice, and yielding ultimately insubstantial results), the dog decides to fast completely: "The way is through fasting, the highest can only be attained through the highest efforts, if it is even attainable, and voluntary *[freiwillig]* fasting is the highest way for us" (*Erzählungen*, 348; *Complete Stories*, 309). The object of his investigations, however, has not changed. "The highest" sought here is still in some sense nothing other than the "high freedom" promised in the expression of absolute knowledge—in the desired disclosure of the one thing fundamentally inexpressible. In other words, the dog has come no further; he still knows nothing of this inexpressible knowledge. The problem, however, is no longer the same, no longer purely a matter of giving expression to the inexpressible. The dog is left only with the here-and-now *(Diesseits)* of the equation. If expression cannot disclose the one thing it ought in principle to indicate, what in fact does it present?

The dog, rather than following the scientific method in eliminating contradiction from its presuppositions, goes the other direction: he emphasizes *(betont)* the contradiction. What continually falls apart in this way is the presupposition that there might be a uniform and direct relationship between the method and its desired end, and ultimately between expression (in accordance with accepted rules of universal comprehensibility) and meaning (as the result of compliance with this teleologically ordered system). His own investigations do nothing but disclose this limit. Insofar as the posited end, in its ideality, seems necessarily to fall away and remain inaccessible to actual means, the discrepancy is always located on the side of actuality—contradictory rules, descriptions, that indicate a hidden ground rather than yield positive results. The same is true of the dog's own experiments. Maintaining the contradictory suppositions of science—albeit in a negative form as the abstention from all means toward the production of nourishment—he discovers only that this, too, yields nothing of the desired results. But a shift has taken place. "The highest," absolute knowledge, is accessible only through an equally "high" way: "free" or "voluntary fasting" *(freiwilliges Hungern)*. One must freely enter into hunger of one's own accord. To fast completely, "the ultimate and most powerful means of my research" (*Erzählungen*, 348; *Complete Stories*, 309), remains impossible. Thus, he can reach no end that is not already fasting itself; there is no end other than the means toward the end.

In the end, the dog speaks of an "instinct" preventing him from falling into the formal generalities of science. Kafka's text, fragmentary and incomplete, breaks off with an eschatological dream of an ultimate science, a science beyond the end of all science: "It was this instinct which, perhaps precisely for the sake of science, but another science, different from the science practiced today, an ultimate science, permitted freedom to be prized above all else. Freedom! Of course, the freedom possible today is a clumsy creature. But nevertheless freedom, nevertheless a possession" (*Erzählungen*, 354; *Complete Stories*, 316). The dog's science, if it is one, is the science of freedom. That is, his "instinct," which forces him to transgress and oppose the scientific method, is already the science of a "freedom" that will arrive only after science, "as it is practiced today," has reached its logical end and has been exceeded. The "freedom" expressed here is already a freedom beyond the *télos* of scientific discovery. The science as practiced today has nothing to do with this freedom. It can only posit a freedom as the concept toward which it is directed and that thus directs and orders its investigations. This dream, however, will never be realized. Science, eternally persisting in its desire for objective universalization, can reach no end. "It rests immanent in itself, has nothing outside itself that is its *télos* but is itself the *télos* for everything outside itself. . . ," to borrow a phrase from de Silentio. Thus, if the ultimate freedom beyond the strictures of scientific form is still, in the dog's case, to be found in his investigation—if this is in fact its goal—it can be understood only from a position prior to the teleoethical discourse of scientific conceptuality. Resisting in advance its disappearance in conceptual form, this freedom can appear, though perhaps not be understood, only as a possession. A possession *(Besitz)*, not a concept *(Begriff)*.

The actuality of freedom—a freedom in actuality—must exist and persist in language. The language of actuality, of this world and in the world of time, can never dissolve entirely into universality. In the third *Octavo Notebook*, Kafka comments: "For everything outside of the sensible world, language can only be used deictically, but never even in an approximately comparative way, since it, corresponding to the sensible world as it does, only deals with possessions and their relationships" ("Oktavheften," 68). Language is nowhere but "in the sensible world." It is, like Abraham, already consigned to actuality and immediacy, unable to find "relief" in its ethicoteleological orientation toward an end in universal conceptuality. Not that an ideal communicability does not continue to structure linguistic expression—it must—but the expression as such remains irreducible to its ideal communication, irreducible to understanding.

The closest Kafka's dog comes to something like "discovery" has nothing to do with where food comes from; indeed, he insists he is not at all interested in this, but is interested only in the dogs themselves, in their "essence" (*Erzählungen*, 333, 353; *Complete Stories*, 290, 315). It has to do rather with the availability of the means for discovery. As in the case of Kafka's assessment of Abraham, having in advance abandoned the principle of universal communicability, the dog nonetheless has a responsibility to interpret *(deuten)* for others. In the middle of his fast, he recalls the belief in a concept of fasting that led him to this means in the first place. He begins with the idea that the possibility of fasting is maintained within the conceptual possibility of an absolutely unlimited freedom. The result, however, is perhaps as surprising as the "way" is by now familiar:

> As far as fasting is concerned, I appeal to the well-known dialogue, in the course of which one of our philosophers expressed the intention to forbid fasting, against which a second advised with the question: "But who would

> ever fast?" and the first let himself be convinced and withdrew the prohibition. But now the question arises again: "Is fasting then not actually forbidden?" The vast majority of commentators denies it, sees fasting as freely given, stands by the second philosopher, and thus fears no dire consequences *[schlimme Folgen]* from an erroneous commentary. Of this I had well assured myself before I began fasting. But now, doubled over in hunger, and in my confusion seeking relief at my back legs and desperately licking them, chewing them, sucking them, right up to my backside, the general interpretation appeared utterly false to me, I cursed the science of commentary, cursed myself for having been led astray; the dialogue contains, of course, as a child must recognize, more than just one prohibition of fasting. The first philosopher wanted to forbid fasting, and what a philosopher wants is already done, thus, fasting was prohibited; the second philosopher not only agreed with him, but furthermore held fasting for impossible, thus laying a second prohibition on top of the first, the prohibition of dog nature itself; the first recognized this and thereupon withdrew the explicit prohibition, that is, he offered the dogs after the interpretation of all that, to use their insight and to forbid fasting for themselves. So here was a threefold prohibition instead of the usual one, and I had violated it. (*Erzählungen*, 349; *Complete Stories*, 310)

This dialogue is by no means unequivocal. Whether or not one is free to fast is by no means decided; the question remains in the end unanswered. To fast is to engage, even to transgress, a limit. For Kafka, this limit is as much epistemological as it is ethical. Or rather, the ethical and epistemological converge at the crossing of this limit. From the presupposition of guaranteed and unobscured freedom—the absolute freedom to do what one chooses, simply to decide for oneself in the absence of any prescriptive norm or prohibition—the narrator, deep in his fast, finds only prohibition, prohibition upon prohibition. What might originally have been only a single prohibition has now become more than one. What takes place in this dialogue is not, as had previously been supposed, the negation of a proposed prohibition, but—no longer restricted only to an economy of polar and mutually exclusive dichotomy of affirmation or negation, yes or no—the possibility of an actual freedom. Through the negation of the conception of an absolute and presumably permissive freedom—which, however, in its inaccessible ideality remains perhaps more restrictive than anything else—the dog perceives, if only momentarily, autonomy: "To forbid fasting for oneself."

Afterword
Freedom and Interpretation

There must be, then, a responsibility for interpretation, for, as Kafka has suggested, the possibility of freedom, unavailable both in and through conceptuality, might exist, if it is indeed today possible, only in the departure from such conceptual determination. It cannot be posited as a kind of goal—even the goal, as we are concerned with it here, of interpretation. Nor could it exist as the "truth" of interpretation. It cannot, in this sense, definitively be deduced or otherwise distilled from actuality. Freedom, in a word, cannot be ideal. To speak of it as transcendent is to speak only of its impossibility, of its inactuality and unavailability, and to situate it in an infinitely remote beyond in which it would only disappear.[1] To speak in this way would be perhaps not really to speak, or even not to speak at all and remain silent. How, then, can one still speak of something unavailable in this way?

It is not enough simply to assert unequivocally that freedom is not an ideal, suggesting that it is only in ideality that it cannot exist, whereas it would easily be available elsewhere in another form. The opposition to conceptuality might at least be clear insofar as conceptuality as such, determined in and by an inevitable and requisite universalization, is, in the end, never itself free, but always bound within a certain obligatory form or formal obligation. Even its absolute idealization would provide no guarantee of its own absolute unboundedness, of its own absolute freedom. The difficulty of freedom, then, amounts to more than the impossibility of its universality. If it is to be possible, we must insist, it must exist in actuality, in the here and now, and not in some beyond.

Yet, on the other hand, is the absolute absence of universality at all conceivable? Each of the authors examined here has, in one way or another, arrived at the same conclusion: No. The difficulty is rather that no universal ideal is as such, purely and simply, available, not that it cannot exist. Unable to assume anything more than finite particularity from the beginning, each of these authors in his own work has neither been able to resolve finite particularity in some universal ideal nor, on the other hand, to understand particularity as such without also noting that there must be something beyond finitude alone. Finitude, in its fragmentary form, can never account for itself. The dilemma, sketched out largely in terms of the various discrepancies between conceptions of universality and particularity, presents a certain problem for any concept of freedom. If freedom is available only in its finite presentation, it will nonetheless always exceed its own presentation; it will always exceed its own finite apprehensibility. And if the goal of all investigation—however it may be conceived and however it may be carried out—is freedom in actuality, then it can occur only in the account of the separation between particularity and universality. Freedom, thus, is given only in interpretation.

What, precisely, we must now ask, is interpretation? And what can its responsibility be? (It is evidently, at least in Kafka's formulation, a responsibility to others—"*den anderen gegenüber*"—that constitutes interpretation's imperative, not, as one might otherwise suspect, a duty to a responsible interpretation of the text, one that would answer, or answer for the text, at every turn.) And if, in the end, the responsibility for interpretation coincides with a notion of "freedom" and autonomy construed precisely—again, this is Kafka's formulation—as a "possession" as opposed to a "concept," what does this mean? If freedom cannot be a "concept," but only a "possession," what, in the end, does one possess? And how can possession take place in the absence of conceptual mediation?

What interpretation means is by no means limited to textual commentary; indeed, a commentary that would seek to "explain" the text it is reading insofar as it would systematically summarize its assumed intentions and thus either exclude or justify aberrant comments within the text would ultimately miss the text it claims to read, resulting instead in no interpretation whatsoever. On the other hand, the interpretation of a text (in Adorno's sense) would begin precisely with the resistance to any such justification; it would have to begin with the moments at which a text exhibits its own failure to conform to an only imagined systematicity, its failure to conform to an inevitably incomplete universality. These would be the moments of paradox or self-contradiction, the moments at which the linguistic presentation disrupts the assumed (philosophical) intentions. Recognizing now the discrepancy between literal, material expression and the "truths" this expression ought ideally to represent, philosophy—understood by Adorno as "language critique" *(Sprachkritik)*—can interpret only what is given as expression without the aid of any pregiven mode of interpretation, without the aid of any complete and systematic methodology. In this sense, philosophical interpretation would expose the continual foundering of universality in a particularity it cannot entirely accommodate and for which it cannot entirely account.

Though Adorno apparently began his reading of Kierkegaard with these discrepancies apparently incompatible with the assumed (philosophical) goal of conceptual universality, he ultimately found that the paradoxical finitude of these expressions remained inseparable from the very finitude that is language. In spite of all universalization seemingly necessary for the regular production of meaning from signs, universal communicability can never overcome the very finitude upon which linguistic expression depends. "Philosophy," in Adorno's sense, is concerned with the interpretation of "signs," which are not given together with the rule of their legibility. In and of themselves incomplete, both materially and temporally finite, they are, as he said, "ruins," without guarantee of their meaning and without any regulative system that would guarantee their legibility. Philosophy's task, then, is interpretive; it can only "decipher" *(enträtseln)* signs. Yet "deciphering" in no way does away with the difficulty. The task is not to deduce a fixed and eternal meaning by repairing the "friability" *(Brüchigkeit)* of signs; it is not to restore a lost totality. On the contrary, the task of philosophy is to read signs only as they appear and only in their own finite occurrence, not to subsume them under another conceptual order. And if words, in their ruination, can never overcome their own finitude, can never leave it behind, then this finitude itself will continually disrupt the possibility of arriving at meaning in any ultimate and definitive sense. Philosophy is thus confronted with what Adorno refers to as its "paradox": it has to seek meaning out of the very elements that preclude any possibility of arriving at an either stable or ideal meaning. This, Adorno suggests, is precisely the point. Interpretation never results in "sense" *(Sinn)*. There is no "result" in this sense; there is only its infinite deferral. Thus, the finitude of "signs" available in interpretation is as much temporal as it is material, ruin and ruination at the same time.

Nevertheless, Adorno does identify a certain "freedom" that is available to "the philosopher" in interpretation: "Today the philosopher is confronted with a fallen language. His material is the ruins of words to which history binds him; his only freedom is the possibility of their configuration towards the force of truth in them" ("Thesen über die Sprache des Philosophen," 368–69). As opposed to an infinite freedom acquired through absolute knowledge, the freedom possible "today" for the philosopher is directly related to a language of "ruins." Unbound by a purely conceptual understanding of the production of meaning in language, it is a freedom to build—or rather "construct" and "re-construct"—"configurations." Figuration, in Adorno's sense, is conceived as an effect of linguistic finitude, and thus, in the absence of any guaranteed meaning, figuration first becomes figuration in interpretation. Figuration, in this sense, can no longer be understood merely as another way of representation. What figures mean they can no longer mean by referring back to any intention. Words in configuration, however, are nonetheless words and cannot be stripped of their finitude and transiency. There is accordingly no guarantee that a figure will be legible. Reading is never more than a possibility.

Unable to overcome its own finitude, figuration, as Adorno suggests, would be the locus of its material transformation, its material transformability. It is, however, a transformability conceivable only as transformation without end. Unable to arrive at either a constant sense or a constant image or figure, figuration would be the nonregulative principle of transformation. And yet, here precisely our task must become more difficult. The particular freedom of figuration is not an absolute freedom. Even Adorno's philosopher is not concerned solely with the infinite production of varying configurations, as if words in configurations could be made to mean anything at all. What, we might say with Kierkegaard, had been the aesthetic future of infinite possibility, "possibilities everywhere," becomes in its ethical obligation narrowly delimited as its own task *(Obgave)*. Every word or sign, every figure or image, is given only in its own finite presentation.

Confronted only with its own inevitable finitude, as both ruin and ruination, language comes unavoidably into contact with its own unfathomable uncertainty. Finitude in language is always doubled; it is always more than merely finite. Every language reaches the internal limit of its requisite actuality. There is no language other than "in the world of time." Yet even here, language never follows a strictly linear chronology. Insofar as its meaning is never accounted for entirely within the temporality of its own occurrence, and insofar as this meaning is always and inevitably exceeded by its own infinite unfathomability, its occurrence inevitably marks not the continuation of a linear, temporal progression, but rather its interruption in the concurrence of more than one temporality. The irreducibility of language to linear temporality opposes and undoes the universalizing capacity of linguistic communication. The paradoxical anachronicity of communication, never as such expressible, is never strictly unequivocal. Language continually exceeds itself in the uncertainty of what cannot be known. And yet—and this is precisely its effect as finite—its encounter cannot be avoided; it is, we might suggest, obligatory. Even finitude itself cannot entirely explain, cannot singularly explain, what language means or why it means what it means. Because it is finite, it cannot. And because it is finite, it cannot avoid its finitude. Why? "In order," Kierkegaard might exclaim, "to live accordingly." Finitude's one command, then, must be: Obey. But obey what? In the end, there is no prescriptive rule that might be followed, but only the imperative obligation to obey—to obey, that is, what cannot be followed, what can appear as neither rule nor regulation. Language's obligation is conceivable only as a responsibility to the unknown and indeterminable.

Precisely in this way, language's obligatory finitude is not an obligation oriented toward an end. It is the asymptotic obligation in the absence of any possible arrival. The difficulty is that the responsibility to a text's inevitable finitude is conceivable only as the obligatory responsibility to this void. To obey what cannot be obeyed is nonetheless imperative. It is the very rule of language, which, necessarily indirect insofar as the secret of its communicability (the paradoxical demand of universalization where universalization alone can never suffice) cannot as such appear. Even in the unavoidable, inexplicable finitude of language, communication must still take place. Only—as is the case with de Silentio's Abraham and Kafka's dogs—language can neither contain nor refer to its own universality, its own universalizability. Language cannot account for its own rule. "Communication" is nonetheless still "universalization," as Kierkegaard's de Silentio continually reminds us. It is simply never reducible to or generalizable as universalization alone. Language must remain silent about the only thing of which it would continually speak; it must remain silent about the secret rule of its comprehensibility. Language itself, in every act of speech, communicates nothing other than its own fundamental incomprehensibility. Every language, that is, calls Abraham to mind. For this reason, then, there must be interpretation.

Interpretation is not a rule, but a responsibility. It cannot overcome or otherwise alter this necessary finitude of language. "Corresponding" *(entsprechend)*, as Kafka says, to the "sensible world" *(sinnliche Welt)*, language speaks only of "possession *[Besitz]* and its relationships." Finitude thus delimits not what language means, but how it means what it means. Interpretation is thus called upon to account for this limit, and yet it must give an account without being able to explain it or explain it away. Explanation as justification or unification would be only deception, a jest; it would, in the end, be only irresponsible. If freedom is understood as the absence of prescriptive delimitation—"For the issue depends on freedom," Kant has explained, "and it is in the power of freedom to pass beyond every specified limit"[2]—and if there can be freedom only where it is not already made to disappear in an absolute beyond of infinite idealization, then there can be freedom only where I respond to it, where I account for it. It can exist only when I ask after it. In the end, the one question that both cannot be answered and cannot not be answered is this: Am I free? It is only a question, but it is all I have.

Notes

1. Kierkegaard Who?

1. Commentaries that interpret Kierkegaard's texts on the basis of their systematic orientation through the proper name of the signatory constitute the norm of Kierkegaard scholarship. Rather than understanding the problem of the name as endemic to a more fundamental problem of language, these normative studies take the answer to the question apparently raised by the question of authorship as the key to each text's correct understanding with regard to the "whole" of Kierkegaard's authorship. Too numerous to be listed here in full, those generally taken as the most "authoritative" include Mark C. Taylor, *Kierkegaard's Pseudonymous Authorship* (1975), and *Journeys to Selfhood: Hegel and Kierkegaard* (1980); Alastair Hannay, *Kierkegaard* (1982); Louis Mackey, *Kierkegaard: A Kind of Poet* (1971), and *Points of View: Readings of Kierkegaard* (1986); Stephen N. Dunning, *Kierkegaard's Dialectic of Inwardness: A Structural Analysis of the Theory of Stages* (1985), George Connell, *To Be One Thing: Personal Unity in Kierkegaard's Thought* (1985); Hermann Deuser, *Kierkegaard: Die Philosophie des religiösen Schriftstellers* (1985); Roger Poole, *Kierkegaard: The Indirect Communication* (1993); and Sylvia Walsh, *Living Poetically: Kierkegaard's Existential Aesthetics* (1994).

2. The insistence that linguistic meaning *must* be universal is most fully developed in Kierkegaard's *Fear and Trembling,* where Abraham's absolute singularity condemns him to a silence that continually "haunts" every purportedly universal meaning. That is, for communication to take place at all, meaning must in some sense be universal, though the radical singularity of the existing subject, in Kierkegaard's account, continually prevents that universality from becoming absolute in the Hegelian sense of "absolute knowledge." Cf. chapter 5 for a discussion of Kierkegaard's *Fear and Trembling* and the limit of universality in language.

3. Though certainly not alone in this assessment of one aspect of Kierkegaard scholarship, this tendency was pointed out most recently by Habib C. Malik, in *Receiving Søren Kierkegaard,* 217.

4. P. A. Heiberg, *Bidrog til et Psykologisk Billede af Søren Kierkegaard i Barudom og Ungdom.*

5. P. A. Rosenberg, *Søren Kierkegaard: Hans Liv, Hans Personligket og Hans Forfatterskab. En Vijlednings til Studiet af Hans Værker.*

6. The essay was first published in Hungarian in 1910 and then included in *Die Seele und die Formen (Soul and form)*, first published in 1911 in German.

7. For this interpretive gesture, Lukács is also affiliated with the early response to Kierkegaard in critical theory. Cf. Michael Theunissen and Wilfried Greve, eds., *Materialien zur Philosophie Søren Kierkegaards*, 76, 79.

8. The first book-length translation of Kierkegaard's work was a volume containing the first nine *Øjeblikket* articles under the title *Christentum und Kirche: "Die Gegenwart," Ein ernstes Wort an unsere Zeit, insbesondere an die evangelische Kirche* (Christendom and church: "The moment," an earnest word to our time, especially to the Protestant Church) (Hamburg, 1861). This was followed in 1862 by Albert Bärthold's rendition of Kierkegaard's *For Self-Examination*, followed by his 1873 translation of Kierkegaard's *Point of View*, which appeared collected with other essays on his significance as a "religious" author under the title *Sören Kierkegaard, Eine Verfasser-Existenz eigener Art.* The theological focus in Germany continued through the 1880s with Bärthold's translations of *Sickness unto Death* (1881), *The Lilies of the Field* (1885), and *Stages on Life's Way* (1886). Christoph Schrempf, who later became the general editor of the first edition of Kierkegaard's *Gesammelte Werke* (1909–22), began translating Kierkegaard with the 1890 publication of *The Concept of Anxiety* and *Philosophical Fragments.* Notably, both Bärthold and Schrempf are credited with solidifying the theological hold on Kierkegaard as guided by their own interests in theology. Both were deeply involved with the church. Schrempf, a pastor, ultimately felt compelled to leave the church after working through his own considerations of Kierkegaard's attack on the church. For a more extensive account of the early history of Kierkegaard translation, cf. Malik, *Receiving Søren Kierkegaard*, 211–82.

9. The first studies of Kierkegaard in French, for example, cite these early German translations. Cf. Malik, *Receiving Søren Kierkegaard*, 352. The inauguration of Kierkegaard's German reception is symptomatic of Kierkegaard reception more generally. Significant for our purposes here, the early English translations of Kierkegaard are generally considered motivated and colored by the religious interests of his first two significant translators, David Swenson and Walter Lowrie. Cf. Malik, 352.

10. Herbert Schnädelbach, *Philosophy in Germany, 1831–1933*, 2. Notably also, Paul Tillich was Adorno's advisor for his habilitation thesis *Kierkegaard: Construction of the Aesthetic.* In a more contemporary context, this tradition of dialectical theology persists in the debates between Hermann Deuser and Klaus M. Kodalle. Cf. Hermann Deuser, *Dialektische Theologie: Studien zu Adornos Metaphysik und zum Spätwerk Kierkegaards* and *Kierkegaard: Die Philosophie des religiösen Schriftstellers;* Klaus M. Kodalle, "Adornos Kierkegaard—Ein kritischer Kommentar," and Deuser's response to Kodalle, "Kierkegaard in der Kritischen Theorie."

11. Malik, *Receiving Søren Kierkegaard*, 283.

12. Roger Poole credits Brandes with the philosophical dismissal of Kierkegaard until well into the twentieth century; cf. Roger Poole, "The Unknown Kierkegaard: Twentieth-century Receptions."

13. Malik, *Receiving Søren Kierkegaard*, 357. The Kassner essay was also noted by Rilke as "exceptional." Cf. chapter 3.

14. Allan Janik, "Haecker, Kierkegaard, and the Early *Brenner*." Janik identifies Haecker as the first "existentialist" of the twentieth century (p. 201). In this regard, Janik applauds Haecker for his central role in shaping the conventional appropriation of Kierkegaard.

15. Although it is generally acknowledged that Heidegger owes a significant debt to Kierkegaard, there has been precious little work concerning the substance of this "influence."

Roger Poole, for example, reserves especial vehemence for Heidegger in particular for "shamelessly" borrowing from Kierkegaard without sufficiently acknowledging his significance. Poole, like others before him, sees little need to analyze the effects of the relationship. Rather, he simply takes for granted that we already know what Kierkegaard says and what he means, founding his assertions on nothing more than claims that Heidegger "imitates" Kierkegaard (Poole, "The Unknown Kierkegaard," 52). Rather than considering Heidegger's "unscrupulous" adoption of a reported Kierkegaard or making of him another sort of "existentialist," however—which ultimately has more to do with Jaspers and Jean-Paul Sartre than it does with either Heidegger or Kierkegaard—a more instructive point of departure might be the apparent commonality of the terms "idle talk" (Heidegger) and "chatter" (Kierkegaard) as problematized in Peter Fenves's recent *"Chatter": Language and History in Kierkegaard.*

16. From Jaspers's *Philosophie* (1932), cited in Schnädelbach, *Philosophy in Germany,* 159.

17. Studies that follow this pattern are numerous. I mention here only a few of the more significant: Taylor, *Kierkegaard's Pseudonymous Authorship* (1975) and *Journeys to Selfhood* (1980); Dunning, *Kierkegaard's Dialectic of Inwardness* (1985); Connell, *To Be One Thing* (1985); and Walsh, *Living Poetically* (1994). Even explicitly "theological" accounts take the problematic of "becoming" a "self" as central to any understanding of Kierkegaard. Cf., for example, Arnold B. Come, *Kierkegaard as Theologian: Becoming My Self* (1997).

18. Karl Jaspers, "The Importance of Kierkegaard," 35–48. Jaspers writes: "Still the question of what the real Kierkegaard was, what he signified historically, and what his present influence is, cannot be answered unequivocally" (p. 36). This does not mean, however, that Jaspers himself renders something other than the existentialist account.

19. Numerous attempts have been made of late to claim Kierkegaard as a kind of protopostmodernist. Kierkegaard's professed lack of "authority" tends to lapse into a celebration of linguistic indeterminacy as linguistic meaninglessness. In one way or another, every attempt to claim or deny a relation to "postmodernism" for Kierkegaard understands the goal of this project as a general freedom from normative determinacy, what Matuštík wants to call the "postmodern suspension of normative discourses" (Martin J. Matuštík, "Kierkegaard's Radical Existential Praxis," 240)—whether linguistic, conceptual, social, or ethical. In this way, and under its own normative gesture, each expresses either praise or horror at a project reduced either to notions of a pure "free play" or, more negatively, to an ultimate "nihilism" encompassing each of these categories. Cf., for example, Michael Weston, *Kierkegaard and Modern Continental Philosophy: An Introduction*; Martin J. Matuštík and Merold Westphal, eds., *Kierkegaard in Post/Modernity*; Merold Westphal, *Becoming a Self: A Reading of Kierkegaard's Concluding Unscientific Postscript*; Mark C. Taylor, *Erring: A Postmodern A/theology*; Poole, *Kierkegaard.* Some caution is advised, however, with regard to the easy deployment of these terms. Relying, as these authors do, on the facile conflation of less compatible philosophies of "postmodernism" in such divergent authors as Foucault, Lyotard, Derrida, Rorty, and Habermas, it is by no means clear what the project of this postmodernism might be unless it is reduced to a kind of slogan about indeterminacy without any more particular investigation of its operations. In this sense, it remains difficult if not impossible to situate Kierkegaard in relation to it. One must ask, furthermore, what one expects to gain in the affiliation to this term, especially given the polemical status of recent debates. On the polemical use of the term "postmodernism," cf. Judith Butler, "Contingent Foundations: Feminism and the Question of 'Postmodernism.'"

20. Although one might be tempted to include Fenves in this same camp of "postmodernists," his repeated insistence that "communication cannot not take place," for example, places him directly opposed to any facile identification of linguistic indeterminacy with sheer emptiness or meaninglessness. Moreover, the possibility that "nothing" might also be communicated in language rather serves to point out significant presuppositions about both language and subjectivity. The significance of "chatter" for any understanding of Kierkegaard, as

Fenves points out, lies in the possibility not that language might not mean anything, but rather that language continues to comply with all rules of coherent, meaningful communication, and yet it still might also convey nothing.

21. Taylor, *Kierkegaard's Pseudonymous Authorship*, vii.

22. For a succinct articulation of this linguistic aporia see Werner Hamacher, "The Second of Inversion: Movements of a Figure through Celan's Poetry," 276–77.

23. The fragment's finitude joins it with a crucial aspect of the fragment in German romanticism as described in Nancy and Lacoue-Labarthe's *The Literary Absolute: The Theory of Literature in German Romanticism:* "Each fragment stands for itself and for that from which it is detached" (p. 44). And, further, the fragment "combines completion and incompletion in itself" (p. 50). By emphasizing the simultaneous temporality of this duality in the fragment, Werner Hamacher arrives at an even more disruptive and paradoxical account: "[A] fragment would each time be precisely the language that is not entirely language, not entirely itself but something other than, and different from, language itself: a fragment would be that which in the face of language passed behind or beyond it; a fragment would be the language in which something other than language itself—nothing, for example—also spoke and, therefore, a language in which at least two languages always spoke—a broken language and the break of language" (Werner Hamacher, *Premises: Essays on Philosophy and Literature from Kant to Celan*, 225).

24. In this sense, this Kierkegaardian passage from *Either/Or* would have much in common with Werner Hamacher's discussion of the imperative indeterminacy of language in his "LECTIO: de Man's Imperative."

25. The definition is supplied by the editors of the English edition of *Either/Or* (p. 629 n. 36).

26. Kevin Newmark defines Kierkegaard's use of *anacoluthon* here as "the interruption of rhetorical 'coherence' by the philosophical thesis of fragmentation articulated in it" (Kevin Newmark, "Secret Agents: After Kierkegaard's Subject," 746). Paul de Man, further, connects *anacoluthon* to Friedrich Schlegel's definition of "irony" as "permantent *parabasis*" (Paul de Man, "The Concept of Irony," 178–79).

27. It is precisely this excess in language through its fragmentation that tends to be misread in the assessment of its indeterminacy. John Smyth, for example, in his otherwise insightful reading of the play of indeterminacy in Kierkegaard's work, interprets the indeterminacy of the fragment in A's account merely as a sign of its "arbitrariness." Indeterminacy and "arbitrariness," however, are not the same thing. By making an indeterminate text an arbitrary one, he elides the difficulty posed by linguistic meaning: the fact that language, no matter how indeterminate, still means what it says. Cf. John Smyth, *A Question of Eros: Irony in Sterne, Kierkegaard, and Barthes*, 256.

28. A note added by the editors of this edition following the word "fulguration" in Kierkegaard's text reads as follows: "A loan word in Danish, meaning a sudden flashing (for example, the flashing of molten gold or silver), and used only once, here, in Kierkegaard's authorship" (*Either/Or* I, 629). It is perhaps precisely because of this notion of "fulguration" and "glinting transiency" that Adorno cites this passage on the fragment in his book on Kierkegaard under the rubric of "reconciliation." Cf. Theodor W. Adorno, *Kierkegaard: Construction of the Aesthetic*, 139–40.

29. As I shall demonstrate, the necessary absence of prior meaning and the consequent imperative of its interpretation is absolutely central to Kierkegaard's understanding of language (cf. esp. chapters 4 and 5). In spite of this, many interpreters of Kierkegaard continually insist on the religious interpretation of his work. In this vein, even Louis Mackey, otherwise praised for his putatively "postmodern" take on Kierkegaard, claims that "unless you know the meaning, the interpretation is worthless," insisting in this case that Climacus's *Philosophical Fragments* is still about "Christianity." Cf. Mackey, *Points of View*, 135.

30. For a suggestive discussion of the relationship between language and alterity, see Pat Bigelow, "The Poetic Poaching of Silence."

31. Accounts of Kierkegaard's "indirect communication" are indeed numerous. Among the most succinct and helpful is Kevin Newmark's discussion from "Taking Kierkegaard Apart," his introduction to Sylviane Agacinski's *Aparté*. Here he explains that "the *form* of communication (which is partly, though not entirely, a question of aesthetics since it is concerned with the outward form or sensuous appearance of the communication) and the *meaning* of the communication (which would at some point become *religious* truth as inwardness) are maintained indissolubly in a relationship of nonadequation ..." (in Sylviane Agacinski, *Aparté: Conceptions and Deaths of Søren Kierkegaard*, 9).

32. The notion of "indirect communication" reflects the crux of Kierkegaard's argument against Hegelian idealism. His objection lies in the insistence that "objectivity" can characterize thought only in abstraction. The moment one recognizes that there must be someone doing the thinking, this ideal objectivity falls apart. Cf. Judith Butler, "Kierkegaard's Speculative Despair."

33. This polemical situation characterizes much of Kierkegaard's later work. The confusion of an illusory "Christendom" with actual "Christianity" is most thoroughly—and polemically—carried out in the series of pamphlets entitled *The Moment*, which was written and published by Kierkegaard at the end of his life. These texts are included in the English translation Søren Kierkegaard, *Attack upon Christendom*. See also his *Practice in Christianity* (also written in 1848, the same time as *Point of View*), *For Self Examination*, and *Judge for Yourself*.

34. For discussions of the ways in which the works themselves refuse such systematic organization, see, for example, Christopher Norris, "Fictions of Authority: Narrative and Viewpoint in Kierkegaard's Writing"; Garff, Joakim, "The Eyes of Argus: The Point of View and Points of View with Respect to Kierkegaard's 'Activity as an Author'"; and Louis Mackey, "Points of View for His Work as an Author: A Report from History."

35. Compare, in this regard, the comments regarding the impossible unity of the signatory/signature as analyzed by Jacques Derrida: "But the condition of possibility of those effects [the presentation of the signatory in the signature] is simultaneously the condition of their impossibility, of the impossibility of their rigorous purity. In order to function, that is, to be readable, a signature must have a repeatable, iterable, imitable form; it must be able to be detached from the present and singular intention of its production. It is its sameness which, by corrupting its identity and its singularity, divides its seal." Jacques Derrida, *Limited Inc.*, 20.

36. *Papirer*, X1 A 250 n.d., 1849.

37. Søren Kierkegaard, *Philosophical Fragments, or A Fragment of Philosophy; Johannes Climacus, or, De Omnibus Dubitandum Est*, 98. "But, humanly speaking, consequences built upon a paradox are built upon the abyss, and the total content of the consequences, which is handed down to the single individual only under the agreement that it is by virtue of a paradox, is not to be passed on like real estate, since the whole thing is in suspense."

38. Newmark, "Secret Agents." Newmark's account of the fragmentation in or of Antigone in *Either/Or*, to which this reading is indebted, reads it as the articulation of Kierkegaard's notion of subjectivity. Cf. esp. 741ff.

39. Kafka, Franz. *Briefe, 1902–1924*; 238.

40. Only one account of Kierkegaard's reception takes account of Adorno's book: Michael Theunissen and Wilfried Greve, eds., *Materialien zur Philosophie Søren Kierkegaards*.

41. Hence, the famous outrage at Heidegger's unacknowledged theft from Kierkegaard. Cf., for example, Poole, "The Unknown Kierkegaard," 52–53.

42. To be guided by a desire for results, Kierkegaard explains, can only lead to a failure in understanding: "But we are curious about the result, just as we are curious about the way a book turns out. We do not want to know anything about the anxiety, the distress, the paradox" (*Fear and Trembling*, 63).

2. Learning to Read

1. Furthermore, this configuration of texts marks an emphatic turn away from the transcendental idealism associated with Adorno's work as a student of Hans Cornelius toward what is commonly identified as his "materialism," which was most notably influenced by his friendship with Walter Benjamin Cf. Rolf Thiedemann, "Editorsche Nachbemerkung."

2. Though rarely discussed, the close proximity of Adorno to Kierkegaard has been suggested. See, for example, Michael Theunissen and Wilfried Greve, *Materialien zur Philosophie Søren Kierkegaards,* 76–83. A notable exception exists in the work of Hermann Deuser, who relates Adorno's "negative dialectics" to Kierkegaard's own conception of a dialectic that continually eludes any sort of resolution in Hegelian *Aufhebung.* Cf. Hermann Deuser, *Dialektische Theologie.* Deuser comments specifically on Adorno's *Kierkegaard* in a short critical response to a critique of Adorno's text by Klaus M. Kodalle. Kodalle's essay criticizes Adorno for missing the theological "core" *(Kern)* of Kierkegaard's authorship, whereas Deuser's response emphasizes Adorno's insistence that even the theological texts are not free of the inherent indeterminacy of the aesthetic. Cf. Klaus M. Kodalle, "Adornos Kierkegaard" and Hermann Deuser, "Kierkegaard in der kritischen Theorie."

3. Adorno was responding here to the few attempts to come to terms with Kierkegaard's work written in German after the turn of the twentieth century, which appeared more or less concurrently with the first translations of Kierkegaard's texts into German. In this context Adorno cites Theodor Haecker, *Søren Kierkegaard und die Philosophie der Innerlichkeit* (1913); August Vetter, *Frömmigkeit als Leidenschaft: Eine Deutung Kierkegaards* (1928); Erich Przywara, S.J., *Das Geheimnis Kierkegaards* (1929); and Christoph Schrempf, *Søren Kierkegaard: Eine Biographie,* Bd. I (1927) and Bd. II (1928).

4. Theodor W. Adorno, *Kierkegaard: Konstruktion des Ästhetischen,* in *Gesammelte Schriften,* II, 9; translated as *Kierkegaard: Construction of the Aesthetic,* 3. All further citations of this work will be noted parenthetically within the text, citing first the German and then the English translation. Translations have been modified in order to render Adorno's German more accurately.

5. More recently, Werner Hamacher has taken this disjunction as his point of departure in writing: "It is not certain that there can be a science of literature" (Werner Hamacher, "'Lectio,'" 181).

6. Cited in Adorno's text: Søren Kierkegaard, *Gesammelte Werke,* II, 149. Adorno's translator Hullot-Kentor follows Walter Lowrie's translation rather than the Hongs': Søren Kierkegaard, *Either/Or,* vol. 2, trans. Walter Lowrie, with revisions and a foreword by Howard A. Johnson (Princeton, N.J.: Princeton University Press, 1971), 182.

7. In Adorno's paraphrase, the concept of subjective communication is based upon Kierkegaard's assumption that "subjective thinking" requires a "doubled reflection"—reflection on the matter *(Sache)* as well as the thinking subject's own self-reflection—and this "doubled reflection" is also constitutive of subjective interiority. "Accordingly, aesthetic means precisely the way in which interiority appears as the How of subjective communication ..." (*Kierkegaard,* 26; 15). Rather than following Kierkegaard's own discussions of the necessary "indirectness" of communication as indicative of a discrepancy between the subject and its possible communications, Adorno insists that the communication of a subject is nothing more than the replication of a subjective interiority in terms of a formal and, ultimately, ideal expression in speech. In Adorno's paraphrase, Kierkegaard's notion of communication looks something like the successful speech act. "Communication" would describe the making universally understandable of any expression of subjective intention.

8. Adorno's general intention in the book on Kierkegaard is, consistent with his critique of idealism elsewhere, to show by way of an identification of Kierkegaard with the principles of idealism the ultimate incompatibility of idealism with "reality." Idealism, in Adorno's view, is nothing more than pure formalism and, as such, necessarily abandons every hope of understanding anything of "reality" in its material and historical appearance. Although

Adorno's critique of formalism is based largely on a discussion of Kant's first *Critique*, Kant's aesthetics elsewhere do not conform so rigidly to Adorno's formalist model. This is most explicitly true of Kant's third *Critique*, the *Critique of Judgment*. Although Adorno cites Kierkegaard's concept of communication as indicative of the idealist limitations of his aesthetics, Adorno's insistence that Kierkegaardian communication *(Mitteilung)* stands at the center of his aesthetics is perhaps less about Kierkegaard than it is about Kant. In the third *Critique*, all aesthetic judgments, both those of the sublime and those of the beautiful, depend upon their "universal communicability" *(allgemeine Mitteilbarkeit)*. Judgments of the sublime, Kant claims, unlike those of the beautiful, are based on reason and a priori principles of "human nature" as ideas, especially those concerning morality. "Hereupon is grounded the necessity of the corroboration of others in our own judgements of the sublime ... (Hierauf gründet sich nun die Notwendigkeit der Beistimmung des Urteils anderer vom Erhabenen zu dem unsrigen)...." Immanuel Kant, *Kritik der Urteilskraft* Werkausgabe, Bd. X, 190, B 112, A 111. Even in the universal communicability of aesthetic judgments, for Kant, there persists something radically incommunicable.

9. Hullot-Kentor uses the Swenson and Lowrie translation: Søren Kierkegaard, *Concluding Unscientific Postscript*, trans. David Swenson and Walter Lowrie (Princeton, N.J.: Princeton University Press, 1968), 68-69.

10. Adorno is certainly not the only philosopher to have desired the disappearance of the questions of philosophy. Wittgenstein, for example, claims in the *Tractatus:* "The answer to the problem of life is evident in the disappearance of the problem" (6.521). Similarly, in the *Philosophical Investigations* he claims that "the clarity for which we strive is nevertheless a *complete* one. But that only means that philosophical problems should disappear *completely*" (§ 133). Ludwig Wittgenstein, *Traktatus logico-philosophicus: Tagebücher 1914–1916* and *Philosophische Untersuchungen.*

11. Theodor Adorno, *Negative Dialektik*, 71; translated as *Negative Dialectics*, 63. All further citations of this edition will be noted parenthetically within the text, citing first the German and then the English translation. Translations have been modified in order to render Adorno's German more accurately.

12. Alexander Garcia Düttmann argues for the paradoxical temporality of Adorno's notion of "interpretation." If there is no temporal progression from question to answer in and through interpretation question and answer both emerge and transpire only within interpretation: "Thus emerge the riddles: they emerge first in interpretation." Therefore, there is nothing outside of interpretation to which the interpretation would refer or that might appear as the result of interpretation. In Düttmann's terms, "interpretation" cannot give knowledge: "The solution is not knowledge over which one would have control after the destruction of the riddle, for such an impression would again produce another riddle. The solution is an experience without knowledge: the riddle does not dissolve into knowledge." Alexander Garcia Düttmann, *Das Gedächtnis des Denkens*, 106–7.

13. Walter Benjamin, *Ursprung des deutschen Trauerspiels*, 141; translated as *The Origin of the German Tragic Drama*, 162. All subsequent citations will be given parenthetically within the text, citing first the German and then the English translation.

14. Similarly, Paul de Man understands allegory primarily in terms of the temporal difference between signs: "The relationship between the allegorical sign and its meaning *(signifié)* is not decreed by dogma.... We have, instead, a relationship between signs in which the reference to their respective meanings has become of secondary importance. But this relationship between signs necessarily contains a constitutive temporal element; it remains necessary, if there is to be allegory, that the allegorical sign refer to another sign that precedes it. The meaning constituted by the allegorical sign can then consist only in the *repetition* (in the Kierkegaardian sense of the term) of a previous sign with which it can never coincide, since it is of the essence of this previous sign to be pure anteriority." Paul de Man, "The Rhetoric of Temporality," in *Blindness and Insight: Essays in the Rhetoric of Contemporary Criticism*, 207.

15. In this sense, allegorical figuration continually excludes the possibility of reducing any expression solely to its occurrence within history, apart from its own self-historicization. The irreducibility of the figure to a nondiscursive history continually thwarts Adorno's own attempts to identify a particular historical moment as the "materiality" that constitutes Kierkegaard's philosophy. Adorno's reading of Kierkegaard isolates the "bürgerliches Intérieur" (bourgeois interior) as the locus of historical concretion. This *Intérieur*, however, is part of the texts Adorno is reading, not an external and extralinguistic "reality" that would inform them. In order for Adorno to identify some of Kierkegaard's figures as indicative of historical, concrete, material reality and others as evidence of Kierkegaard's more seductive tendencies, the "traps" laid for the unsuspecting reader, Adorno has to distinguish between claims that otherwise appear identical. Some statements mean what they say; others do not.

The identification of this *Intérieur*, however, has generally been acknowledged only for its desired function as the locus of historical concretion. Adorno himself cited this *Intérieur* as of primary significance. In his well-known letter to Walter Benjamin of August 2, 1935—one of the few discussions of his work on Kierkegaard outside of the published texts—Adorno formulated his criticism of Benjamin by way of the notion of the *Intérieur* as exemplified in the book on Kierkegaard. This was the only thought in the book that he discussed. Its importance for him was primarily conceived in terms of the "dialectical image" of the nineteenth century: "Now I am myself the last person to be unaware of the relevance of the immanence of consciousness for the nineteenth century, but the concept of the dialectical image cannot simply be derived from it; rather, the immanence of consciousness itself, as *intérieure*, is the dialectical image for the nineteenth century as alienation. And there I shall have to leave the stake which the second chapter of my Kierkegaard book enjoys in this new game." Theodor Adorno and Walter Benjamin, *The Complete Correspondence, 1928–1940*, 106.

For more general discussions of the function of such instances of historical concretion in Adorno's work, see Gillian Rose, *Melancholy Science: An Introduction to the Thought of Theodor W. Adorno*, esp. 63–64, and Susan Buck-Morss, *The Origin of the Negative Dialectics*, 111–21.

16. Hullot-Kentor cites Søren Kierkegaard, *Fear and Trembling and the Sickness unto Death*, trans. Walter Lowrie (Princeton N.J.: Princeton University Press, 1974), 169.

17. Even in the late *Negative Dialectics*, Adorno characterizes his interest in his early work as primarily one of separating the particularity of individual "subjects" from a universalizing—and, hence, oppressive—"subjectivity." From the "Preface": "Ever since the author began to trust his own intellectual impulses, he took it as his task to break through the illusion of constitutive subjectivity with the power of the subject" (*Negative Dialectics*, 10, xx). Rainer Nägele, for example, acclaims Adorno for the insight that "subjectivity" and "subjects," though mutually incompatible, remain unthinkable in isolation: "Subjectivity, for Adorno, is both the resistance against and the principle of domination. Any philosophy that does not acknowledge this double role and instead claims an absolute subject, from Hegel to existentialism, remains locked in contradiction." Rainer Nägele, "The Scene of the Other," 59.

18. Hullot-Kentor cites Søren Kierkegaard. *Stages on Life's Way*, trans. Walter Lowrie (Princeton, N.J.: Princeton University Press, 1940), 90.

19. Hullot-Kentor cites Søren Kierkegaard, *Either/Or*, vol. 2, trans. Walter Lowrie (Princeton, N.J.: Princeton University Press, 1971), 179-80.

20. It should be noted, however, that Adorno's notion of "idealism" as it appears in his texts is largely the by-product of his polemics. Virtually no philosopher after Kant and Hegel is spared Adorno's rebuke of hidden idealist tendencies. Adorno's accusation generally appears as one of a certain subjective universalization at the expense of historical particularization. The accusation is most emphatically against those philosophers who might otherwise display the greatest affinities with Adorno's own work—especially against Heidegger and, most significant for this reading of Adorno, against Kierkegaard. Thus, the point here is neither to correct Adorno's polemical definition of "idealism" nor to rescue those philosophers accused of

idealist tendencies from Adorno's polemical attack, but rather to follow the more affirmative and productive traits of Adorno's critique, which, in turn, rather betray stronger affinities than mere condemnation.

21. Hullot-Kentor cites Søren Kierkegaard, *Either/Or*, vol. I, trans. David Swenson and Lillian Marvin Swenson (Princeton, N.J.: Princeton University Press, 1971), 188.

22. Hullot-Kentor cites Søren Kierkegaard, *Training in Christianity and the Edifying Discourses Which 'Accompanied' It*, trans. Walter Lowrie (Princeton, N.J.: Princeton University Press, 1972), 185-86.

3. Affirmation

1. Kierkegaard's essay had only just been translated into German by Theodor Haecker and published in the journal *Der Brenner* (1915), vol. 5, 15–55. On the early translations of Kierkegaard into German, see Allan Janik, "Haecker, Kierkegaard, and the Early *Brenner*. The Rilke letters cited here are contained in the collection *Briefe*, Bd. 2. Page references refer to this collection. All translations have been prepared for this volume. English versions of Rilke's letters can also be found in *Letters of Rainer Maria Rilke*, vols. 1 and 2, trans. Jane Bannard Greene and M. D. Herter Norton (New York: W. W. Norton, 1947).

2. The comment on Kassner's essay appears in a letter to Mathilke Vollmoeler written on July 23, 1906. Comments on Rilke's familiarity with particular texts of Kierkegaard are to be found in William Small's *Rilke-Kommentar zu den Aufzeichnungen des Malte Laurids Brigge*, p. 16, and in Wolfgang Leppmann's *Rilke—Sein Leben, seine Welt, sein Werk*, p. 233. Attempts to understand the relationship between Rilke and Kierkegaard have been few. There have been perhaps only two. Otto Friedrich Bollnow discussed Rilke's affinity to "existential philosophy" in terms of a connection to Kierkegaard and developed an understanding of Rilke as "existentialist" specifically in terms of Rilke's representations of death (Bollnow, *Existenzphilosophie*, 83–94). In a more recent essay, Irina Frowen treated the relationship simply as one of "influence," making of Rilke only a slightly different "existentialist" than Kierkegaard and would himself somehow exemplify the "aesthetic" in "poetic existence" (Irina Frowen, "Rilkes 'Ölbaum-Garten' zwischen Kierkegaard's 'Entweder-Oder'"). Her essay attempts a schematic reading of Rilke's poem through Kierkegaardian "stages of existence." In her insistance upon the connection between Rilke and Kierkegaard as one of a common existentialism, she is simply following Bollnow, to whom she refers without other discussion. Both Bollnow and Frowen take Rilke as "exemplary" of a Kierkegaardian "poetic existence." Bollnow, moreover, finds Rilke disappointingly restricted to the "aesthetic stage" or "artistic life-form" that *Existenzphilosophie*, he believes, far surpasses.

3. Søren Kierkegaard, "At a Graveside," 79. The Danish reads: "Døden har ingen Forstilling og agter ikke paa Forstillinger."

4. Discussions of figuration tend to focus on this formation of the figure, accepting figuration as in principle limitless, always able to establish epistemological familiarity by way of similarity or some other related correspondence. *The New Princeton Encyclopedia of Poetry and Poetics*, for example, calls figuration "the transmutation of ideas into images." Figuration thus produces a "speculative reality" in which, analogous to Freudian dream interpretation, a "latent meaning, lying beneath the aesthetic surface," is rendered "manifest" and "palpable" (Alex Preminger and T. V. F. Brogan, *The New Princeton Encyclopedia of Poetry and Poetics*, 408–9). The essentially providential interpretation of figures has been most clearly identified by Auerbach, who, tracing figural interpretation back to "the historical situation that drove St. Paul to preach among the Gentiles," claims that phenomenal presentation is taken as representation of a transcendental reality both "present" and yet to come in some future time: "the individual earthly event is not regarded as a definitive self-sufficient reality, nor as a link in a chain of development in which single events or combinations of events perpetually give rise to new events, but viewed primarily in immediate vertical connection with a divine order which encompasses it, which on some future day will itself be concrete reality; so that the

earthly event is a prophecy or *figura* of a part of a wholly divine reality that will be enacted in the future. But this reality is not only future; it is always present in the eye of God and in the other world, which is to say that in transcendence the revealed and true reality is present at all times, or timelessly" (Erich Auerbach, "Figura," 72).

5. Rilke connects this image of death as "bluish distillate" indirectly to Tolstoy's "The Death of Ivan Ilyitsch" in his letter to Lotte Hepner of November 8, 1915. Here, he says of Tolstoy's comprehension of death, and "The Death of Ivan Ilyitsch" in particular: "His [Tolstoy's] enormous experience of Nature (I hardly know anyone who so passionately devoted himself to studying Nature) made him astonishingly able to think from a sense of the whole and to write out of a feeling for life which was so permeated with the finest particles of death, that death seemed to be contained everywhere in it as an odd spice in the strong flavor of life—but for that very reason this man could be so deeply, so frantically frightened when he discovered that somewhere there was pure death, that bottle full of death or that hideous cup with the handle broken off and the senseless inscription 'Faith, love, hope,' out of which one was compelled to drink bitterness of undiluted death" (*Briefe* vol. 2, 57–58).

6. The only definition of *Absud* given in the Grimm *Deutsches Wörterbuch* is the Latin *decoctum*. The absence of any exemplary quotations here underscores the rarity of this word.

7. Grimm's discussion of *wunderlich* defines it first as the oldest adjectival form of *Wunder* and traces its history prior to *wunderbar*, which eventually replaced it in the sixteenth century. The replacement of *wunderlich* by *wunderbar* then restricts *wunderlich* solely to the sense of *sonderbar*.

8. This image might be said to become legible as a figure of death in Rilke's own description as related by Marie von Thurn und Taxis in *Erinnerungen* (Recollections). Here it is used, in a description of this poem, in referring to a suddenly appearing falling star witnessed by Rilke in Toledo in 1911: "The falling star—he [Rilke] had seen it then in Toledo. He went at night over a bridge, and suddenly a magnificent meteor fell with tearing speed over the entire firmament, from its zenith to the dark horizon—and disappeared. That was marvelous death." (Maria von Thurn und Taxis, *Erinnerungen*, 81.) In other words, the figure in the poem is not legible as death at all—at least not as explained by this recollection.

9. This is not the only time Rilke presents commands in the infinitive. The seventh *Duino Elegy*, for example, has them as well in a passage virtually parallel to the one from the poem "Death":

> O einst tot sein und sie wissen unendlich,
> alle die Sterne: denn wie, wie, wie sie vergessen!
>
> O to be dead once and to know them without end,
> all the stars: then how, how, how to forget them!
>
> (*Werke in Drei Bänden* I, 466)

10. Some of the work in this direction has already been done. In his essay on Paul de Man, Werner Hamacher points out that de Man, in his discussion of metaphor, shows that the desired metaphorical completion is always thwarted by its own contingency. See Hamacher, "Lectio."

11. In another essay about death, Kierkegaard claims not that there is no detectable distinction among the dead, but that the scale of distinction is dramatically reduced. The world leader and the infant who died at birth are now distinguished only by the measurable differences between their respective gravestones. See Søren Kierkegaard, "The Work of Love in Remembering One Dead."

12. A's discussion of "either/or" appears in the "Diapsalmata" at the beginning of *Either/Or*, vol. I, under the heading "Either/Or, *An Ecstatic Discourse*." He insists that the inevitable result of any decision is always only regret. The passage begins: "Marry, and you

will regret it. Do not marry, and you will also regret it. Marry or do not marry, you will regret it either way. Whether you marry or you do not marry, you will regret it either way. Laugh at the stupidities of the world, and you will regret it; weep over them, and you will also regret it. Laugh at the stupidities of the world or weep over them, you will regret it either way" (Kierkegaard, *Either/Or* I, 38).

13. Similarly, John Smyth argues that death's indeterminacy ironizes Socratic irony by indiscriminately imposing a kind of "*radical* or *mortal play*" into an otherwise free, aesthetic indeterminacy: "For death is the sign and site not only of a necessary indeterminacy but also, evidently, of a certain necessary closure" (John Smyth, *A Question of Eros*, 188). But how death would function as a sign remains an open question.

14. This is perhaps the most literal, direct connection to the Apollo poem and already indication enough of the relevance of Robert Hass's otherwise unspecified assertion that the "true provenance" of the Apollo sonnet is death. Robert Hass, "Looking for Rilke," 245.

15. This is the main distinction that, according to Taylor, separates Kierkegaard's notion of self from that of Hegel. See Mark C. Taylor, "Self in/as Other."

16. *Forklare* means both "to transfigure," as the translation here renders the term in English, and also "to explain." This already suggests a possible limitation within Judge William's notion of ethics that does not become apparent until Kierkegaard's later essay on death, in which death is the limit to all "explanation" *(Forklaring)*.

17. "Enten-Eller det er in Talismand, hvormed man kan tilintetgjøre hel Verden." *Journals and Papers* I, 756 (*Papirer* III B 179:27) n.d, 1842.

18. The word "*überholen*" is taken here literally as "metaphor" in the sense of *metaphérein*, to transfer or carry over.

19. In a recent reading of the paragraphs in Heidegger's *Sein und Zeit* concerning the "Being unto death" *(Sein zum Tode)*, Jacques Derrida goes somewhat further than Rilke does here and argues for an "originary mourning" within the "existential analysis of death." In this context, he explains: "For, conversely, if death is indeed the possibility of the impossible and therefore the possibility of appearing as such of the impossibility of appearing as such either, then man, or man as *Dasein*, never has a relation to death as such, but only to perishing, to demising, and to the death of the other, who is not the other. The death of the other thus becomes again 'first,' always first. It is like the experience of mourning that institutes my relation to myself and constitutes the egoity of the *ego* as well as every *Jemeinigkeit* in the *différance*—neither internal nor external—that structures this experience. The death of the other, this death of the other in 'me,' is fundamentally the only death that is named in the syntagm 'my death,' with all the consequences that one can draw from this" (Jacques Derrida, *Aporias*, 76).

20. Rilke's insistence upon the "Yes" of death crosses over into a theophilosophical discourse. Franz Rosenzweig discusses the "Yes" at the beginning of his *Der Stern der Erlösung* (The star of redemption): "That is the power of the Yes, that it applies everywhere, that unlimited possibilities of reality lie within it. It is the originary word of language, one of those through which the—not exactly sentences, but rather first the words from which sentences are formed, words as sentence parts as such, shorthand signs of a sentence, although it can be used as such, but rather it is the silent accompaniment of all sentence parts, the confirmation, the 'sic,' the 'amen' behind every word. It gives every word in the sentence its right to existence, it installs it in the sentence where it might dwell, it 'posits.' The first Yes in God grounds the whole infinity of divine essence. And the first Yes is 'in the beginning'" (Franz Rosenzweig, *Der Stern der Erlösung*, 29). Michel de Certeau describes the "Yes" as a performative speech act: "This act does not postulate a reality or a knowledge anterior to that which it says. Even in its linguistic form it has the force of a beginning. Among the performatives, it fits more precisely into the class of the 'commissives.' The examples which Austin gives of this class (I promise, am determined to, pledge myself, dedicate myself to, declare my intention, etc.) bring up in review the terms which mark the social manifestation of the initial *volo* in mystical texts"

(Michel de Certeau, *La Fable mystique, XVIe–XVIIe siècle,* 237). Jacques Derrida, furthermore, comments on both of these texts: "The arche-originary *yes* resembles an absolute performative. It does not describe and does not state anything, but engages a kind of arche-engagement, a kind of alliance or consent or promise lost in its acquiescence to the utterance which it always accompanies, albeit silently, and even if this utterance is radically negative. Since this performative is presupposed as the condition of possibility for all other performatives, it is not one performative among others.... It is not, *stricto sensu,* an act, it is not assignable to any subject nor to any object. If it opens the eventness of an event, it is not itself an event" (Jacques Derrida, "A Number of Yes"). Death's Yes in Rilke's discussion is not simply a performative in the sense of a promise; death's Yes is an imperative. It is not a promise I make and with which I freely obligate myself. It is given to me by death; it obliges me.

21. On this point, the similarity between Rilke and Kierkegaard could be extended to include Rilke's *The Notebooks of Malte Laurids Brigge,* which includes a virtually verbatim quotation of Kierkegaard's "At a Graveside." Kierkegaard illustrates the unsettling force of death's affirmation by reiterating the response to every question of death as "Yes, it is possible." In Rilke's Malte, each of his speculations about God, history, and the world is answered with the same statement: "Yes, it is possible" *(Ja, es ist möglich)* (*Werke in Drei Bänden* III, 127–28). Kierkegaard explains: "Every condition that wants to make the certainty of death into a conditional certainty for the wisher, every agreement that wants to make the certainty of death into a conditional certainty for the person making up his mind, every arrangement that wants to condition the certainty of death as to time and hour for the one who is acting, every condition, every agreement, every arrangement runs aground on this statement" ("At a Graveside," 95).

4. The Other Proposition

1. Pat Bigelow takes this as the "basic insight" of the *Philosophical Fragments,* which he describes in terms of "sameness" and "otherness." Thus, "the same cannot be posited except as other than the other, and the same can only be posited" (Bigelow, *Kierkegaard and the Problem of Writing,* 180).

2. Hegel has defined *necessity* as the "union" of possibility and actuality. G. W. F. Hegel, *Encyclopädie der philosophischen Wissenschaft, Erster Theil, Die Logik, Werke* VI, para. 147. This union, if it is one, Climacus suggests, is anything but stable.

3. In another context, Werner Hamacher has described the work of "or" on the philosophy of Jean-Luc Nancy as the possibility of the impossible as opened up in the possibility of possibility: "This premodal making possible of possibilities, which takes place in the *or,* is always then in play when it is a question of decision between different ways of speaking, thinking and acting, a question of decision between them and their omission, and it is there in play above all where it is a question of the decision between the possibilities of Being and of not-Being: every *or* that stands before the choice between the one possibility and the other, opens these possibilities and thus also the possibility of a decision between an *or* and *no or [keinem oder]. Or* thus opens possibilities of decision, not so that in this way the decision should have already happened, but it sets up at the same time the possibility of such a decision not being made, or a decision being made against any further decision. In the *or* that releases all decisions, all decisions are also kept on and held up, because in every individual case it also makes possible the decision against decision and against the possibility of decision. Every *or* also says *or without or*" (Werner Hamacher, "Ou, séance, touche de Nancy, ici (II)," in *Paragraph* 17:2 (July 1994), 103).

4. This argument, even in its most general formulation, forms the basis of Kierkegaard's critique of Hegelian speculation. The universalization of speculative thought must ignore or forget the very existence of the one thinking. For a more detailed discussion of this problematic, see Judith Butler, "Kierkegaard's Speculative Despair."

5. For the Danish edition, cf. *Papirer* IV, 61.

6. Using the pseudonym "Anti-Climacus," Kierkegaard insists, in his *Practice in Christianity*, echoing the essay "At a Graveside," discussed earlier: "In the grave there is rest, but *beside* the grave there is no rest; it says: up to here and no further" (Søren Kierkegaard, *Practice in Christianity*, 18).

7. Climacus explicitly cites four of Plato's early dialogues: *Protagoras, Gorgias, Meno,* and *Euthydemus.* Cf., for example, *Meno,* in which Socrates claims: "The soul, then, as being immortal and having been born again many times, and having seen all things that exist, whether in this world or in the world below, has knowledge of them all; and it is no wonder that she should be able to call to remembrance all that she ever knew about virtue, and about everything; for as all nature is akin, and the soul has learned all things, there is no difficulty in a man eliciting out of a single recollection all the rest—the process generally called 'learning'—if he is strenuous and does not faint; for all inquiry and all learning is but recollection" (81*c-d*). Plato, *The Dialogues of Plato*, vol. I, 278.

8. Hegel's own account of the role of recollection in speculation is perhaps most evident in the discussion of "absolute knowledge" as the fulfillment of *Geist* as *Erinnerung:* "Since its accomplishment consists in Spirit knowing what it is, in fully comprehending its substance, this knowledge means its concentrating itself on itself *(Insichgehen)*, a state in which Spirit leaves its external existence behind and gives its embodiment over to Recollection *(Erinnerung)*. In thus concentrating itself on itself, Spirit is engulfed in the night of its own self-consciousness; its vanished existence is, however, conserved therein; and this superseded existence—the previous existence, but born anew from the womb of knowledge—is the new existence, a new world, and a new embodiment of Spirit. Here it has to begin all over again at its immediacy, as freshly as before, and thence rise once more to the measure of its stature, as if, for it, all that preceded were lost, and as if it had learned nothing from the experience of the spirits that preceded. But re-collection *(Er-Innerung)* has conserved that experience, and is the inner being, and, in fact, the higher form of the substance. While, then, this phase of Spirit begins all over again its formative development, apparently starting solely from itself, yet at the same time it commences at a higher level. The realm of spirits developed in this way, and assuming definite shape in existence, constitutes a succession, where one detaches and sets loose the other, and each takes over from its predecessor the empire of the world.... The goal, which is Absolute Knowledge or Spirit knowing itself as Spirit, finds its pathway in the recollection of Spirits as they are in themselves and as they accomplish the organization of their spiritual kingdom. Their conservation, looked at from the side of their free existence appearing in the form of contingency, is *History;* looked at from the side of their intellectually comprehended organization, it is the *Science* of the ways in which knowledge appears. Both together, or History (intellectually) comprehended *(begriffen)*, form at once the recollection and the Golgotha of Absolute Spirit, the reality, the truth, the certainty of its throne, without which it were lifeless, solitary, and alone" (Georg Wilhelm Friedrich Hegel, *Phänomenologie des Geistes, Werke,* Bd. 3, 590–91; English translation from *The Phenomenology of Mind*, 807–8.)

9. Jean-Paul Sartre, similarly, points out that "Kierkegaard takes as his point of departure the person seen as non-knowledge" in order to develop an understanding of the transition from non-knowledge to knowledge as the "transformation of being into meaning." Jean-Paul Sartre, "The Singular Universal," 245, 254.

10. The Danish expression concerns the difference between *omskabe* and *omdanne.* Although the root verbs, *skabe* and *danne*, mean respectively "create" and "form," the prefix *om–* in either case suggests, beyond the simple repetition of the English prefix "re–"—as in "recreate" and "reform"—also an "otherwise." That is, *omskabe* describes not simply a second creation, but a recreation from already present material; it is not a recreation in a void. "Recreate" is chosen here to preserve the literal sense of the Danish *omskabe*, whereas the Hongs have chosen to render the term as "transform," which appears to be still too close to the counterterm *omdanne.* One might, given the specificity of Climacus's usage (and, as I shall demonstrate in subsequent passages, Climacus opts for a decidedly literal usage) and the

apparent lack of preexisting English equivalents, one might want to produce an altogether new term in English—*transcreation* or perhaps *metagenesis.*

11. Naming is rather the reversal of defining. As Peter Fenves has shown, this naming points out a difference between language and concepts: "Each name in the language of names becomes in the train of 'the god' a *pseudo*-name, not precisely a false name but a name that denies its nominal status and a concept that denies its conceivability" (Fenves, "*Chatter,*" 128). In a certain sense, the entire project of the *Philosophical Fragments* hinges upon the process of naming. Every concept upon which the argument of the text is developed harkens back to its own moment of naming, introduced in each case by "Let us call. . . ." Fenves quite correctly identifies the foundering of recollection that this process points out, "for there is nothing to recall, indeed no words upon which to call, until the command 'Let us call something *x*' has been carried out" (127). Although there is nothing to recall here other than the moment of naming itself, it would perhaps still be somewhat shortsighted to insist, as Fenves does, that the linguistic act of naming is only self-referential and that "the language of names recalls itself to itself." Language, for Climacus, is always about more than a simple intralinguistic referential failure. Something else is always at stake. The difficulty lies in understanding how this nonlinguistic something else plays itself out within a language to which it is always irreducible.

12. In the well-known footnote in *The Concept of Anxiety,* Kierkegaard under the pseudonym "Vigilius Haufniensis" claims similarly, in elaboration of his comment that "the speaker is language and also . . . it is Adam himself who speaks": "But this much is certain, that it will not do to represent man himself as the inventor of language." Søren Kierkegaard, *The Concept of Anxiety,* trans. Reidar Thomte (Princeton, N.J.: Princeton University Press, 1980), 47.

13. Peter Fenves has related the discrepancy between the part and the whole as it appears in this text to its very title, *Philosophical Fragments* (*Smuler,* "crumbs") and, by extension to the Kierkegaardian problematic of "chatter" *[snak]*: "The crumbs on which philosophy snacks are not philosophical fragments. Whereas each fragment, according to the presentation of this 'genre' in early romanticism, refers to the whole of which it was once part, no crumb of bread, or of any other food, can claim a referential function, except perhaps the crumbs that fell from the transubstantiated bread of the Last Supper. But even these crumbs, if there were any, would refer to what cannot be incorporated, what cannot be saved, whatever in sum recedes from reference because of its unaccountable, endless insignificance" (Fenves, "*Chatter,*" 139).

14. With regard to this passage in the *Fragments,* Bigelow identifies the "radical breach of thinking with the immediacy of the world" as the source and destination of all thought. Furthermore, he identifies this breach as the single, central thought of Kierkegaard's work (Bigelow, *Kierkegaard and the Problem of Writing,* 54–55.)

15. On the *Philosophical Fragments* as the exploration of the limits of language, see Louis Mackey, "A Ram in the Afternoon: Kierkegaard's Discourse of the Other," in *Points of View: Readings of Kierkegaard,* 102–40; and Bigelow, *Kierkegaard and the Problem of Writing,* 93–102.

16. In fact, the concept of "repetition" in general for Kierkegaard emerges through the critique of "recollection," even though "repetition" as such is not formalized in the *Philosophical Fragments.* In his discussion of "repetition" as a principle common to both Kierkegaard and Nietzsche, Gilles Deleuze understands repetition as the proliferation of "non-conceptual difference" under the appearance of similarity. Following Kierkegaard and Nietzsche, Deleuze opposes repetition to "all forms of 'generality'"—"not only the generalities of habit but also to the particularities of memory." Using Freud's connection between the repetition compulsion and the drives, Deleuze forms a functional understanding of repetition as a kind of unconscious, "the unconscious of the free concept, of knowledge or of memory, the unconscious of representation." Gilles Deleuze, *Difference and Repetition,* 5, 7, 14.

17. Similarly, irony takes its place as a tool of philosophy for Kierkegaard by introducing

difference as the disruption of habit. Irony, as Agacinski has shown, is the "non-dialectizable negativity" that resists and interrupts the otherwise habitual functioning of "the System," of Hegelian *Aufhebung*, and so on. Agacinski, *Aparté*, 35–47. For Kierkegaard's own account of the particularly disruptive freedom of irony, see the chapter "Observations for Orientation" in his dissertation *The Concept of Irony with Constant Reference to Socrates*, 246–58.

18. In another context, Kierkegaard, now as Anti-Climacus, suggests that "offense" is always, in every case, unavoidable. Cf. Kierkegaard, *Practice in Christianity*, 76.

19. The Danish *anden/andet* means both "second" and "other." Although the expression "Discipelen paa anden Hand" is idiomatically equivalent to the English "the Follower at second hand," Climacus is more explicit about how this term *anden* is to be understood. *Anden* is not a numeric term. It is not possible, as Climacus explains, "to speak of a follower at fifth, at seventh hand, etc." (*Philosophical Fragments*, 90).

20. Kierkegaard, *Papirer* V B 6:22 *n.d.*, 1844; cited in the "Supplement" of the Hong translation of the *Philosophical Fragments*, 214.

21. The description from Gesenius's *Hebräische Grammatik* is helpful: "The Hebrew language is no longer familiar with the living use of case endings, but either does not overtly mark case relationships of the noun at all . . . or uses prepositions; however, the genitive relationship is marked primarily through the close proximity ('dependance' *[Anlehnung]*) of the *Nomens regens* on the *Nomens rectum*. The noun, namely, which in the genitive serves to more closely define a *Nomens regens* immediately preceding it, remains entirely unchanged in form; conversely, the near co-utterance *[Zusammensprechung]* of the governing noun with the governed noun has the immediate result that the sound transfers to the latter and the resulting reduction in emphasis on the preceding word is in general followed by further alterations. . . . Thus, only the noun immediately preceding the genitive is changed, and the grammatical language says of such a noun that it stands in dependance *[in der Anlehnung]* or in the *Status constructus*; on the other hand, of a noun which is not followed by a genitive, it stands in the primary form *[Hauptform]* or in the *Status absolutus*." Wilhelm Gesenius, *Hebräische Grammatik* (1896), 341–42. The first edition of this work had been published in Halle in 1813.

22. This argument is elaborated in Kierkegaard/Johannes Climacus's *Concluding Unscientific Postscript to the Philosophical Fragments* (55–60) and has also been discussed earlier in this volume in the context of Adorno's assessment of the place of "communication" in Kierkegaardian philosophy.

23. Ludwig Wittgenstein, *The Blue and Brown Books*, 9. The entirety of the *Blue Book* is devoted to the understanding of these differing grammars in ways strikingly similar to that seen in Climacus's discussion of "faith."

24. For an alternate discussion of Kierkegaard's understanding of "authority," see Cavell, Stanley. "Kierkegaard's *On Authority and Revelation*," in *Must We Mean What We Say?* 163–79.

5. Abraham

1. All references to the biblical account of Abraham's sacrifice are taken from the King James version of the Old Testament.

2. In an alternate translation, Speiser offers a somewhat more elusive account of this verse, removing the direct object of the verb "to see": "On Yahweh's mountain there is vision." This translation, Speiser claims, is left "intentionally neutral." (Genesis, in *The Anchor Bible)*, trans. Epraim Avigdor Speiser.

3. The oldest and most famous accounts of Abraham's faith are certainly those of St. Paul (Romans 4; Hebrews 11). With regard to de Silentio's *Fear and Trembling*, a concise discussion of more traditional understandings of and commentary on Abraham's sacrifice is to be found in Louis Jacobs, "The Problem of the *Akedah* in Jewish Thought," and Pailin, David A. "Abraham and Isaac: A Hermeneutical Problem before Kierkegaard."

4. Readings of *Fear and Trembling* that reiterate this hierarchical schematization are

legion. To indicate but a few of the better known accounts: Mark C. Taylor, *Kierkegaard's Pseudonymous Authorship* (1975), 244–47, and *Journeys to Selfhood* (1980), 252–61; Alastair Hannay, *Kierkegaard* (1982), 74–79; Louis Mackey, *Points of View* (1986) 55–61; and Edward F. Mooney, *Knights of Faith and Resignation* (1991), 94–95.

5. Virtually every reading of Kafka that takes up his commentary on Abraham remains bound up in an attempt to decide what sort of "influence" might have been brought to bear or whether there was an "influence" in the first place. See, for example, Bert Nagel, *Kafka und die Weltliterature: Zusammenhänge und Wechselwirkungen* (1983), 278–98; Wolfgang Lange, "Über Kafkas Kierkegaard-Lektüre und einige damit zusammenhängende Gegenstände" (1986). Such interpretations, however, invariably falter in their summary acceptance of the most conventional accounts of Kierkegaard, thus rendering any question of influence moot from the start. Questions of influence cannot be answered with the generic account of an author's commonly held meaning. Not only do such accounts tell us little about the author's work in the first place, but they do little to inform us of how a particular individual may have approached the work.

6. The paradoxical ground of ethics as described in *Fear and Trembling* is perhaps most clearly drawn out in a recent reading of this text by Jacques Derrida. He insists, in short, that every ethical act necessarily involves the transgression of its own ethical presuppositions. Cf. Jacques Derrida, *The Gift of Death*, 53–81.

7. Kafka first encountered Kierkegaard in 1913 during the period in which he was breaking off his first engagement with Felice Bauer. His familiarity with Kierkegaard at this time was essentially biographical and consisted almost entirely of a familiarity with his diaries. Kafka writes, referring to a collection of excerpts from Kierkegaard's journals: "Today I received Kierkegaard's *Buch des Ritters (Book of the Knight)*. As I suspected, his case, in spite of essential differences, is very similar to my own; at least he lies on the same side of the world. He corroborates me like a friend" (*Tagebücher*, August 21, 1913). Only several years later, in 1917, did he begin to read Kierkegaard more extensively. Mention of Kierkegaard and Kierkegaard's work can be found from this point on in Kafka's letters and diaries. From these remarks and the books found in what remains of Kafka's library, one can assume familiarity with at least the following texts, including both the pseudonymous texts and the theological discourses: *Fear and Trembling*, *Either/Or* I and II, *The Concept of Anxiety*, *Sickness unto Death*, "The Thorn in the Flesh," *Stages on Life's Way*, *Attack upon Christendom*, and *Repetition*. For a discussion of the books in Kafka's library, see Jürgen Born, *Kafkas Bibliotek* (Frankfurt am Main, Fischer, 1990), 114–16, 210.

8. One need only read Kafka's "Die Sorge des Hausvaters" ("The Cares of the Family Man"), however, to note how problematic this apparent coincidence is: "It would be tempting to believe that this creature *[Gebilde]* might once have had some purposeful form and now it is only broken. This does not appear to be the case; at least there is no indication of it; nowhere are there any breaks or fissures to see which might indicate anything of the kind; the whole thing appears senseless, but in its own way complete. Moreover, nothing more can be said about it, since Odradek is exceptionally mobile and cannot be grasped." And: "In vain I wonder what will come of him. Can he die? Everything that dies once had a kind of goal *[Ziel]*, a kind of activity, upon which it wore itself out; that does not apply to Odradek." (*Kafka, Sämtliche Erzählungen*, 139–40, and *The Complete Stories*, 428–29). As elsewhere, the English translations available are cited for purposes of reference; the translations have been modified in order more accurately to reflect the original.

9. Precisely this insistence upon the possibility of misunderstanding with regard to faith is taken up in one of the sketches of Abraham included in Kafka's 1921 letter to Robert Klopstock: "But another Abraham. One who wants a to sacrifice thoroughly correctly and has utterly the correct sense for it, but cannot believe *[glauben]* that he was intended, he, the disgusting old man and his child, the filthy boy. He does not lack true faith, this faith he has, he would make the sacrifice in the correct frame of mind, if he could only believe that he was

intended. He's afraid that, while he embarks as Abraham with his son, he will, however, be transformed into Don Quixote along the way. The world at that time would have been appalled at Abraham, if it had watched; he, however, is afraid the world will laugh itself to pieces at the sight. It is not the laughableness itself which he fears—of course, he is also afraid of it, especially his laughing along—but mainly he's afraid that this laughableness will make him even older and more disgusting, his son even dirtier, even less worthy of really having been called. An Abraham who comes uncalled! It's like when the best student is to be honored with a prize at the end of the year and in the expectant silence the worst student because of *[infolge]* a hearing mistake comes forward from the last filthy row and the class erupts in laughter. And it is perhaps no mistake at all, his name really was called, the reward of the best should in the teacher's view simultaneously be the punishment of the worst.

"Terrible things. Enough." (*Briefe*, 333–34)

10. This point is perhaps most emphatically articulated in the narrative "Ein Brudermord" ("A Fratricide"), in which the murdered corpse refuses to dissolve into the ideal elation the act was expected to bring about. Immediately after the act, Schmar, the murderer, behaves as follows: "'Done,' says Schmar and throws the knife, the superfluous, bloody ballast, against the nearest house front. 'The bliss of murder! The relief, the release from the flowing of another's blood! Wese, old nightbird, friend, alehouse crony, you are seeping away in the dark street. Why are you not just a blood-filled bubble so that I might sit on you and you would disappear utterly and completely. Not everything is fulfilled, not all flowering dreams bear fruit, your weighty remains lie here, already inaccessible to every kick. What is the silent question you thus pose supposed to mean?'" (Kafka, *Erzählungen*, 145; *Complete Stories*, 403–4)

11. Kafka presents the same thought in the third *Octavo Notebook:* "We are not only sinful because we have eaten from the tree of knowledge, but also because we have not yet eaten of the tree of life. Sinful is the position in which we find ourselves independent of guilt" ("Oktavheften," 74).

12. Peter Fenves reads the breach of this promise as of primary significance for *Fear and Trembling*, claiming that the breach of this promise "made by the being that is supposed to ground itself, destroys the schemata of intelligibility and the concepts of comprehensibility through which meaning is secured." Cf., *"Chatter,"* 174.

13. Similarly, in an essay on Heidegger and the attempt to distinguish another notion of temporality from the "vulgar concept of time" that has been virtually pervasive throughout the history of Western philosophy, Derrida suggests in the end that there is nothing but the "vulgar concept of time" (Jacques Derrida, "Oussia and Gramme").

14. There are numerous instances of precisely this temporalizing excess in Kafka's work. Here I will name only two, which give some indication of the potential range of its appearance. "Das nächste Dorf" ("The Next Village") most directly identifies the excessive temporality of spatial separation as that which makes the distance toward a desired end insurmountable. On the other hand, the havoc wrought by the uncontrollable discrepancy between the temporal and the spacial is perhaps most painfully evident in the unpredictable misconnections of "Eine alltägliche Vervirrung" ("A Daily Confusion"), also in the third *Octavo Notebook.*

15. The dating and publication history of this narrative are given in Hartmut Binder, *Kafka Kommentar zu sämtlichen Erzählungen*, 256–57. "Der Aufbruch" ("The Departure") is in the same notebook, together with "Ein Hungerkünstler" ("A Hunger Artist") and "Forschungen eines Hundes" ("Investigations of a Dog"). The narrative was originally untitled.

16. The English translation in *The Complete Stories* follows the shorter version of the narrative found in the collection *Beschreibung eines Kampfes*, 86. This version ends with: "'Away from here–that is my destination.'"

17. Though it has not often been discussed in the secondary literature, when it has been, it has tended to be read as explicitly autobiographical either by equating particular formulations in the text with events in Kafka's own life (cf., for example, Binder) or by

thematizing the dog's investigations in terms of significant and unsettling concerns from Kafka's own life. The latter readings tend to identify the central thematic concern of a narrative about dogs, via a certain turn of phrase that takes the pejorative epithet of "dogs" as "Jews" to identify and represent "Jews" as "dogs." (Cf., for example, Marthe Robert, *As Lonely as Franz Kafka.*) Robert furthermore suggests that the "Investigations" were written at a point when Kafka felt he would have to abandon work on his novel *The Castle*, thus, for our purposes, suggesting a connection between the "Investigations" and the impossibility of writing, the impossibility of completing a task of writing. One might rather take this text as an account of Kafka's own writing, an exploration of what it means to write in general and, specifically, what it means to write in the absence of resolution or conclusion; writing without the possibility of success; writing, so to speak, in the face of disaster.

18. Each of these suggested meanings of *verreden* is given in Grimm's *Deutsches Wörterbuch der deutschen Sprache.* The English translators opted for the more idiomatic "got it all wrong," which certainly carries part of the meaning, though it loses the reference to speech that is so important to this investigation.

19. On the basis of the way in which the text breaks off, prior to the completion of subsequent investigations mentioned by the narrator, it has been suggested that Kafka never completed the text. See, for example, Binder, *Kafka Kommentar zu den sämtlichen Erzählungen*, 261–64.

20. Kierkegaard, under the pseudonym Vigilius Haufniensis, begins the *Concept of Anxiety* with a warning against the illusory capacity of dialectical negation, and seeks rather to prevent the negative from "becoming an illusion"—to prevent it, that is, from disappearing altogether.

21. Søren Kierkegaard, *Samlede Værker*, Bd. 5 (Copenhagen: Gyldendal, 1962), 271. The English translation of this passage replaces *desultorisk* with the more palatable *salient*, thus reinscribing Abraham's incomprehensibility within a coherent methodological form.

22. The etymology is taken from the *Oxford English Dictionary.*

23. In his account of the same passage, Kevin Newmark makes this "calling to mind" of Abraham, in every language a reminder of Abraham's faith, into a reminder of Abraham's singularity. Newmark, however, situates his reading of Kierkegaard within the context of Hegel's account of language (in the *Phänomenologie des Geistes* and the *Enzyklopädie*) as the mediation of a radical break with or sacrifice of sensory perception on the way toward thought, "a radical sacrifice or break with the immediacy of the objective world that comprises at the same time the promise of a meaningful future" (383). From this he concludes: "What every tongue reminds us, then, is that its own promise of future meaning is predicated on the original sacrifice of a natural relationship to the world. All language necessarily recalls Abraham's story insofar as it repeats a severance of generic ties; no longer immediately related to the world by the certitude of representation, or resemblance, every tongue celebrates its semiotic independence from the slavish constraints of sensory perception" (383–84). However, the "slavish constraints" of which Kierkegaard's de Silentio speaks are not (as in Hegel) identified as "sensory perception"; it is the very institution of universalization that is language in its *promise* of a future meaning. De Silentio does not believe that language can "promise" in this sense at all; it can never be assured of "future meaning." Kevin Newmark, "Between Hegel and Kierkegaard: The Space of Translation."

24. Jean Wahl, one of the few readers to take seriously Kafka's cryptic commentary on Kierkegaard, points this out: "We therefore discover two incommunicable spheres in the world of Kafka: the incommunicable of the particular, and the incommunicable of the general. For Kierkegaard on the other hand, only the particular is incommunicable, while the general is communicable (which is the social and moral order). For Kafka the general becomes an unattainable ideal and a mysterious driving force." Jean Wahl, "Kierkegaard and Kafka," 265.

Afterword

1. Here I refer to one of the few contemporary philosophers to address more or less directly the difficulty of thinking through freedom. If one were to conceive of freedom only as absolutely unbounded in an ideal sense, writes Jean-Luc Nancy, "I would keep the surprise and experience of freedom for a beyond that I would pretend to attain in disappearing. But the experience is already taking place, as I have continually said, and all philosophy has said it without ever being able to say it (except by cheating . . .)." Jean-Luc Nancy, *The Experience of Freedom*, 149.

2. Immanuel Kant, *Critique of Pure Reason* (Transcendental Dialectic, book I, sec. I).

Works Cited

Adorno, Theodor. "The Actuality of Philosophy." *Telos,* Spring 1977, 120–33.

———. "Die Aktualität der Philosophie." In *Gesammelte Schriften* I, 325–44.

———. *Gesammelte Schriften,* vols. I–XX. Frankfurt am Main: Suhrkamp, 1979.

———. "Die Idee der Naturgeschichte." In *Gesammelte Schriften* I, 345–65.

———. *Kierkegaard: Construction of the Aesthetic.* Trans. Robert Hullot-Kentor. Minneapolis: University of Minnesota Press, 1989.

———. *Negative Dialectics.* Trans. E. B. Ashton. New York: The Seabury Press, 1973.

———. *Negative Dialektik.* Frankfurt am Main: Suhrkamp, 1966.

———. "Thesen über die Sprache des Philosophen." In *Gesammelte Schriften* I, 366–71.

——— *Kierkegaard: Konstruction des Aesthetischen.* In Gesammelte Schriften, II.

Adorno, Theodor, and Walter Benjamin. *The Complete Correspondence, 1928–1940.* Ed. Henri Lonitz. Trans. Nicholas Walker. Cambridge, Mass.: Harvard University Press, 1999.

Agacinski, Sylviane. *Aparté: Conceptions and Deaths of Søren Kierkegaard.* Trans. Kevin Newmark. Tallahassee: Florida State University Press, 1988.

Auerbach, Erich. "Figura." In *Scenes from the Drama of European Literature,* 11–76.

———. *Scenes from the Drama of European Literature.* Minneapolis: University of Minnesota Press, 1984.

Baldwin, Birgit. "Irony, The 'Little, Invisible Personage': Reading Kierkegaard's Ghosts." *Modern Language Notes* 104 (1989), 1124–41.

Benjamin, Walter. *Briefe,* Bd. I–II. Ed. Gershom Scholem and Theodor W. Adorno. Frankfurt am Main: Suhrkamp, 1966.

———. *Gesammelte Schriften.* Ed. Rolf Tiedemann and Hermann Schweppenhäuser. Frankfurt am Main: Suhrkamp, 1977–85.

———. *The Origin of German Tragic Drama.* Trans. John Osborne. London: NLB, 1977.

———. *Ursprung des deutschen Trauerspiels.* Ed. Rolf Thiedemann. Frankfurt am Main: Suhrkamp, 1955.

Bigelow, Pat. *Kierkegaard and the Problem of Writing.* Tallahassee: Florida State University Press, 1987.

Binder, Hartmut. *Kafka Kommentar zu sämtlichen Erzählungen.* Munich: Winkler, 1975.

Bollnow, Otto Friedrich. *Existenzphilosophie.* Stuttgart: Kohlhammer, 1955.

Bonß, Wolfgang. "Empirie und Dechiffrierung von Wirklichkeit." In *Adorno Konferenz.* Frankfurt am Main: Suhrkamp, 1983, 201–25.

Bové, Paul. "The Penitentiary of Reflection: Sören Kierkegaard and Critical Activity." In *Kierkegaard and Literature,* ed. Ronald Schleifer and Robert Manckley. Norman: University of Oklahoma Press, 25–57.

Buck-Morss, Susan. *The Origin of the Negative Dialectics.* New York: The Free Press, 1977.

Butler, Judith. "Contingent Foundations: Feminism and the Question of 'Postmodernism.'" In *Feminists Theorize the Political,* ed. Judith Butler and Joan W. Scott. New York and London: Routledge, 1992, 3–21.

———. "Kierkegaard's Speculative Despair." In *Routledge History of Philosophy,* vol. VI, ed. Robert C. Solomon and Kathleen M. Higgins. London and New York: Routledge, 1993, 363–95.

Cavell, Stanley. *Must We Mean What We Say?* Cambridge: Cambridge University Press, 1969, 163–79.

Come, Arnold B. *Kierkegaard as Theologian: Becoming My Self.* Montreal, Kingston, London and Buffalo: McGill-Queens University Press, 1997.

Connell, George. *To Be One Thing: Personal Unity in Kierkegaard's Thought.* Macon, Ga.: Mercer University Press, 1985.

de Certeau, Michel. *La Fable mystique, XVIe–XVIIe siècle.* Paris: Gallimard, 1982.

Deleuze, Gilles. *Difference and Repetition.* Trans. Paul Patton. New York: Columbia University Press, 1994.

de Man, Paul. *Aesthetic Ideology,* ed. Andrzej Warminski. Minneapolis: University of Minnesota Press, 1996.

———. *Blindness and Insight: Essays in the Rhetoric of Contemporary Criticism.* Intro. by Wlad Godzich. Minneapolis: University of Minnesota Press, 1983.

Derrida, Jacques. *Aporias.* Trans. Thomas Dutoit. Stanford, Calif.: Stanford University Press, 1994.

———. *The Gift of Death.* Trans. David Wills. Chicago: University of Chicago Press, 1995.

———. *Limited Inc.* Evanston, Ind.: Northwestern University Press, 1988.

———. *Margins of Philosophy.* Trans. Alan Bass. Chicago: University of Chicago Press, 1982.

———. "A Number of Yes." Trans. Brian Holmes. *Qui Parle* 2:2 [fall 1988], 120–33.

Deuser, Hermann. *Dialektische Theologie: Studien zu Adornos Metaphysik und zum Spätwerk Kierkegaards.* Munich: Grünewald, 1980.

———. *Kierkegaard: Die Philosophie des religiösen Schriftstellers.* Darmstadt: Wissenschaftliche Buchgesellschaft, 1985.

———. "Kierkegaard in der kritischen Theorie." In *Die Rezeption Søren Kierkegaards in der deutschen und dänischen Philosophie und Theologie: Text und Kritik,* Sonderreihe, Bd. 15. Copenhagen and Munich: Wilhelm Fink Verlag: 1983, 101–13.

Dunning, Stephen N. *Kierkegaard's Dialectic of Inwardness: A Structural Analysis of the Theory of Stages.* Princeton, N.J.: Princeton University Press, 1985.

Düttmann, Alexander Garcia. *Das Gedächtnis des Denkens.* Frankfurt am Main, Suhrkamp, 1991.

Fenves, Peter. *"Chatter": Language and Historty in Kierkegaard.* Stanford, Calif.: Stanford University Press, 1994.

———. "Image and Chatter: Adorno's Construction of Kierkegaard." *Diacritics* 22:1 (Spring 1992), 100–14.

Frowen, Irina. "Rilkes 'Ölbaum-Garten' zwischen Kierkegaards 'Entweder-Oder.'" In *Blätter der Rilke-Gesellschaft*, vols. 16 and 17, 1989 and 1990, 177–87.

Garff, Joakim. "The Eyes of Argus: The Point of View and Points of View with Respect to Kierkegaard's 'Activity as an Author.'" In *Kierkegaardiana* 15 (Copenhagen: Reitzel, 1991).

Genesis. In *The Anchor Bible*, vol. I. Intro., trans., and notes by E. A. Epraim Avigdor Speiser. Garden City, N.Y.: Doubleday, 1964, 161–66.

Gesenius, Wilhelm. *Hebräische Grammatik*, Völlig umgearbeitet von E. Kautzsch, 26. Auflage. Leipzig: Vogel, 1896.

Grimm, Jacob, and Wilhelm Grimm. *Deutsches Wörterbuch*. Ed. Akademie der Wissenschaften der DDR in Zusammenarbeit mit der Akademie der Wissenschaften zu Göttingen. Leipzig: S. Hirzel, 1983.

Haecker, Theodor. *Søren Kierkegaard und die Philosophie der Innerlichkeit*. Innsbruck: Brenner Verlag, 1913.

Hamacher, Werner. "LECTIO: de Man's Imperative." In *Reading de Man Reading*, ed. Lindsay Waters and Wlad Godzich. Minneapolis: University of Minnesota Press, 1989, 171–201.

———. "Ou, séance, touché de Nancy, ici (II)." *Paragraph* 17:2 (July 1994).

———. *Premises: Essays on Philosophy and Literature from Kant to Celan*. Trans. Peter Fenves. Stanford: Stanford University Press, 1996.

———. "The Second of Inversion: Movements of a Figure through Celan's Poetry." *Yale French Studies* 69 (1985), 276–311.

Hannay, Alastair. *Kierkegaard*. London: Routledge and Kegan Paul, 1982.

Hass, Robert. "Looking for Rilke." In *Twentieth Century Pleasures*.

———. *Twentieth Century Pleasures*. New York: Ecco Press, 1984.

Hegel, Georg Wilhelm Friedrich. *Encyclopädie der philosophischen Wissenschaft, Erster Theil, Die Logik*. *Werke*, vol. VI. Ed. Eva Moldenhauer und Karl Markus Michel. Frankfurt am Main: Suhrkamp, 1986.

———. *Phänomenologie des Geistes*, *Werke* Bd. 3. Frankfurt am Main: Suhrkamp, 1970.

———. *The Phenomenology of Mind*, 2nd ed. Trans. J. B. Baillie. London and New York: Humanities Press, 1931.

Heiberg, P. A. *Bidrog til et Psykologisk Billede af Søren Kierkegaard i Barudom og Ungdom*. Copenhagen, 1895.

Huyssen, Andreas. "Paris/Childhood: The Fragmented Body in Rilke's *Notebooks of Malte Laurids Brigge*." In *Modernity and the Text: Revisions of German Modernism*. New York: Columbia University Press, 1989, 113–41.

Huyssen, Andreas, and David Bathrick, eds. *Modernity and the Text: Revisions of German Modernism*. New York: Columbia University Press, 1989.

Jacobs, Louis. "The Problem of the *Akedah* in Jewish Thought." In *Kierkegaard's Fear and Trembling—Critical Appraisals*, ed. Robert L. Perkins, Tuscaloosa: University of Alabama Press, 1981, 1–9.

Janik, Allan. "Haecker, Kierkegaard, and the Early *Brenner*: A Contribution to the History of the Reception of *Two Ages* in the German-Speaking World." In *International Kierkegaard Commentary*, vol. 14: *Two Ages*. Macon, Ga.: Mercer University Press, 1984, 189–222.

Jaspers, Karl. "The Importance of Kierkegaard." In *Søren Kierkegaard: Modern Critical Views*, ed. Harold Bloom. New York and Philadelphia: Chelsea House Publishers, 1989.

Kafka, Franz. *Beschreibung eines Kampfes*. Frankfurt am Main: Fischer, 1954.

———. *Briefe, 1902–1924*. Ed. Max Brod. New York: Schocken Books, Inc., 1958.

———. *The Complete Stories*. Ed. Nahum N. Glatzer. New York: Schocken Books, 1971.

———. *Hochzeitsvorbereitungen auf dem Lande*. Ed. Max Brod. Frankfurt am Main: Fischer, 1953.

———. *Sämtliche Erzählungen*. Ed. Paul Raabe. Frankfurt am Main: Fischer, 1969.

———. *Tagebücher*. Ed Hans-Gerd Koch, Michael Müller, und Malcolm Pasley. Frankfurt am Main: S. Fischer, 1990.

Kant, Immanuel. *Critique of Pure Reason*. Trans. Norman Kemp Smith. New York: St Martin's Press, 1965.

———. *Kritik der Urteilskraft. Werkausgabe*, Bd. X. Ed. Wilhelm Weischedal. Frankfurt am Main: Suhrkamp, 1977.

Kierkegaard, Søren. "At a Graveside." In *Three Discourses on Imagined Occasions*, 71–102.

———. *Attack upon Christendom*. Trans. Walter Lowrie. Princeton, N.J.: Princeton University Press, 1944.

———. *The Concept of Anxiety*. Trans. Howard V. Hong and Edna Hong. Princeton, N.J.: Princeton University Press, 1980.

———. *The Concept of Irony with Constant Reference to Socrates*. Trans. Howard V. Hong and Edna Hong. Princeton, N.J.: Princeton University Press, 1989.

———. *Concluding Unscientific Postscript to Philosophical Fragments*. Trans. Howard V. Hong and Edna H. Hong. Princeton, N.J.: Princeton University Press, 1992.

———. *Either/Or*, vols. I and II. Trans. Howard V. Hong and Edna H. Hong, Princeton, N.J.: Princeton University Press, 1987.

———. *Fear and Trembling/Repetition*. Trans. Howard V. and Edna H. Hong. Princeton, N.J.: Princeton University Press, 1983.

———. *For Self-examination: Judge for Yourself!* Trans. Howard V. Hong and Edna H. Hong. Princeton, N.J.: Princeton University Press, 1990.

———. *Journals and Papers*. Vols. 1–7. Ed. and trans. by Howard V. Hong and Edna H. Hong, assisted by Graegor Malantschukv. Bloomington: Indiana University Press, 1967–78.

———. *Kierkegaard's Attack upon "Christendom," 1854–1855*. Princeton, N.J.: Princeton University Press, 1944.

———. *Papirer*. 2. forøgede Udg. ved Niels Thulstrup. Udg. af Det danske Sprog og Litteraturselskab og Søren Kierkegaard Selskabet., Bd. 1–16. København: Gyldendal, 1968–78.

———. *Philosophical Fragments/Johannes Climacus*. Trans. and ed. Howard V. Hong and Edna H. Hong. Princeton, N.J.: Princeton University Press, 1985.

———. *Practice in Christianity*. Trans. Howard V. Hong and Edna H. Hong. Princeton, N.J.; Princeton University Press, 1991.

———. *The Point of View of My Work as an Author*. Trans. Walter Lowrie. New York: Harper and Brothers, 1962.

———-. *Samlede vaerker*. Ed. A. B. Drachmann, J. L. Heiberg, og H. O. Lange. Copenhagen: Gyldendal, 1962–64, Bd. 1–20.

———. *Three Discourses on Imagined Occasions*. Trans. and ed. Howard V. Hong and Edna H. Hong. Princeton, N.J.: Princeton University Press, 1993.

———. "The Work of Love in Remembering One Dead." In *Works of Love*, part 2.

———. *Works of Love*. Trans. Howard and Edna Hong. New York: Harper and Row, 1962.

Kirmmse, Bruce. *Kierkegaard in Golden Age Denmark*. Bloomington: Indiana University Press, 1990.

Kodalle, Klaus M. "Adornos Kierkegaard—Ein kritischer Kommentar." In *Die Rezeption Søren Kierkegaards in der deutschen und dänischen Philosophie und Theologie: Text und Kritik*, Sonderreihe, Bd. 15. Copenhagen and Munich: Wilhelm Fink Verlag, 1983, 70–100.

Kroner, Richard. "Kierkegaards Hegelverständnis." In *Materialien zur Philosophie Søren Kierkegaards*, ed. Michael Theunissen and Wilfried Greve. Frankfurt am Main: Suhrkamp, 1979.

Lange, Wolfgang. "Über Kafkas Kierkegaard-Lektüre und einige damit zusammenhängende Gegenstände." In *Deutsche Vierteljahresschrift für Literaturwissenschaft und Geistesgeschichte* 60:2 (June 1986), 286–308.

Leppmann, Wolfgang. *Rilke—Sein Leben, seine Welt, sein Werk*. Bern: Scherg, 1993.

Lowrie, Walter. *Kierkegaard.* New York: Harper, 1962.

Mackey, Louis. *Kierkegaard: A Kind of Poet.* Philadelphia: University of Pennsylvania Press, 1971.

———. *Points of View: Readings of Kierkegaard.* Tallahassee: Florida State University Press, 1986.

Malik, Habib C. *Receiving Søren Kierkegaard.* Washington, D.C.: The Catholic University of America Press, 1997.

Matuštík, Martin J. "Kierkegaard's Radical Existential Praxis." In *Kierkegaard in Post/ Modernity,* ed. Martin J. Matuštík and Nerold Westphal.

Matuštík, Martin J., and Merold Westphal, eds. *Kierkegaard in Post/Modernity.* Bloomington and Indianapolis: University of Indiana Press, 1995.

Mooney, Edward F. *Knights of Faith and Resignation.* Albany: State University of New York Press, 1991.

Nagel, Bert. *Kafka und die Weltliterature: Zusammenhänge und Wechselwirkungen.* Munich: Winkler, 1983.

Nägele, Rainer. "The Scene of the Other." *Boundary 2* II:I (Fall 1982), 54–79.

Nancy, Jean-Luc. *The Experience of Freedom.* Trans. Bridget McDonald. Stanford, Calif.: Stanford University Press, 1993.

Nancy, Jean-Luc, and Philippe Lacoue-Labarthe. *The Literary Absolute: The Theory of Literature in German Romanticism.* Trans. Phillip Barnard and Cheryl Lester. Albany: State University of New York Press, 1988.

Newmark, Kevin. "Between Hegel and Kierkegaard: The Space of Translation." *Genre* 16 (Winter 1983), 373–88.

———. "Secret Agents: After Kierkegaard's Subject." *Modern Language Notes* 112:5 (1997), 719–52.

———. "Taking Kierkegaard Apart." Intro. to *Aparté: Conceptions and Deaths of Søren Kierkegaard,* by Sylviane Agacinski, trans. Kevin Newmark.

Norris, Christopher. *The Deconstructive Turn.* New York: Methuen, 1984.

———. "Fictions of Authority: Narrative and Viewpoint in Kierkegaard's Writing." In *The Deconstructive Turn,* 85–106.

The Oxford English Dictionary. 2nd ed, Prepared by J. A. Simpson and E. S. C. Weiner. Oxford: Clarendon Press; New York: Oxford University Press, 1989.

Pailin, David A. "Abraham and Isaac: A Hermeneutical Problem before Kierkegaard." In *Kierkegaard's Fear and Trembling—Critical Appraisals,* ed. Robert L. Perkins. Tuscaloosa: University of Alabama Press, 1981, 10–42.

Pawel, Ernst. *Nightmare of Reason: A Life of Franz Kafka.* New York: Farrar, Straus and Giroux, 1984.

Plato. *The Dialogues of Plato.* 2 vols. Trans. B. Jowett. New York: Random House 1967.

Poole, Roger. *Kierkegaard: The Indirect Communication.* Charlottesville and London: The University Press of Virginia, 1993.

———. "The Unknown Kierkegaard: Twentieth-century Receptions." In *The Cambridge Companion to Kierkegaard,* ed. Alastair Hannay and Gordon D. Marino. Cambridge: Cambridge University Press, 1998.

Preminger, Alex, and T. V. F. Brogan, eds. *The New Princeton Encyclopedia of Poetry and Poetics,* Princeton, N.J.: Princeton University Press, 1993.

Ricoeur, Paul. "Philosophie après Kierkegaard." *Revue de théologie et de philosophie* 3 (1963), 303–16.

Rilke, Rainer Maria. *Briefe.* Wiesbaden: Insel-Verlag, 1950.

———. *Werke in Drei Bänden.* Frankfurt am Main: Insel, 1993.

Robbins, Jill. *Prodigal Son/Elder Brother: Interpretation and Alterity in Augustine, Petrarch, Kafka, Levinas.* Chicago: University of Chicago Press, 1989.

Robert, Marthe. *As Lonely as Franz Kafka.* Trans. Ralph Manheim. New York: Schocken Books, 1986.

Rose, Gillian. *Melancholy Science: An Introduction to the Thought of Theodor Adorno.* New York: Columbia University Press, 1978.

Rosenzweig, Franz. *Der Stern der Erlösung.* Frankfurt am main: Suhrkamp, 1988.

Sartre, Jean-Paul. "The Singular Universal." In *Kierkegaard: A Collection of Critical Essays*, ed. J. Thompson. New York: Anchor Books, 1972, 230–65.

Schleifer, Ronald, and Robert Manckley, eds. *Kierkegaard and Literature.* Norman: University of Oklahoma Press, 1984.

Schnädelbach, Herbert. *Philosophy in Germany, 1831-1933.* Trans. Eric Matthews. London and New York: Cambridge University Press, 1984.

Schrader, George. "Kant and Kierkegaard on Duty and Inclination." In *Kierkegaard: A Collection of Critical Essays*, ed. J. Thompson. New York: Anchor Books, 1972, 324–41.

Schweppenhäuser, Hermann. *Kierkegaards Angriff auf die Spekulation.* Frankfurt am Main: Suhrkamp, 1967.

Small, William. *Rilke-Kommentar zu den Aufzeichnungen des Malte Laurids Brigge.* Chapel Hill: University of North Carolina Press, 1983.

Smyth, John V. *A Question of Eros: Irony in Sterne, Kierkegaard, and Barthes.* Tallahassee: Florida State University Press, 1986.

Søren Kierkegaard Selskaben, ed. *Søren Kierkegaards Bibliotek.* Copenhagen: Munksgaard, 1957.

Stahl, August, ed. *Rilke—Kommentar zum lyrischen Werk.* Munich: Winkler Verlag, 1978.

Steinacker, Peter. "Verborgenheit als theologisches Motiv in der Ästhetik." *Neue Zeitschrift für systematische Theologie und Religionsphilosophie* 23 (1981), 254–71.

Sussman, Henry. *Franz Kafka: Geometrician of Metaphor.* Madison, Wisc.: Coda Press, 1979.

———. *The Hegelian Aftermath.* Baltimore: Johns Hopkins University Press, 1982.

Taylor, Mark C. *Erring: A Postmodern A/theology.* Chicago: University of Chicago Press, 1984.

———. *Journeys to Selfhood: Hegel and Kierkegaard.* Berkeley: University of California Press, 1980.

———. *Kierkegaard's Pseudonymous Authorship.* Princeton, N.J.: Princeton University Press, 1975.

———. "Self in/as Other." In *Kierkegaardiana*, vol. XIII. (Copenhagen: Nunksgaard, 1984, 63–71.

Theunissen, Michael. *Der Begriff Ernst bei Kierkegaard.* Freiburg: Alber, 1958.

———. "Negativität bei Adorno." In *Adorno Konferenz.* Frankfurt am Main: Suhrkamp, 1983.

———. *The Other.* Boston: MIT Press, 1987.

Theunissen, Michael, and Wilfried Greve, eds. *Materialien zur Philosophie Søren Kierkegaards.* Frankfurt am Main: Suhrkamp, 1979.

Thildemann, Rolf. "Editorsche Nachbemerkung" to *Gesammelte Schriften*, by Theodor Adorno, I, 381–84.

Thompson, Josiah. *Kierkegaard: A Critical Biography.* New York: Knopf, 1974.

———, ed. *Kierkegaard: A Collection of Critical Essays.* Garden City, N.Y.: Doubleday, 1972.

Thurn und Taxis, Marie. *Erinnerungen an Rainer Maria Rilke.* Munich, 1933.

Thusltrup, Niels. *Kierkegaard's Relation to Hegel.* Trans. George L. Stengren. Princeton, N.J.: Princeton University Press, 1980.

Wahl, Jean. "Kierkegaard and Kafka," trans. Lienhard Bergel. In *The Kafka Problem*, ed. Angel Flores. New York: Octagon, 1963.

Walsh, Sylvia. *Living Poetically: Kierkegaard's Existential Aeshtetics.* University Park: Pennsylvania State University, 1994.

Weston, Michael. *Kierkegaard and Modern Continental Philosophy: An Introduction.* London and New York: Routledge, 1994.

Westphal, Merold. *Becoming a Self: A Reading of Kierkegaard's Concluding Unscientific Postscript.* West Lafayette, Ind.: Purdue University Press, 1996.

Wittgenstein, Ludwig. *The Blue and Brown Books.* Oxford: Basil Blackwell, 1958.

———. *Traktatus logico-philosophicus: Tagebücher 1914–16,* and *Philosophische Untersuchungen*, Werkausgabe Bd. I. Frankfurt am Main: Suhrkamp, 1989

Index

Geoffrey A. Hale received a Ph.D. in German from The Johns Hopkins University and studied at the Free University in Berlin through a Fulbright scholarship. He has published essays on philosophy, literature, and psychoanalysis.